THE LAW OF COPYRIGHT

Second Edition

Revised and Updated by

Margaret C. Jasper, Esq.

Oceana's Legal Almanac Series:
Law for the Layperson

2000
Oceana Publications, Inc.
Dobbs Ferry, N.Y.

You may order this or any other Oceana publications by visiting Oceana's Web Site at http://www.oceanalaw.com

Library of Congress Cataloging-in-Publication Data

Jasper, Margaret C.
    The law of copyright / by Margaret C. Jasper.—2nd ed.
        p. cm. — (Oceana's legal almanac series. Law for the layperson, ISSN 1075-7376)
    Rev. ed. of: The law of copyright / Mavis Fowler. 1996.
    ISBN 0-379-11337-6 (cloth : alk. paper)
        1. Copyright—United States—Popular works.
    I. Fowler, Mavis. Law of copyright. II. Title. III. Series.

    KF2995 .J37 1999
    346.7304'82—dc21

                                            99-58626

Oceana's Legal Almanac Series: Law for the Layperson
ISSN 1075-7376

©2000 by Oceana Publications, Inc.

Manufactured in the United States of America on acid-free paper.

To My Husband Chris

Your love and support
are my motivation and inspiration

-and-

In memory of my son, Jimmy

ABOUT THE AUTHOR

MARGARET C. JASPER is an attorney engaged in the general practice of law in South Salem, New York, concentrating in the areas of personal injury and entertainment law. Ms. Jasper holds a Juris Doctor degree from Pace University School of Law, White Plains, New York, is a member of the New York and Connecticut bars, and is certified to practice before the United States District Courts for the Southern and Eastern Districts of New York, and the United States Supreme Court. Ms. Jasper has been appointed to the panel of arbitrators of the American Arbitration Association and the law guardian panel for the Family Court of the State of New York, is a member of the Association of Trial Lawyers of America, and is a New York State licensed real estate broker and member of the Westchester County Board of Realtors, operating as Jasper Real Estate, in South Salem, New York.

Ms. Jasper is the author and general editor of the following legal almanacs: Juvenile Justice and Children's Law; Marriage and Divorce; Estate Planning; The Law of Contracts; The Law of Dispute Resolution; Law for the Small Business Owner; The Law of Personal Injury; Real Estate Law for the Homeowner and Broker; Everyday Legal Forms; Dictionary of Selected Legal Terms; The Law of Medical Malpractice; The Law of Product Liability; The Law of No-Fault Insurance; The Law of Immigration; The Law of Libel and Slander; The Law of Buying and Selling; Elder Law; The Right to Die; AIDS Law; The Law of Obscenity and Pornography; The Law of Child Custody; The Law of Debt Collection; Consumer Rights Law; Bankruptcy Law for the Individual Debtor; Victim's Rights Law; Animal Rights Law; Workers' Compensation Law; Employee Rights in the Workplace; Probate Law; Environmental Law; Labor Law; The Americans with Disabilities Act; The Law of Capital Punishment; Education Law; The Law of Violence Against Women; Landlord-Tenant Law; Insurance Law; Religion and the Law; Commercial Law; Motor Vehicle Law; Social Security Law; The Law of Drunk Driving; The Law of Speech and the First Amendment; Employment Discrimination Under Title VII; Hospital Liability Law; and Home Mortgage Law Primer.

TABLE OF CONTENTS

INTRODUCTION

This almanac explores the law of copyright under which authors obtain certain defined and exclusive rights to their works for a limited period of time. In general, to be covered by copyright, a work must be original and in a concrete "medium of expression." These requirements are discussed more fully in this almanac.

A copyright gives the owner the exclusive right to reproduce, distribute, perform, display, or license his or her work, including the exclusive right to produce or license the production of derivatives of the work. A discussion of the seven basic rights guaranteed by copyright in the United States is set forth in this almanac.

Limited exceptions to the right of exclusivity, such as the right of "fair use," is also explored, as well as the duration of copyright protection and the subject of "public domain"—i.e., works which can be used freely by anyone for any purpose. Copyright infringement—i.e., the unauthorized use of a copyright protected work—and the author's rights in case of infringement are also set forth in this almanac.

The U.S. Copyright Act (17 U.S.C. §§ 101 - 810) is the Federal legislation which guarantees authors copyright protection. The Copyright Act was enacted by Congress by virtue of their constitutional power to "promote the progress of science and useful arts, by securing for limited times to authors and inventors the exclusive right to their respective writings and discoveries." (U.S. Constitution, Article 1, Section 8, Clause 8). Given the scope of the Federal legislation and its provision precluding inconsistent state law, the field is almost exclusively under Federal jurisdiction.

Because changing technology has led to an ever expanding understanding of the word "writings". The Copyright Act now also encompasses architectural design, software, the graphic arts, motion pictures, and sound recordings. The scope of this coverage is explained in more detail in this almanac.

The federal agency charged with administering the Copyright Act is the Copyright Office of the Library of Congress. The U.S. Copyright Office accepts applications for copyright registration. Nevertheless, under current law, works are copyrighted as soon as they are created, whether or not a copyright notice is attached and whether or not the work is registered. Copyright notice and the registration process are further discussed in this almanac.

There are two primary international treaties which also impact on copyright law: (1) The Berne Convention for the Protection of Literary and Artistic Works; and (2) The Universal Copyright Convention (UCC). The United States is a party to both treaties. The Berne treaty is administered by the World Intellectual Property Organization (WIPO), an international organization headquartered in Geneva, Switzerland. The UCC is administered by UNESCO, a United Nations agency. The provisions and protections provided under the Berne Convention and the UCC, and additional copyright-related treaties, are also discussed herein.

The Appendix provides resource directories, applicable statutes, and other pertinent information and data. The Glossary contains definitions of many of the terms used throughout the almanac.

CHAPTER 1:

HISTORICAL AND LEGISLATIVE DEVELOPMENT OF U.S. COPYRIGHT LAW

Early English Copyright Law

Modern day copyright law originated in England with the passage of the Statute of Anne by the British Parliament in 1710. Prior to the enactment of the Statute of Anne, the Stationer's Company, a group of London booksellers and printers, had been granted a publishing monopoly by Royal decree in an effort to regulate dissemination of writings unfavorable to the Crown. The Stationer's monopoly ended in 1695, when its official license expired, paving the way for competition by new publishers and printers.

In an effort to protect their monopoly, the Stationer's Company petitioned the government to regulate this competition on the basis that it would create economic disaster. In response, the Statute of Anne was enacted, which, among other things, continued the Stationer's rights in existing works for 21 years, until 1731. Despite this provision, the Stationer's monopoly over book publishing was effectively eliminated by the Statute of Anne.

The stated purpose of the Statute of Anne was to enhance public welfare by the dissemination of knowledge, and encourage authors to compose and write "useful work." The statute provided that:

1. A new work had to be created in order to obtain a copyright.

2. The length of the copyright term was subject to time limitations. This created a "public domain" for literature.

3. The rights granted to the copyright owner to print, publish and sell the work were limited in that the copyright owner did not control the use of the work once it has been purchased. Thus, although the statute provided for the "author's copyright," in practice, this provision afforded only a limited benefit because authors still had to "assign" their work to a bookseller or publisher in order to have the work printed and published—a necessary prerequisite to payment.

Under the statute, new works were protected for 14 years from the date of first publication, which would then revert to the author and could be extended to a second term of 14 years, if the author lived to its commencement.

The Stationer's Company continued for many years to maintain that their rights were perpetual. However, their position was finally rejected in 1774 when the House of Lords ruled that the copyright term was finite, and once it ended the work was in the public domain.

Early American Copyright Law

Copyright law in the United States is derived from the English copyright law and common law. The framers of the U.S. Constitution made copyright law purely federal: "The Congress shall have power . . . to promote the progress of science and useful arts, by securing for limited times to authors and inventors the exclusive right to their respective writings and discoveries." (U.S. Constitution, Article 1, Section 8, Clause 8). Congress subsequently enacted the Copyright Act of 1790.

In order to be protected, the 1790 Act required registration of works eligible under the Act with the clerk of the district court having venue over the author or proprietor of the work. It also required the author or proprietor to deliver a copy of the work within six months of its publication to the Secretary of State. Today, the U.S. Copyright Office—a department of the Library of Congress—registers claims to copyright, and otherwise administers the provisions of the Copyright Act.

Since its original enactment, The Copyright Act has been revised numerous times. The scope of the Act has been broadened, and protection for new and developing technology has been incorporated.

For example, copyright protection was extended to prints in 1802, and to musical compositions in 1831. Copyright protection was also extended to dramatic compositions in 1856, to photographs in 1865, and to paintings, drawings, sculptures, and models or designs for works of the fine arts in 1870.

Copyright terms have also changed over the years. For example, the 1831 amendment extended the initial fourteen year term, which was renewable for another fourteen years, to provide for one twenty-eight year initial term, and a renewal privilege of fourteen years available only to the author or the author's widow and children. Copyright duration was again recently extended under The Sonny Bono Copyright Term Extension Act of 1998, which is more fully discussed in Chapter 4 of this almanac.

The most massive revisions to U.S. Copyright Law took place in 1909 and 1976, as further set forth below.

The Copyright Act of 1909

A major revision of the U.S. Copyright Act was completed in 1909. The scope of the law was broadened to include copyright protection for all works of authorship. The 1909 Copyright Act required that all copies of a published work bear a copyright notice, and that the notice be in a certain form and location. If the notice was incorrect, or omitted, the work would be deemed to have entered the public domain and be free for all to copy.

The 1909 Copyright Act provided for an initial twenty- eight year copyright term, and further extended the number of years in a renewal term from 14 to 28 which, when added to the initial 28 year term, provided for a total of 56 years of copyright protection.

The 1909 Copyright Act also established that copyright protection began at the moment of publication rather than as of the date of filing for registration, and provided a system of registration for published works and certain unpublished works. However, most unpublished works could only be protected under state common law.

In addressing new categories of materials available for copyright protection, Congress also addressed the difficulty of balancing the public interest with proprietary rights. For example, in expanding copyright protection to music, Congress was concerned with balancing the rights of the consumer with the right of the composer to earn an adequate return on his or her work.

The 1909 Act did not contain the amendments necessary to permit the United States to join The Berne Convention for the Protection of Literary and Artistic Works—the principal international copyright convention ratified in 1886. For example, the Act required that published works which did not contain a formal notice would fall into the public domain whereas the Berne Convention required no such formalities. In addition, the Act's copyright term was shorter than that provided for by the Berne Convention.

The Copyright Act of 1976

Because there was much dissatisfaction with the 1909 Act, a major revision of the Copyright Act was again undertaken in 1976. The 1976 Act preempted all previous U.S. copyright law, and covered topics such as the scope and subject matter of works covered; exclusive rights; copyright term; copyright notice and registration; and copyright infringement, fair use, and the defenses and remedies to infringement. For example:

(1) The 1976 Act relaxed notice requirements. Thus, between 1978 and March 1, 1989, omission of a proper copyright notice for works pub-

lished under the Act was not automatically fatal to the copyright, and could be cured.

(2) The 1976 Act abolished common law copyrights. After 1977, all rights in copyrights are determined by the Copyright Act.

(3) The 1976 Act permits registration of both published and unpublished works.

(4) Under the 1976 Act, registration is required as a prerequisite to bringing an action for infringement for U.S. works.

(5) The 1976 Act provided a minimum registration period of seventy-five years. If a person is named as the author in the application for registration, the life of the registration was the life of the author, or last surviving author, plus fifty years.

(6) The 1976 Act empowered authors, or certain heirs of the author, to revoke transfer of copyright within a given five year window, beginning no earlier than the thirty-fifth year following publication, or registration if it was an unpublished work, provided that at least a two-year notice is given.

The 1976 Act also addressed technological developments and their impact on what works might be copyrighted. In addition, Federal copyright protection was extended for the first time to unpublished works thus preempting state common law.

The 1976 Act further addressed library rights and provided a major exception to the prohibition on copying copyrighted materials. Thus, materials used "for purposes such as criticism, comment, news, reporting, and teaching," including the making of multiple copies for classroom use, were permitted under the Act. Congress also appointed The National Commission on New Technological Uses of Copyrighted Works (CONTU) for the purpose of establishing guidelines for the "minimum standards of educational fair use" under the 1976 Act.

Selected provisions of The Copyright Act of 1976 are set forth in Appendix 1 and referenced throughout the almanac.

The 1976 revision was also deemed necessary because the United States sought to join The Berne Convention, and amendments were necessary to bring the U.S. into accord with international copyright law. In that connection, the existing dual 28-year copyright terms were replaced with a single "life of author plus 50 years" term.

Nevertheless, because certain provisions in the law were not amended, such as notice formalities, it was not until the Congress enacted the Berne

Convention Implementation Act of 1988, that the impediments for U.S. entry into the Berne convention were removed.

The Berne Convention is discussed in more detail in Chapter 8 of this almanac. Selected Provisions of the Berne Convention are set forth in Appendix 2.

Post-1976 Legislative Developments

Since passage of the 1976 Act, there have been a number of significant legislative developments, as outlined below.

In 1980, a new section was added to the Act which defined copyright protection in computer programs.

In 1984, the Semiconductor Chip Protection Act was passed in order to afford protection to new forms of technology. This Act is discussed in more detail in Chapter 7 of this almanac.

In 1988, The Berne Convention Implementation Act amended those aspects of the 1976 Act which conflicted with the Berne Convention, such as the notice requirement, permitting the United States to gain entry.

In 1990, Congress amended the Copyright Act to prohibit commercial lending of computer software. The amendment contained an exception for libraries and noted that libraries could lend software provided the copy of the computer program on loan by the library affixed a copyright warning to the package.

In 1990, Congress also amended the Copyright Act to ensure that state universities would not be immune from being sued for monetary damages in federal court. State and private universities are now subject to the same copyright regulations, and may likewise be sued for copyright infringement. However, because the eleventh amendment to the U.S. Constitution precludes states from being sued in federal courts, the Supreme Court is considering the constitutionality of this amendment.

In 1990, Congress further amended the 1976 Act granting protection to architectural works and giving new rights covering the visual arts.

In 1992, an Amendment to Title 17, Section 304 of the Copyright Act made copyright renewal automatic, which dramatically curtailed the entry into the public domain of works protected by copyright before 1978.

In 1992, Congress further addressed the fair use doctrine as it pertained to unpublished works, and imposed new criminal penalties for copyright infringement.

In 1992, Congress also enacted provisions which covered home audio taping using digital media. The Audio Home Recording Act of 1992 is discussed in more detail in Chapter 7 of this almanac.

In 1993, Congress abolished the Copyright Royalty Tribunal and replaced it with arbitration panels to make royalty determinations. Under the 1976 Act, the Copyright Royalty Tribunal had been established to determine whether copyright royalty rates in connection with sound recordings of music, and performances on jukeboxes and cable television were reasonable and made any necessary adjustments.

In 1993, Congress also did away with the compulsory license for jukeboxes and replaced it with a voluntary negotiated license. Under the 1976 Act, a jukebox owner was required to obtain a compulsory license to perform copyrighted music publicly on a phonorecord player. The owner was required to file an application, affix the certificate to the machine, and pay an annual royalty fee to the Register of Copyrights for later distribution by the Copyright Royalty Tribunal to the copyright owners.

In 1995, Congress sought to further protect sound recordings by enacting the Digital Performance Right in Sound Recordings Act, which affords the exclusive right to perform publicly a sound recording by means of a digital transmission. Copyright owners of sound recordings were thus granted protection against unauthorized performances of their works.

In 1996, the TRIPS Agreement was enacted as part of the Final Act of the Uruguay Round of the General Agreement on Tariffs and Trade (GATT). Under the TRIPS Agreement, works of foreign origin which were in the public domain in the United States were restored to copyright effective January 1, 1996.

GATT and its successor, the World Trade Organization (WTO) are discussed more fully in Chapter 8 of this almanac.

In 1996, a new section was added to the Copyright Act which permits government agencies and nonprofit organizations who provide special services to the disabled, to reproduce copyrighted material in Braille, audio or digital text for use by the disabled.

In 1997, the No Electronic Theft Act was passed under which the government is allowed to prosecute individuals who "give away" copies of copyrighted works without the permission of the copyright owner, in addition to the prosecution of those who "sell" copies as under the existing law.

In 1998, Congress extended the basic copyright term to "life plus 70 years," and the term for anonymous, pseudonymous, and works made for hire to 95 years from the date of publication.

In 1998, Congress also passed the Digital Millennium Copyright Act, which is further discussed in Chapter 7 of this almanac.

CHAPTER 2:

THE COPYRIGHT REGISTRATION PROCESS

The United States Copyright Office

The United States Copyright Office is the only office that can accept copyright applications and issue certificates of registration. Beginning with the Copyright Act of 1909, copyright registrations gradually rose in number from approximately 100,000 per year in the early 1900's to 450,000 in 1977. The yearly number of registrations has continued to grow. In 1988 approximately 600,000 copyright registrations were issued by the Copyright Office.

Copyright registration application forms may be obtained from the U.S. Copyright Office in person, by mailing in a request, or by calling the 24-hour forms hotline: (202) 707- 9100. Some public libraries also carry application forms. Forms may also be downloaded from the Copyright Office website which is provided in the bibliography of this almanac.

Submitting a photocopy of the copyright form is permissible provided the copy looks like an original, i.e., the form is photocopied back to back and head to head on a single sheet of 8-1/2 by 11 inch white paper. In other words, the copy must look just like the original.

The mailing address for the United States Copyright Office is: U.S. Copyright Office, Library of Congress, 101 Independence Avenue, S.E.,Washington, D.C. 20559-6000. The Copyright Office is located in the James Madison Memorial Building, Room LM-401, of the Library of Congress. Hours of service are 8:30 a.m. to 5:00 p.m. eastern time, Monday through Friday, except Federal holidays. The Public Information Office telephone number is (202) 707-3000/(TTY) (202) 707-6737.

The Copyright Office does not maintain a mailing list. The Copyright Office sends periodic e-mail messages via NewsNet, a free electronic mailing list. Important announcements and new or changed regulations are published in the Federal Register and most updates also appear on the Copyright Office website.

Registration

Registration of one's work with the U.S. Copyright Office is generally voluntary. Nevertheless, registration is recommended for a number of reasons. Many choose to register their works because they wish to have the facts of their copyright on public record and obtain a certificate of registration.

Perhaps more importantly, if one wishes to bring a lawsuit for infringement of a U.S. work, the work must be registered. Registered works may also be eligible for statutory damages and attorney's fees in successful litigation. Further, if registration occurs within five years of publication, it is considered prima facie evidence in a court of law.

To register a work, the applicant must submit the following:

1. A completed application form for the type of work being registered, as further set forth below;

2. A non-refundable filing fee; and

3. A non-returnable copy or copies of the work to be registered— known as the "deposit," as further discussed below.

Generally, each work requires a separate application, unless it falls under the category of a "collection."

The required copy or copies of the work to be registered must be submitted with the application and will not be returned. Upon their deposit in the Copyright Office, under Sections 407 and 408 of the Copyright law, all copies, phonorecords, and identifying material, including those deposited in connection with claims that have been refused registration, become the property of the United States Government.

Deposits

A deposit refers to the copy or copies of the work to be registered that must be submitted with the copyright application. Section 408(b) sets forth the number of deposits required according to the type of work being registered, as set forth below:

1. For an unpublished work, one complete copy or phonorecord;

2. For a published work, two complete copies or phonorecords of the best edition;

3. For a work first published outside the U.S., one complete copy or phonorecord as so published;

4. For a contribution to a collective work, one complete copy or phonorecord of the best edition of the collective work.

In certain cases, such as works of the visual arts, identifying material such as a photograph may be used instead.

Copies of all works under copyright protection that have been published in the United States are required to be deposited with the U.S. Copyright Office within three months of the date of first publication

Because there are so many different software formats, the Copyright Office generally requires a printed copy or audio recording of the work being submitted for deposit. The Copyright Office does accept CD-ROM versions of the work. The deposit requirement consists of the best edition of the CD-ROM package of any work, including the accompanying operating software, instruction manual and a printed version, if included in the package.

Computer Programs

Where a computer program is more than fifty pages in length, the entire program does not need to be deposited with the Copyright Office. Instead, only the first twenty-five and last twenty-five pages of a printout of the source code version of the program must be sent to the Copyright office with the application. These sections may include the copyright notice.

Nevertheless, when an applicant seeks to register a revised computer program, and the revisions are not contained in the first or last twenty-five pages of the source code, the fifty pages which include the revised code along with the copyright notice should instead be submitted with the application.

Sometimes computer programs include trade secrets and other confidential information. If this information is located in the first or last twenty-five pages of the source code, the applicant will obviously not want to deposit these pages, thereby divulging confidential information. As a result, the Copyright Office will consider a request from the applicant to deposit other pages of the code, or less than the fifty pages which are generally required.

Collections

A registrant may register unpublished works as a collection on one application with one title for the entire collection if certain conditions are met. It is not necessary to list the individual titles in the collection, although one may do so by completing a continuation sheet.

Processing Time

The time the Copyright Office requires to process an application varies, depending on the amount of material the Office is receiving. One may generally expect a certificate of registration within approximately 8 months following submission. Nevertheless, copyright registration is deemed effective on the day the necessary registration materials and fee are received in the Copyright Office.

If the registrant wants to know when the Copyright Office receives their material, he or she should send the package by registered or certified mail and request a return receipt from the post office. In the event further information is needed, the Copyright Office will call or write.

The Copyright Office generally does not provide status information for submissions that were received less than eight months prior to the request. If it is imperative that the registrant have this information sooner, they may pay an hourly fee and request that the Certifications and Documents Section conduct an in-process search.

Application Forms

The Copyright Office uses different application forms for registering a work depending on the subject matter. The most commonly used forms are set forth below:

1. Form PA - Form PA is used to register published and unpublished works of the performing arts, including musical and dramatic works, pantomimes and choreographic works, motion pictures and other audiovisual works

A sample Form PA is set forth at Appendix 3.

2. Form SE - Form SE is used to register serials, i.e., works issued or intended to be issued in successive parts bearing numerical or chronological designations and intended to be continued indefinitely, including periodicals, newspapers, magazines, newsletters, annuals, journals, etc.

A sample Form SE is set forth at Appendix 4.

3. Form SR - Form SR is used to register published and unpublished sound recordings.

A sample Form SR is set forth at Appendix 5.

4. Form TX - Form TX is used to register published and unpublished nondramatic literary works, including books, poetry, essays, lectures, and computer programs, etc.

A sample Form TX is set forth at Appendix 6.

5. Form VA - Form VA is used to register published and unpublished works of the visual arts, including architectural, pictorial, graphic, and sculptural works.

A sample Form VA is set forth at Appendix 7.

6. Form GR/CP - Form GR/CP is an adjunct application which is used to register a group of contributions to periodicals, and is used in conjunction with basic application Form TX, PA or VA.

A sample Form GR/CP is set forth at Appendix 8.

One must be careful to use the correct form when filing their application for copyright registration. For example, Form PA is used for the registration of music and/or lyrics, as well as other works of the performing arts, even if the song is submitted on a cassette. However, Form SR is used for registering the performance and production of a particular recording of sounds.

The appropriate application form needed to register a claim for copyright in a derivative work also depends upon the type of work for which registration is sought. It does not depend upon the preexisting or public domain material that may have been used to create the derivative work.

For example, to register a claim for a screenplay based on a novel, one must use Form PA, for performing arts, not Form TX, which is used to register original novels. To register a sound recording based on previously registered words and music, use Form SR, not Form PA, which is used to register original words and music.

Completing the Application

Detailed instructions for completing each space of the copyright application accompany each form. Nevertheless, registration is often delayed because of mistakes or omissions in filling out the form. Following are some of the common items which cause an application to be rejected or delayed.

Author Information

The application requires the registrant to provide the name of the author of the work. Ordinarily, the author is the person who actually created the work. If the work or any contribution to it is a work made for hire, the employer is considered the author. Do not name the author of previously published or registered work(s), or public domain material incorporated into a derivative work, unless that person is also the author of the new material.

Nature of Authorship

The application requires the registrant to provide the "nature" of his or her authorship, i.e. to specify what the author(s) created. Examples include "music," "words," "arrangement," "screenplay," "compilation and editorial revision," "translation," "new text," "dramatization," "artwork," etc.

Year of Creation

The application requires the registrant to provide the year the work was created. The year of creation is the year in which the new work—i.e., the particular version for which registration is sought—was fixed in a copy or phonorecord for the first time, even if other versions exist or if further changes or additions are planned.

Date of Publication

If the work has been "published," as defined under copyright law, the application requires the registrant to provide the date—i.e., the month, day and year—the work the applicant is seeking to register was first published.

Copyright Claimant

The application requires the registrant to provide the name of the copyright claimant. The copyright claimant is either the author of the work, or a person or organization who has obtained from the author all of the rights he or she initially owned.

When the claimant named is not the author, a brief transfer statement is required to show how the claimant acquired the copyright. Examples of generally acceptable transfer statements are "by written agreement," "by assignment," "by written contract," and "by will." It is not necessary to attach copies of the transfer documents to the application.

When the name of the claimant is not the name of the author, but the two names identify one person, the relationship between the names should be explained, for example: "Jones Publishing Company, solely owned by John Jones" or "John Jones d/b/a Jones Recording Company."

Previous Registration and Derivative Work

If the work being registered, or another version of the work being registered, has been previously registered with the Copyright Office, the applicant must state why he is seeking another registration of the work, and give information concerning the prior registration, such as the date and certificate of registration number, etc.

If the work being registered contains a substantial amount of material that (i) was previously published; (ii) was previously registered in the U.S. Copyright Office; (iii) is in the public domain; or (iv) is not included in the claim, the applicant should briefly describe the preexisting material that has been recast, transformed, or adapted in the applicable space, e.g., the title of the previous work. The applicant should then describe all new copyrightable authorship covered by the copyright claim for which registration is sought. If the claim for copyright is in the compilation only, the applicant should so state.

Fee Deposit Accounts

The Copyright Office maintains a system of Deposit Accounts for the convenience of those who frequently use its services. The system allows an individual or firm to establish a Deposit Account in the Copyright Office and to make advance deposits into that account. Deposit Account holders can charge copyright fees against the balance in their accounts instead of sending separate remittances with applications and other requests for services.

Deposit accounts do not operate in the same way as commercial charge accounts and cannot be overdrawn or used as a form of advance credit. When an account is opened, the initial deposit must be at least $250 and all subsequent deposits into the account must be $250 or more.

The deposit account holder must maintain a sufficient balance to cover all charges against the account. The Copyright Office sends account holders monthly statements showing deposits, charges, and balances. Funds must be available in a deposit account for the payment of copyright fees before an application for registration can be accepted or other services performed.

It is important for account holders to keep detailed records of deposits and charges to make sure that the Copyright Office is not forced to delay action on a particular application because of insufficient funds in the deposit account. A copyright registration is effective on the date of receipt in the Copyright Office of all the required elements in acceptable form, including the fee. If a deposit account has become depleted, the effective date of receipt cannot be calculated until funds replenishing the account are received. This is significant because the effective date of registration may have important legal consequences in certain instances.

Further, if there are insufficient funds in the accounts, deposit account holders may have to resubmit claims to copyright by sending another application and additional deposit copies of the work to be registered, as the first deposit copies may have already been transferred to other departments of the Library of Congress and will no longer be available to the Copyright Office, in accordance with regulations based on Sections 407 and 408 of the Copyright Act.

In order to charge fees against a deposit account, the exact name and number of the account must be given on all applications for registration or requests for services. The copyright registration filing fee and the renewal claim filing fee charged by the Copyright Office are nonrefundable filing fees charged for processing a copyright application. These fees are retained for all applications, whether or not registration of copyright is ultimately accomplished.

A schedule setting forth current Copyright Office fees and fee increases is set forth at Appendix 9.

Obtaining Copies of Registration Documents

Copyright registration documents should be kept in a safe place. However, if the registration certificate becomes lost, destroyed or misplaced, a duplicate may be obtained from the U.S. Copyright Office. In order to obtain a copy of one's copyright registration documents, including the application and submitted work, one must contact the Certifications and Documents Section of the Copyright Office and pay the applicable fee.

The Copyright Office will not honor a request for a copy of someone else's work without written authorization from the owner or from his or her designated agent if that work is still under copyright protection, unless the work is involved in litigation. Written permission from the copyright owner or a litigation statement is required before copies will be made available.

Public Domain Records

The Copyright Office does not compile nor maintain a list of works which are in the public domain. A search of their records, however, may reveal whether a particular work has fallen into the public domain. For an hourly fee, the Copyright Office will conduct a search of their records by the title of a work, an author's name, or a claimant's name. In addition, an individual may search the records in person without paying a fee.

Copyright Renewal Applications

For works originally copyrighted between January 1, 1950 and December 31, 1977, the statute now in effect provides for a first term of copyright protection lasting for 28 years, with the possibility of renewal for a second term of 47 years. Thus, if a valid renewal registration is made for a work, its total copyright term is 75 years.

For example, if a work was first copyrighted in 1960, the first term expired in 1988, but if it had been renewed at the proper time, the copyright will be extended an additional 47 years, and will not expire until 2035.

The present copyright law does away with renewal requirements for works first copyrighted after 1977.

Time Limitations for Copyright Renewal

The present copyright statute provides that, in order to renew a copyright, the renewal application and fee must be received in the Copyright Office "within one year prior to the expiration of the copyright." It also provides that all terms of copyright will run through the end of the year in which they would otherwise expire.

Thus, since all copyright terms will expire on December 31st of their last year, all periods for renewal registration will run from December 31st of the 27th year of the copyright, and will end on December 31st of the following year.

To determine the time for renewal:

1. Ascertain the date of the original copyright for the work. In the case of works originally registered in unpublished form, the date of copyright is the date of registration. For published works, copyright begins on the date of first publication.

2. After determining the original copyright date, add 28 years to the year the work was originally copyrighted to determine the calendar year during which the copyright will be eligible for renewal, and December 31st of that year will be the renewal deadline. For example, a work originally copyrighted on April 26, 1963, will be eligible for renewal between December 31, 1990, and December 31, 1991.

Persons Eligible to Claim Copyright Renewal

Only certain persons who fall into specific categories named in the copyright law can claim renewal. Except in the case of four specific types of works, the law gives the right to claim renewal to the individual author of the work, regardless of who owned the copyright during the original term. If the author is deceased, the statute gives the right to claim renewal to certain of the author's beneficiaries, such as widow and children, executors, or next of kin, depending on the circumstances.

The owner of the copyright at the time of renewal is entitled to claim renewal only in four specified instances:

1. A posthumous work—i.e., a work as to which no copyright assignment or other contract for exploitation has occurred during the author's lifetime.

2. A periodical, cyclopedic, or other composite work.

3. A work copyrighted by a corporate body otherwise than as assignee or licensee of the individual author.

4. A work copyrighted by an employer for whom such work was made for hire.

Renewal Application

In order to renew a copyright, the application and fee must be received in the Copyright Office during the renewal period and before the renewal deadline. If an acceptable application and fee are not received before the renewal deadline, the work falls into the public domain and the copyright cannot be renewed. The Copyright Office has no discretion to extend the renewal time limits.

CHAPTER 3:

COPYRIGHT PROTECTED WORKS

In General

Copyright is a form of intellectual property law. An author's original work is considered protected under copyright law the moment it is created and fixed in a tangible form so that it is perceptible either directly or with the aid of a machine or device. Thus, even if a particular work is not readable to the eye, such as a music CD, if it can be perceived with the aid of a machine or a device—i.e., a CD player—it is protected.

Applicable Law

In understanding one's rights in a particular work, it is important to first determine whether the work is covered under the present day copyright law, or whether it is still covered under the 1909 Act.

The 1976 Act specifies that, but for a limited number of exceptions, its provisions are effective as of January 1, 1978. Therefore, any cause of action in copyright arising prior is governed by the 1909 Act. Since there is a three-year statute of limitations in which such an action could be brought, the 1909 law can be applicable in such cases until 1981.

Further, a transitional Section 103 of the 1976 law also provided that no work that had fallen into the public domain before January 1, 1979 could be renewed under the 1976 law. Thus, if publication occurred before January 1, 1978, the provisions of the 1909 Act will generally prevail.

Original Works of Authorship

Copyright law protects original "works of authorship." Works of authorship generally fall into the following eight categories provided the work has been fixed in a tangible, material form:

1. Literary works;

2. Musical works, including any accompanying words;

3. Dramatic works, including any accompanying music;

4. Pantomimes and choreographic works;

5. Pictorial, graphic and sculptural works;

6. Motion pictures and other audiovisual works;

7. Sound recordings; and

8. Architectural works.

Facts, Ideas, Systems and Methods

Copyright does not protect facts, ideas, systems, or methods of operation. For example, an individual may express his or her ideas in a writing or drawing and claim copyright in that specific description, but copyright will not protect the idea itself as revealed in the written or artistic work. Once the author reveals the work to the public, the underlying idea is in the public domain, and the author can only control the specific "form" in which his or her idea was expressed, e.g., the song, the poem, the movie, etc.

Photographs

While copyright law may protect an author's original photograph, it does not protect the subject matter of the photograph. Thus, a photographer may copyright his own photographs of an event, but this does not bar the publication of another photographer's pictures of the same event.

Names, Titles and Slogans

Names, titles, slogans and short phrases are generally not protected by copyright law. For example, the name of a musical group is not protected by copyright. However, in some cases, these items may be protected under trademark law as trademarks.

Copyright protection may be available for logo art work that contains sufficient authorship. In some circumstances, an artistic logo may also be protected as a trademark. For further information on obtaining a trademark, the reader is advised to contact the U.S. Patent & Trademark Office at (800) 786-9199 for further information.

Government Works

Under the Copyright Act, works of the United States Government are not copyright protected. Thus, any booklets, manuals, reports or other works created by government employees in the course of their employment are in the public domain.

Phonorecords or Copies

Under the law, although creation and fixation of a work in a tangible form may take place in a number of ways, the Act generally categorizes tangible forms as either "phonorecords" or "copies." A phonorecord refers to a sound recording—an object upon which "sound" is fixed. All other material objects are categorized as "copies."

Live Musical Performances

The unauthorized fixation of live musical performances was not protected until passage of the anti-bootleg provisions under the Uruguay Round Agreements Act (URAA) in 1994. Prior to the URAA, musical artists had limited recourse against those who recorded and distributed their live performances without permission. Under the URAA, civil and criminal remedies were enacted to try and stop this illegal practice. The Copyright Act was amended to provide musical artists with the right to bring a civil lawsuit for the unauthorized making, fixation and trafficking in sound recordings and music videos, and to make it illegal to fix sounds or images of a live musical performance in a copy or phonorecord, and to copy, distribute or transmit the unauthorized copy or phonorecord.

This anti-bootlegging provision establishes the first departure from the general rule in that an infringement remedy is permitted for a work that was not fixed by the author in a tangible form.

Federal Preemption vs. Common Law Copyright

All state laws concerning copyright, whether statutory or common law, were federally preempted—i.e., in effect, terminated—by the 1976 Act. After January 1, 1978, only the federal courts retained jurisdiction over the copyright of works "fixed in a tangible form."

However, unless and until a work is "fixed" in a tangible medium of expression—e.g., either as copy or a phonorecord—its common law copyright does not terminate, and its federal statutory copyright does not begin. Thus, the following three areas were left unaffected by the preemption.

1. Works that do not come within the subject matter of federal copyright law;

2. Causes of action arising under state law before January 1, 1978;

3. Violations of rights not equivalent to any of the exclusive rights under copyright, such as unfair competition, deceptive trade practices and misappropriation.

In addition, some jurisdictions have held that an oral work may be protected under common law copyright if the speaker clearly intended to create a property interest in the work, but those circumstances must be narrowly defined.

Copyright Ownership

Under the copyright law, the creator of the original expression in a work is its author. The author is also the owner of the copyright unless there is a written agreement by which the author assigns the copyright to another person or entity. In the case of a "work made for hire," as further discussed below, the employer or commissioning party is considered to be the author. The author is free to assign their copyright to anyone. For example, many publishers require assignment of copyright as a condition of publication.

Where two or more persons contribute to the work, and intend at the time the work is created that all contributors will be joint owners of the whole finished work, they would be considered joint authors and co-owners of the copyright.

Original Work

Originality is a constitutional requirement for copyright protection. An original work is one which is independently created by the author, although the work is not necessarily unique. Thus, in order to prevail in an infringement action, the copyright owner must prove that the infringing work (i) is substantially similar to the author's work; and (ii) was actually copied from the author's work.

For example, an artistic reproduction that makes an exact copy of a preexisting artistic work would not be sufficiently original to grant copyright in the reproduction. However, if the author contributes something recognizably different to the underlying work, it would qualify as original even if the contribution may be considered minimal.

Derivative Work

A derivative work—i.e., a work based upon one or more preexisting works—is also protected under copyright law. Because a derivative work generally involves substantial use of a prior work, unless the use falls under the doctrine of "fair use," the author of a derivative work must either use a preexisting work that is in the public domain, or obtain permission from the author of the preexisting work, to avoid infringement.

A Sample Request for Permission to Use Copyrighted Material is set forth at Appendix 10.

Under the Copyright Act, copyright cannot be claimed for any part of a derivative work that has used preexisting material unlawfully. Thus, the person seeking to use the copyrighted material generally requests that the copyright owner issue a license for that use.

A sample Non-Exclusive Copyright License is set forth at Appendix 11.

Further, the derivative author's copyright extends only to those original components he or she contributed to the preexisting work, not to the preexisting work itself.

Compilations

A compilation is defined as "a work formed by the collection and assembling of preexisting materials . . . in such a way that the resulting work as a whole constitutes an original work of authorship." Like derivative works, compilations also make substantial use of preexisting material. However, a compilation does not change the preexisting material but instead "compiles" the material. An example of a compilation is a website directory wherein lists of public website addresses are assembled in some orderly fashion. Again, to be copyrightable, the compilation must satisfy the standard of originality,—i.e., there must be some meaningful distinction between the preexisting work and the compilation.

Exclusive Rights

Under the Copyright Act, the owner of the copyright has the exclusive rights to do and to authorize any of the following:

(1) to reproduce the copyrighted work in copies or phonorecords;

(2) to prepare derivative works based upon the copyrighted work;

(3) to distribute copies or phonorecords of the copyrighted work to the public by sale or other transfer of ownership, or by rental, lease, or lending;

(4) in the case of literary, musical, dramatic, and choreographic works, pantomimes, and motion pictures and other audiovisual works, to perform the copyrighted work publicly;

(5) in the case of literary, musical, dramatic, and choreographic works, pantomimes, and pictorial, graphic, or sculptural works, including the individual images of a motion picture or other audiovisual work, to display the copyrighted work publicly; and

(6) in the case of sound recordings, to perform the copyrighted work publicly by means of a digital audio transmission.

The copyright owner is permitted to transfer any one or more of his or her exclusive rights. For example, the owner may choose to sell their reproduction rights to one entity but their display rights to another. They may also "bundle" all of the exclusive rights together and sell or license them to one person or entity.

Transfer of Ownership

Like any other property, the ownership of a copyright in a work may be transferred, in whole or in part, by any means of conveyance or by operation of law. In addition, ownership may be bequeathed by will or pass as personal property by the applicable laws of intestate succession. Nevertheless, the assignment of copyright does not make the new copyright owner an author under the law, as does the work for hire doctrine.

A sample Assignment of Copyright is set forth at Appendix 12.

Work Made for Hire

A "work made for hire" is a work prepared by an employee within the scope of his or her employment, or a work ordered or commissioned by another party. In the latter case, the agreement that the work is "made for hire" must be documented in writing and signed by the author before the work begins. Work made for hire agreements may include: (I) contributions to a collective work; (ii) part of a movie or other audiovisual work; (iii) a translation; (iv) a supplementary work; or (v) a compilation.

When a work qualifies as a work made for hire, the employer or commissioning party is considered to be the author and owner of the copyright, unless the parties have expressly agreed otherwise in a signed, written instrument.

Nevertheless, the mere fact that the creator is employed by another is not sufficient to create a work made for hire situation. The employee must be performing work that is within the scope of his or her employment for the employer to claim ownership of the work and be considered the author of the work for copyright purposes.

A sample Work Made For Hire Agreement is set forth at Appendix 13.

Formalities of Copyright

As set forth above, the Copyright Act of 1909 required certain formalities, such as publication and notice, in order for the work to be copyright protected.

Publication

Publication was the starting point for determining the copyright duration. Under the 1976 Act, copyright protection began with "creation" of the work instead of publication, thus minimizing the impact of publication on copyright.

Under present copyright law, the term "publication" refers to the distribution of copies or phonorecords of a work to the public by sale or other transfer of ownership, or by rental, lease, or lending. The offering to distribute copies or phonorecords to a group of persons for purposes of further distribution, public performance, or public display also constitutes publication. However, a public performance or display of a work does not in and of itself constitute publication.

Generally, publication occurs on the date on which copies of the work are first made available to the public. Publication is not necessary for copyright protection, and occurs at the discretion and initiative of the copyright owner.

The Copyright Notice

A copyright notice is an identifier placed on copies of the author's work to inform the world of copyright ownership. This notice should be placed in a prominent place on the work, such as on the cover page or title page, so as to give reasonable notice of the claim or copyright.

Under the 1909 Act, omission of the copyright notice on a work had severe consequences. Even if the omission was inadvertent, the author could lose his or her copyright in the work and the work could end up in the public domain.

In 1988, Congress enacted the Berne Convention Implementation Act which amended the Copyright Law to bring its provisions into compliance with international copyright law as set forth in the Berne Convention. A significant formality which was removed was the requirement of notice. Thus, while use of a copyright notice was once required as a condition of copyright protection, it is now optional.

Nevertheless, works that were subject to the 1909 Act and published without notice remain permanently in the public domain, as do works which similarly fell into the public domain under the 1976 Act prior to March 1, 1989. Works which were publicly distributed between January 1, 1978 and March 1, 1989 still retained the formal notice requirement, although it is less strict than under the 1909 Act, and omission of notice can be cured under certain circumstances. For works created after March 1, 1989, absence of a notice means virtually nothing, although some suggest that there may nonetheless be some benefit in displaying a copyright notice on one's work.

For example, innocent infringement of a work without notice is a defense to an action for actual or statutory damages. The burden is on the innocent infringer to prove that he did not have actual notice of the copyright and that he was misled by the lack of notice. The presence of a copyright notice on the work makes it more difficult for the infringer to sustain their burden of proof.

Content of Notice

The three requirements for a valid copyright notice under Section 401(b) include:

1. The copyright symbol;
2. The year of publication; and
3. The copyright owner's name.

The Copyright Symbol

The copyright symbol may be © or the word "Copyright," or the abbreviation "Copr." Most computers include a key that can place a copyright symbol in the text. Nevertheless, the U.S. Copyright Office will accept other designations, including Copywritten; Copyright Pending; Copyright applied for; Copyright registered; Registered U.S. Copyright Office; and Copy.

Year of Publication

It is not difficult to determine the year of publication when a first edition is involved. However, for subsequent editions, it is wise to include not only the date of publication of the first edition but the date of publication of later ones as well. This is because the later edition may be deemed "a new version" by the Copyright Office. If this happens then the publication date of the later edition must be included. However, if it is not considered to be a new version, the publication dates of prior versions must be included in the notice.

In cases involving compilations, or derivative works incorporating previously published material, the year of first publication of the compilation or derivative work is sufficient.

The Copyright Owner's Name

The name of the person or entity who owns the copyright must also be included in the copyright notice.

Unpublished Works

Since notice requirements depend upon the publication date, it has never been necessary to include notice on unpublished works. Moreover, including notice on an unpublished work does not keep an infringer from asserting copyright infringement. However, it is advisable to use a notice so that potential infringers are aware and any "innocent infringement" defenses will be less credible.

Because an unpublished work does not have a date of publication, no date should be included in the notice. Instead, following the copyright symbol and the author's name, a statement that "this work is unpublished," or "work in progress" should be added.

Miscellaneous Notice Provisions

All Rights Reserved

The phrase "all rights reserved" is required in some foreign countries, e.g., Bolivia and Honduras. Nevertheless, there is no harm in including this phrase in a copyright notice even if one does not intend to distribute the work in those countries.

Warnings

It is also advisable to include a warning on one's copyright protected work. A common example of such a warning states:

Except as permitted under the Copyright Act of 1976, as amended, no part of this book may be reproduced in any form or by any electronic or mechanical means, including the use of information storage end retrieval systems, without permission in writing from the copyright owner. Requests for permission should be addressed to the publisher.

Another shortened version of this warning states:

Except as permitted under the Copyright Act of 1976, as amended, this book may not be reproduced in whole or in part in any manner.

Defective Notice

When a notice of copyright is defective because the name or date has been incorrectly stated, the result, while fatal under the 1909 Act is not so under the 1976 Act. In addition, notice is not even required under the Berne Convention. Thus, defective notice, as set forth below, only applies to works published before March 1, 1989, the effective date of the Berne Convention Implementation Act of 1988.

If the work was published in the U.S. before 1978, it had to include a valid copyright notice or the copyright was automatically forfeited and the work entered the public domain. Thus, anyone thereafter could exercise any of the five exclusive rights of a copyright owner with impunity as those rights were no longer exclusive to the original author.

The harshness of this approach was recognized and addressed in the 1976 Act, which gave the copyright owner an opportunity to correct a notice error or omission. This meant that a work was not in the public domain as long as it was (i) registered in the U.S. Copyright Office, and (ii) a reasonable effort was made to add valid notice to all copies of the work which were distributed after discovery of the notice error or omission. If these two conditions were met within 5 years of publication, the work would not enter the public domain.

Further, the validity of ownership of the copyright is protected where the registration has been made in the name of the true owner or where "a document executed by the person named in the notice and showing the ownership of the copyright has been recorded" in spite of defective notice.

Defects due to wrongly stated dates include antedated and postdated notice. When the year in the notice is earlier than the year of first publication, however, the statutory term is computed from the year given in the notice. This applies to anonymous works, pseudonymous works, and works made for hire. When the year in the notice is later than the year of first publication, it is treated as if the notice had been omitted and is governed by Section 405 of the Act.

When the name or date is omitted from the notice, Section 406(c) provides that the work is considered by statute to have been published without any notice.

CHAPTER 4:

COPYRIGHT DURATION AND THE PUBLIC DOMAIN

In General

Since the first copyright law was enacted, much consideration has been given to how long copyright protection should last. Under Article 1, Section 8 of the U.S. Constitution, Congress stated that laws should be passed to protect the writings of authors for "limited times." The concern has been that, although the author is clearly entitled to receive an adequate return on his or her work, it should not be to the extent that the copyright owner maintains a monopoly over the work.

Nevertheless, the duration of copyright protection has gradually increased over the years. Under the original Copyright Act, the term was 14 years, renewable for an additional 14 years. The 1831 amendment extended the original 14-year term to 28 years with a limited 14 year renewal provision. Under the 1909 Act, the copyright term was 28 years from the date of publication, with the possibility of an additional 28-year renewal, for a total of 56 years protection.

The term was again extended under the 1976 Act, which set forth a "life plus 50 years" term, applicable to works created after January 1, 1978. Perhaps the most important reason for increasing the copyright term was so that the United States could gain entry into the Berne Convention which required the longer copyright term. Others reasons given for extending the copyright term included: (i) a longer life expectancy for authors; (ii) the right for authors and their dependents to earn a fair return on the work; (iii) basing the term on "life plus 50 years" was a more certain measurement than "date of publication;" and (iv) the 1909 Act's renewal system was burdensome and costly to administer.

As set forth below, the copyright term was extended an additional 20 years in 1998 with the enactment of the Sonny Bono Copyright Term Extension Act.

A table setting forth the copyright duration and public domain rules is set forth at Appendix 14.

The Sonny Bono Copyright Term Extension Act

The Sonny Bono Copyright Term Extension Act was signed into law on October 27, 1998 and amended those provisions of U.S. Copyright Law concerning duration of copyright protection. The Act basically extends copyright terms for most works created after January 1, 1978 for an additional 20 years. Following are the specific provisions of the Act.

Works created after January 1, 1978

For works created after January 1, 1978, copyright protection will endure for the life of the author plus an additional 70 years.

In the case of a joint work, the term lasts for 70 years after the last surviving author's death.

For anonymous and pseudonymous works and works made for hire, the term will be 95 years from the year of first publication or 120 years from the year of creation, whichever expires first.

Works Created But Not Published or Registered Before January 1, 1978

For works created but not published or registered before January 1, 1978, the term endures for life of the author plus 70 years, but in no case will expire earlier than December 31, 2002.

If the work is published before December 31, 2002, the term will not expire before December 31, 2047.

Pre-1978 Works Still in Original or Renewal Term

For pre-1978 works still in their original or renewal term of copyright, the total term is extended to 95 years from the date that copyright was originally secured.

Public Domain

The public domain includes those works that have become common property of the world and can be used or reproduced freely by all. Thus, the public domain includes most of the world's masterpieces. Because material in the public domain is unprotected by law, its reproduction is in no way piracy. Nevertheless, arrangements, abridgments, or other special versions of works in the public domain may have enough originality for ownership by the individual who created the revised version. Such revisions can be copyrighted, but the original work remains the property of everyone.

In addition, an author's idea, theme, format, plot, setting, characters, and title are also in the public domain because they are incapable of being owned. The person who copies them acts fully within his or her rights because each of the elements is bound to be unoriginal. It is only the specific treatment given it that can be unique, and accordingly, this specific treatment is all that the law protects.

Ideas and Information

An idea is generally only protected by silence, not the law. There is no copyright protection available for an idea until its reduction to concrete and tangible form. Thus, the idea for a new building must become an architectural sketch, and the scientific theory must be developed in a learned monograph. Until such time as the idea is fixed in a tangible form, anyone else can use the idea to his or her own profit if he learns about it. Thus, one should keep his or her ideas, e.g., for a screenplay, a secret until it is written. At that point, the written text will be protected. Others may be entitled to write stories based on that idea, but they cannot copy another's version. Thus, an Alabama Court held:

> It must be understood, however that where the information is accessible to others there can be no ownership of the information itself, but only of the memorial thereof—the collective form into which it has been cast by the labor of the claimant.

Themes

A theme or motif in art is also in the public domain. Thus, a drama on dual personality has been held not to infringe a copyrighted play dealing with the same subject matter. In another case, a copyrighted story about wild horses was held not to have been infringed by a motion picture with the same theme, which the court defined as "the underlying thought which impresses the reader of a literary production, or the text of a discourse."

Only the means of expressing a theme or idea can be protected. In a famous case, the Court described the matter in these words:

> Just as a patent affords protection only to the means of reducing an inventive idea to practice, so the copyright law protects the means of expressing an idea; and it is as near the whole truth as generalization can usually reach that, if the same idea can be expressed in a plurality of totally different manners, a plurality of copyrights may result, and no infringement will exist.

Plots

Plots are as incapable of ownership as ideas or themes. In fact, one critic, Polti, wrote that only thirty-six dramatic plots exist. The courts have gone even further, saying that specific incidents, effects and atmosphere, even similar phrases in dialogue were not copyrightable.

Characters

If an author's characters are undistinguished they will fall into the public domain. However, if they are genuine human beings artistically portrayed, the author owns them. Thus, it is the author's ability to create the character that will determine the extent of an author's copyright.

Copyright Restoration

Under Section 104A, depending upon how a particular work entered the public domain, copyright protection may be restored under certain circumstances.

For example, the restoration of U.S. copyright protection to Mexican and Canadian works under the General Agreement on Tarriffs and Trade (GATT) is part of a trend toward the relaxing of U.S. formality requirements. Before this, changes were only prospective and did not restore copyright protection.

GATT is discussed more fully in Chapter 8 of this almanac.

CHAPTER 5:

COPYRIGHT INFRINGEMENT

In General

If an individual uses a copyrighted work without authorization, the owner may be entitled to bring a copyright infringement action against that person. Section 501(a) of the Copyright Act defines an infringer as anyone who:

> 1. Violates any of the exclusive rights of the copyright owner as provided by Sections 106 through 118, or of the author as provided in Section 106(a), or

> 2. Imports copies or phonorecords into the U.S. in violation of Section 602; or

> 3. Is an infringer of the copyright or rights of the author.

Infringement or piracy is generally defined as "substantial" copying of protected material without the owner's consent. There is no absolute test for infringement. Where infringement is charged, the court or jury may study both works, phrase by phrase, line by line or stroke by stroke, to see whether substantial copying in fact took place. Paraphrasing as well as verbatim copying may constitute infringement.

The plaintiff in an infringement case must prove that the defendant had "access" to the work allegedly infringed. If the defendant produces something identical with the plaintiff's work by mere chance, there is no infringement. Thus, one Court held:

> Borrowed the work must indeed not be, for a plagiarist is not himself *pro tanto* an author; but if by some magic a man who had never known it were to compose anew Keats's Ode on a Grecian Urn, he would be an 'author' and, if he copyrighted it, others might not copy that poem, though they might of course copy Keats's.

Although there are circumstances where a quote or a sample may be used without permission under the fair use doctrine, the U.S. Copyright Office recommends that permission should nonetheless be obtained. The doctrine of fair use is more fully discussed in Chapter 6 of this almanac.

Determining Whether a Work is Copyright Protected

When seeking to use a particular work, one must first determine whether that work is copyright protected. In general, the following works would not be protected and may be freely used:

1. Works that lack originality;

2. Comprehensive compilations of facts, such as the phone book;

3. Unoriginal reprints of public domain works;

4. Works in the public domain;

5. Freeware;

6. U.S Government works;

7. Facts; and

8. Ideas, processes, methods, and systems described in copyrighted works.

Nevertheless, even if it is determined that the work is not protected under copyright law, it may nonetheless be protected under some other law, such as patent or trademark law. Thus, this possibility should be explored by the individual seeking to use the material.

Copyright Notice

The presence or absence of a copyright notice no longer carries the significance it once did because the law no longer requires a formal notice. Older works published without a notice may be in the public domain, but for works created after March 1, 1989, absence of a notice is meaningless, and does not indicate that a particular work is not protected nor that it may be freely used without permission.

Prospective Use of Exclusive Rights

If it is discovered that the work sought to be used is copyright protected, one must then decide whether they wish to exercise any of the copyright owner's "exclusive rights," such as:

1. Make a copy of the work;

2. Use the work as the basis for a new work, i.e., create a derivative work;

3. Electronically distribute or publish copies of the work;

4. Publicly perform the work; or

5. Publicly display the work.

Infringement Exclusions

If it is decided that the individual does want to exercise one or more of the copyright owner's exclusive rights, one must then determine whether their intended use is excluded from liability for infringement. This may occur if:

1. The fair use doctrine applies; or

2. The intended use falls under the library's special rights; or

3. The use is authorized as an educational performance or display as set forth in Section 110 of the copyright law.

Obtaining Permission to Use Copyrighted Material

If an exemption does not excuse infringement and eliminate the need to ask permission or pay fees to exercise the owner's rights, the person seeking to use the copyrighted work must obtain permission from the copyright owner. If one knows who the copyright owner is, he or she may contact the owner directly.

A sample Request for Permission to Use Copyrighted Material is set forth at Appendix 10.

In order to avoid an infringement action, the person seeking to use the copyrighted material may request that the copyright owner issue a license permitting the intended use. A Sample Non-Exclusive Copyright License is set forth at Appendix 11.

Nevertheless, there is no requirement that permission be given in writing. If permission is given orally, it is important to document the conversation and send a confirmation letter to the copyright owner detailing your exact intended use of the copyrighted material.

Copyright Owner Unknown

If the copyright owner cannot be located, or does not respond to a request for permission, this does not eliminate the liability for copyright infringement. The U.S. Copyright Office now provides online searching of some of its registration records and will perform a professional search for a fee, to assist individuals in obtaining accurate copyright ownership information.

Finding the Copyright Owner of a Particular Type of Work

Following are some guidelines to follow in trying to determine the copyright owner of a particular type of work:

Books or Journals

If the work is part of a book or a journal article, one may contact the Copyright Clearance Center ("CCC"). The CCC now offers an experimental electronic permission service and a well-established photocopy-based academic permission service. If the work is registered with the CCC, one can generally obtain permission within 24 to 36 hours.

Freelance Articles

If the work being sought is one that may have been written by a freelance writer, such as a contribution to a periodical, e.g., a magazine or newspaper, permission may be obtained through UnCover. UnCover handles rights for the Publication Rights Clearinghouse, a collective-licensing agency representing such writers' groups as The National Writers Union (NWU), the Canadian Science Writers' Association (CSWA), the Periodical Writers Association of Canada, the Society of Children's Book Writers and Illustrators, and the United States Section of the International Association of Art Critics.

Musical Works

If the intended use is performance of a musical work, performing rights societies, such as Ascap, BMI or Sesac may cover the use. If one seeks to record and distribute a musical composition that has previously been recorded by another, or wishes to synchronize music with visual images, e.g., such as a television commercial, they should contact The Harry Fox Agency, 711 Third Ave., NY, NY 10017 (212) 370-5330.

Playrights

Information concerning playrights may be obtained by contacting one of the following:

1. Samuel French, Inc., 45 West 25th Street, NY, NY 10010-2751, Phone: 212-206-8990, Fax: 212-206-1429

2. Anchorage Press, P.O. Box 8067, New Orleans, LA 70182, Phone: 504-283-8868, Fax: 504-866-0502

3. Baker's Plays, 100 Chauncy Street, Boston, MA 02111-1783, Phone: 617-482-1280, Fax: 617-482-7613.

4. Dramatists Play Services, Inc., 440 Park Avenue South, NY, NY 10016, Phone: 212-683-8960, Fax: 212-213-1539

4. Music Theatre International, 545 Eighth Avenue NY, NY 10018-4307, Phone: 212-868-6668, Fax: 212-643-8465

News Archives

If the work one seeks to use is from a newspaper or other news organization, one should check the internet which accesses many of the largest news organizations. Oftentimes, the organization has placed archives of their back issues online.

Movies

The Motion Picture Licensing Corporation grants public performance rights for movies.

Changed Owners

Sometimes the apparent copyright owner is no longer the real copyright owner due to an assignment or some other transfer. The Copyright Office now provides online searching of some of its registration records and performs professional searches for a fee.

Authority to Render Permission

It is important to make sure that the person rendering permission to use a work is authorized to do so. This is particularly important whenever ownership is not certain, or where a business entity is the copyright owner. Thus, one should inquire of the author whether he or she retained the copyright or whether it was assigned to a publisher.

Permission should be obtained, in writing, and should clearly describe the scope of permission. Vaguely worded permissions may not cover the intended use. In addition, one should describe precisely how they intend to use the work. As stated above, if one is unable to obtain written permission, but receives oral permission, he or she should describe to the copyright owner precisely how they intend to use the work, and should document the conversation in a confirmation letter to the copyright owner.

Royalties

The collection of royalties paid in return for permission to use copyrighted material is usually a matter of private agreement between an author and publisher or other users of the author's work. The Copyright Office plays no role in the execution of contractual terms or business practices. There are copyright licensing organizations and publications rights clearinghouses that distribute royalties for their members which may assist an individual seeking to use copyrighted material in meeting this obligation.

Remedies for Copyright Infringement

A party may seek to protect his or her copyrights against unauthorized use by filing a civil lawsuit in Federal district court. In cases of willful infringement for profit, the U.S. Attorney may initiate a criminal investigation.

The penalties for infringement are very harsh, and are set forth in Section 504 of the Copyright Act:

Section 504. Remedies for infringement: Damages and profits

(a) In General.—Except as otherwise provided by this title, an infringer of copyright is liable for either—

(1) the copyright owner's actual damages and any additional profits of the infringer, as provided by subsection (b); or

(2) statutory damages, as provided by subsection (c).

(b) Actual Damages and Profits.—The copyright owner is entitled to recover the actual damages suffered by him or her as a result of the infringement, and any profits of the infringer that are attributable to the infringement and are not taken into account in computing the actual damages. In establishing the infringer's profits, the copyright owner is required to present proof only of the infringer's gross revenue, and the infringer is required to prove his or her deductible expenses and the elements of profit attributable to factors other than the copyrighted work.

(c) Statutory Damages.—

(1) Except as provided by clause (2) of this subsection, the copyright owner may elect, at any time before final judgment is rendered, to recover, instead of actual damages and profits, an award of statutory damages for all infringements involved in the action, with respect to any one work, for which any one infringer is liable individually, or for which any two or more infringers are liable jointly and severally, in a sum of not less than $500 or more than $20,000 as the court considers just. For the purposes of this subsection, all the parts of a compilation or derivative work constitute one work.

(2) In a case where the copyright owner sustains the burden of proving, and the court finds, that infringement was committed willfully, the court in its discretion may increase the award

of statutory damages to a sum of not more than $100,000. In a case where the infringer sustains the burden of proving, and the court finds, that such infringer was not aware and had no reason to believe that his or her acts constituted an infringement of copyright, the court in its discretion may reduce the award of statutory damages to a sum of not less than $200. . .

Willful infringement basically means that the infringer knew he or she was infringing and did it anyway. In addition, because ignorance of the law is no excuse, even though the infringer didn't know that he or she was infringing, they are still liable for damages. It is only the amount of the award that may be affected by their lack of knowledge and intent.

Further, pursuant to Section 505 of the Copyright Act, remedies for infringement may, in the discretion of the court, include costs and attorney's fees:

Section 505. Attorneys Fees and Costs

In any civil action under this title, the court in its discretion may allow the recovery of full costs by or against any party other than the United States or an officer thereof. Except as otherwise provided by this title, the court may also award a reasonable attorney's fee to the prevailing party as part of the costs.

CHAPTER 6:

FAIR USE

In General

Individuals are liable to the copyright owner if they infringe upon their copyrighted material—i.e., if they use copyright protected material beyond what could reasonably be considered "fair use" without obtaining permission.

The fair use doctrine was first set forth in 1841 in *Folsom V. Marsh*. *Folsom* involved the use of George Washington's private letters in the creation of a fictionalized biography of the President, without the permission of the owner of the letters. The court held that there was no infringement. In handing down the decision Justice Storey stated:

> In short, we must often, in deciding questions of this sort, look to the nature and objects of the selections made, the quantity and value of the materials used, and the degree in which the use may prejudice the sale or diminish the profits, or supersede the objects, of the original work.

Thus, in determining whether a particular use of copyrighted material would constitute "fair use," one must examine the following factors as first set forth in *Folsom*:

(1) The character of the use.

(2) The nature of the work to be used.

(3) The quantity of the work to be used.

(4) The effect the intended use would have in the marketplace for the original.

In determining what constitutes "fair use," one must consider that the courts have repeatedly said that no single factor is determinative, i.e., there is no one fact about the copying at issue that will, by itself, make it fair or unfair. All four factors must be examined, weighed and balanced.

Under the fair use doctrine, it is permissible to use limited portions of a work including quotes, for purposes such as commentary, criticism, news reporting, and scholarly reports. There are no legal rules permitting the use of a specific number of words, a certain number of musical notes, or percentages of a work. Whether a particular use qualifies as fair use depends on all the circumstances.

Good Faith Fair Use Defense

As set forth in Section 504 of the Copyright Act, if an individual reasonably believes that the material he or she copied fell within the "fair use" exception, even if it did not, the court may choose not to award damages to the copyright owner under the "good faith fair use doctrine."

The relevant portion of Section 504 states:

Section 504. Remedies for infringement: Damages and profits

***

(c) Statutory Damages. -

(2) . . . The court shall remit statutory damages in any case where an infringer believed and had reasonable grounds for believing that his or her use of the copyrighted work was a fair use under section 107, if the infringer was:

(i) an employee or agent of a nonprofit educational institution, library, or archives acting within the scope of his or her employment who, or such institution, library, or archives itself, which infringed by reproducing the work in copies or phonorecords; or

(ii) a public broadcasting entity which or a person who, as a regular part of the nonprofit activities of a public broadcasting entity (as defined in subsection (g) of section 118) infringed by performing a published nondramatic literary work or by reproducing a transmission program embodying a performance of such a work.

***

Fair Use in the Library and Archives

Libraries, like individuals, have rights under Section 107 of the Copyright Act to make fair use of copyrighted works. These rights are most commonly exercised in the Reserve Room, where teachers place reading materials on reserve for students to access on their own time. For example, if there are not enough copies to fulfill the needs of the students, the library may be asked to copy the reading materials so that more children can have access to the material. Such copying must conform with fair use principles.

Under Section 107, the practice of making multiple copies for classroom use is an example of fair use, but the provision also requires the user to at least consider the four factors that are set out in the statute before deciding whether a particular use is fair, including:

(1) The purpose and character of the use, including whether such use is of a commercial nature or is for nonprofit educational purposes;

(2) The nature of the copyrighted work;

(3) The amount and substantiality of the portion used in relation to the copyrighted work as a whole; and

(4) The effect of the use upon the potential market for, or value of, the copyrighted work.

In addition to the defense of fair use, certain exemptions are conferred upon libraries with respect to making or distributing single copies for non-commercial purposes. These institutions must be open to the public or to persons doing work in a single specialized field, and a notice of copyright must appear on the copies.

Thus, a purely commercial enterprise could not establish a collection of copyrighted works, call itself a library or archive, and engage in for-profit reproduction and distribution of photocopies.

Even if the requisite conditions are met, photocopying by libraries and archives is exempt only in the following instances:

1. Reproduction of unpublished works for the purpose of preservation and security.

2. Reproduction for the purpose of replacement of damaged, deteriorating, lost, or stolen copies if additional unused copies cannot be obtained at a fair price.

3. Reproduction for patrons who obtain no more than a single copy of no more than one article or a small part of a work, and such copy becomes the property of the user for purposes of study or research, and a copyright warning is prominently displayed.

4. Reproduction of an entire work or a substantial part of it if a copyrighted work cannot be obtained at a fair price, and if the copy becomes the property of the user for study and research and a copyright warning is displayed.

For example, many librarians have had an occasion to make a copy of a book that is very hard to find because it is out of print. Under Section 108 of the Copyright Act, the librarian would only be permitted to copy the rare book if her own collection originally contained the book but it was damaged, deteriorating, lost or stolen.

Patron Requests

If a patron requests part of a book or an article that the library has in its collection, the library must comply with the following provisions of Section 108(d):

(1) The copy must become the property of the patron;

(2) The library should have no notice that the copy will be used for a purpose other than private study, scholarship or research;

(3) The library should have both a display and order form containing a "Warning of Copyright."

If a patron requests that a whole work be copied, the library must comply with the provisions of Section 108(e):

(1) Determine that a copy cannot be obtained at a fair price;

(2) The copy must become the property of the patron;

(3) The library should have no notice that the copy will be used for a purpose other than private study, scholarship or research;

(4) The library should have both a display and order form containing a "Warning of Copyright."

Warning of Copyright

Sections 108(d)(2) and 108(e)(2) require that a warning of copyright be given to patrons in the form set forth in the Copyright Office Regulations. The regulation places responsibility upon the library to provide patrons with specific information about the circumstances under which the library can legally provide the patron with copies and the patron's legal responsibility to use the copies within those boundaries.

Nevertheless, the regulations do not place any burden upon the library to determine whether a patron is making a proper request, nor do they require the patron to provide a declaration of compliance. The library is, however, permitted to deny requests that it believes would violate the law.

The regulation does require that the warning of copyright be placed on printed order forms supplied by the library. Further, if the library provides a form for fax or e-mail orders, the copyright warning should also be included on such form.

Library Photocopy Machines and Computers

Section 108(f)(1) relieves the library of responsibility for unsupervised patron use of copying equipment located in the library provided the library displays a notice on or near the copy station warning patrons that the unauthorized making of a copy of a copyrighted work may be an infringement of the copyright law, according to Section 108(f)(1).

Unlike the form of warning for patrons who request that the library make a copy for them, there is no particular form of notice mandated in this instance. Further, this exemption applies only to the institutions and their employees. The individual user making such an unauthorized copy may be liable.

Audiovisual News Programs

Section 108(f)(3) permits libraries to make a limited number of copies of audiovisual news programs. Unlike other sections of the law that permit copying for patrons, this section does not require that the copy become the property of the patron, so the library can retain and lend its copies.

Audiovisual news programs include local, regional and national network newscasts, interviews concerning current events and on-the-spot news coverage of news events. The provision was not, however, intended to apply to news magazines and documentaries.

Library Reprographic Rights

Section 108(f)(4) states that nothing in that section affects any contractual obligations "assumed at any time by the library or archives when it obtained a copy or phonorecord in its collection."

Interlibrary Loans

Section 108(g) attempts to balance the interests of publishers and libraries regarding interlibrary loan arrangements. The members of the National Commission on New Technological Uses of Copyrighted Works ("CONTU") negotiated guidelines that described what amounts of copying would be "such aggregate quantities as to substitute for a subscription to or purchase of such work."

Reproduction for the Blind

As set forth below, in 1996, Congress added Section 121 to the Copyright Act providing for the reproduction of copyrighted work for the blind or disabled.

SECTION 121. Limitations on exclusive rights: reproduction for blind or other people with disabilities

(a) Notwithstanding the provisions of sections 106 and 710, it is not an infringement of copyright for an authorized entity to reproduce or to distribute copies or phonorecords of a previously published, nondramatic literary work if such copies or phonorecords are reproduced or distributed in specialized formats exclusively for use by blind or other persons with disabilities.

(b)(1) Copies or phonorecords to which this section applies shall—

(A) not be reproduced or distributed in a format other than a specialized format exclusively for use by blind or other persons with disabilities;

(B) bear a notice that any further reproduction or distribution in a format other than a specialized format is an infringement; and

(C) include a copyright notice identifying the copyright owner and the date of the original publication.

(b)(2) The provisions of this subsection shall not apply to standardized, secure, or norm-referenced tests and related testing material, or to computer programs, except the portions thereof that are in conventional human language (including descriptions of pictorial works) and displayed to users in the ordinary course of using the computer programs.

(c) For purposes of this section, the term—

(1) "authorized entity" means a nonprofit organization or a governmental agency that has a primary mission to provide specialized services relating to training, education, or adaptive reading or information access needs of blind or other persons with disabilities;

(2) "blind or other persons with disabilities" means individuals who are eligible or who may qualify in accordance with the Act entitled "An Act to provide books for the adult blind", approved March 3, 1931 (2 U.S.C. § 135a; 46 Stat. 1487) to receive books and other publications produced in specialized formats; and

(3) "specialized formats" means braille, audio, or digital text which is exclusively for use by blind or other persons with disabilities.

Landmark Fair Use Doctrine and Infringement Cases

The following landmark cases established important principles concerning the fair use doctrine and copyright infringement principles.

Folsom v. Marsh (1841)

The *Folsom* case is a landmark case representing the source of the fair use doctrine in the United States. *Folsom* involved the use of George Washington's private letters in the creation of a fictionalized biography without the permission of the owner of the letters. The court found that there was not an infringement and in handing down the decision Justice Storey stated: "In short, we must often, in deciding questions of this sort, look to the nature and objects of the selections made, the quantity and value of the materials used, and the degree in which the use may prejudice the sale or diminish the profits, or supersede the objects, of the original work."

Williams and Wilkins Co. v. National Library of Medicine (1973)

In this case, plaintiffs, Williams and Wilkins Co., publishers of specialized medical journals, sued the National Library of Medicine (NLM) and the National Institute of Health (NIH), charging that the agencies had infringed copyrighted journals by making unauthorized photocopies of articles featured within those publications and distributing them to medical researchers.

The court felt that medicine, and medical research would be harmed by finding an infringement, and since the Copyright Act was at that time under revision by Congress, it was better to allow the status quo to continue in the interim.

Encyclopedia Britannica Educational Corp. v. Crooks (1983)

The Board of Cooperative Educational Services ("BOCES"), a consortium of public school districts, was sued by Encyclopedia Britannica (EB) for systematically taping educational programs that were broadcast on public television stations and making copies available to member schools. The court found that the actions of the school board would have a detrimental effect on the market of the commercially produced programs and that the use was not a fair use.

Maxtone-Graham v. Burtchaell (1986)

In this case, the defendant, Burtchaell, wrote a book that aimed to educate the public about abortions. He sought and was denied permission to excerpt from a book by plaintiff, Maxtone-Graham, that contained interviews with women about their experiences with pregnancy and abortion. The court found in favor of the defendants on their "fair use" defense.

Salinger v. Random House (1987)

In *Salinger*, the second circuit appeals court found that use—not copying but quoting or paraphrasing—of unpublished materials in an unauthorized biography of J.D. Salinger was not fair use.

Feist Publications v. Rural Telephone Service Co., Inc. (1991)

In *Feist*, the Supreme Court found that the compilation of a telephone directory by Feist was not an infringement even though it was compiled from the information in the Rural Telephone Service White Pages. The information in the white pages was not copyrightable because it was public information.

Basic Books, Inc. v. Kinko's Graphics Corp. (1991)

A Federal District Court in New York ruled that *Kinko's Graphic Corporation* infringed copyrights, and did not exercise fair use, when it photocopied "coursepacks" that included book chapters, and then sold them to students for classwork. The court found that most of the fair use factors worked against *Kinko's* in this case, especially given *Kinko's* profit motive in making the copies. Additionally, the court found that the classroom guidelines did not apply to *Kinko's*. The court did not rule that coursepacks cannot constitute fair use in other circumstances.

American Geophysical Union v. Texaco (1992-1995)

The *Texaco* case resulted from a class action suit brought by six scientific publishers on behalf of other publishers registered with the Copyright Clearance Center. In July 1992, a U.S. District judge ruled in the seven-year old copyright case that a Texaco scientist violated the U.S. Copyright Law when he copied articles without providing the appropriate fee to the publishers. Texaco argued that the copying fell within fair use.

The court ruled that the profit motive of the company was a relevant consideration in the analysis of the purpose of the use. They also found against Texaco in considering the amount of the work used focusing on the article as the "whole work" rather than the journal it came from. They also held that the market was affected because Texaco could have paid royalties through the CCC.

In 1994, the U.S. Court of Appeals for the Second Circuit upheld the lower court decision.

In April 1995, Texaco petitioned the U.S. Supreme Court to review the case.

On May 15, 1995, Texaco and a steering committee representing the publishers announced that they had agreed upon terms to settle the case.

The Association of Research Libraries and 14 other academic and library organizations joined together to submit *amicus*—i.e., "friend of the court"—briefs in the case to elucidate and reaffirm the fair use rights that the Copyright law prescribes for scholars and researchers in the pursuit of research and education.

Texaco, which conceded no wrongdoing in the proposed settlement, agreed to pay a seven figure settlement and retroactive licensing fee to the CCC. In addition, Texaco will enter into standard annual license agreements with the CCC during the next five years.

Playboy Enterprises v. Frena (1993)

The defendant, Frena, was sued by Playboy Enterprises when one of their photographs was digitized and placed on an electronic commercial bulletin board system by one subscriber and downloaded by another subscriber. In that case, the court held that the Playboy's distribution rights were infringed.

Campbell v. Acuff-Rose Music, Inc. (1994)

In the *Campbell* case, the Supreme Court ruled that a rap parody of Roy Orbison's song, "Pretty Woman," was a fair use. The court found that a commercial use could be a fair use especially when the markets for an original work and a transformative work may be different.

Religious Technology Center v. Netcom (1995)

A federal judge in California ruled that Netcom may be held liable for copyright infringement because the company did not remove copyrighted materials posted by a subscriber. Nevertheless, the judge further held that Netcom may only be liable for "contributory" copyright infringement, not "direct or vicarious infringement."

Princeton University v. Michigan Document Services, Inc. (1996)

The Sixth Circuit Court of Appeals ruled that an off-campus, for-profit photocopy shop may, as a matter of fair use, make coursepacks that include substantial portions of copyright protected books and sell them to students. On April 9, 1996 the judges of the Sixth Circuit Court of Appeals voted to rehear this case en banc. The effect of that vote is to vacate the previous decision from the Sixth Circuit, leaving in force a previous injunction issued by the District Court. The case was reheard June 12, 1996.

In May 1996, an *amicus* brief was filed in the case on behalf of the educational community by the Attorney General of the State of Georgia, the National School Board Association, the Georgia and California School Boards Associations, and the American Association of School Administrators. ARL filed a letter with the U.S. Court of Appeals for the Sixth Circuit to express its strong support for the important basic principles expressed in the brief of these amici. The American Library Association joined ARL in filing this letter. The ARL-ALA letter calls on the court to take note of the broader issues raised in the case and the significant public interests affected. "If the public did not have the ability to exercise . . . fair use rights," the letter states, "education, scholarly research and the progress of science and the arts would be severely inhibited, and the usefulness—and inevitably the value—of the copyrighted works concerned would be substantially diminished."

CHAPTER 7:

TECHNOLOGICAL ADVANCES

In General

Technology has advanced by light years since the U.S. Copyright Law was originally enacted, and has witnessed the advent of silent films, sound, motion pictures, radio, television, computers, satellites, analog audio and video tape recordings, photocopying and microreprography, and digital and laser recordings.

This list is far from exhaustive. It does not include technological advances presently developing and yet to come, which will bring about even further improvements and expansion in the dissemination of information and entertainment, and the need to address copyright issues in the context of the new technologies.

Clearly, the early copyright law did not anticipate these new developments and, therefore, could not contend with them. Thus, amendments to the law are necessary to provide protection for these new and developing technologies. Some of the most significant amendments dealing with new technology are discussed below.

Semiconductor Chips

Semiconductor chips are basically tiny, integrated circuits contained within a silicon base material. These microchips are used to run all types of electronic equipment, including televisions, appliances, medical devices, etc. The microchip is a three-dimensional pattern made up of layers of "masks" which, when in its final configuration, allows the chip to function. The mask is based on an engineer's drawings of the electronic circuitry.

The creation of a mask is time-consuming and expensive, however, illegal copying of a mask is relatively easy. The infringer merely removes the casing from the microchip and takes pictures of the individual layers, thereby quickly reaping a financial benefit from what may have taken years of costly engineering research and development. Thus, in order to ensure that the creator of the mask receives an adequate return on their work, Congress stepped in and enacted legislation to protect microchip producers.

The Semiconductor Chip Protection Act of 1984

The Semiconductor Chip Protection Act was passed in 1984. Prior to this enactment, microchips had little or no protection. They are so easy to figure out once they are produced, trade secret protection is unavailable. They do not meet the requirement for patentability and, although the U.S. Copyright Office extends copyright protection to the underlying electronic circuitry drawings, pursuant to Section 113(b), it did not extend any protection to the actual manufactured chip.

The text of the Semiconductor Chip Protection Act of 1984 is set forth at Appendix 15.

Under the Act, the mask work sought to be registered must meet the standard of originality set forth in copyright law. Thus, protection would not be available for a common design but would extend to an original work that is independently created.

The owner of a mask work must apply for registration of a claim of protection for the work within two years of the first date of "commercial exploitation" of the mask work anywhere in the world. Under Section 908(a) of the Act, if the owner does not apply for registration, protection of the mask work will terminate.

Under Section 901(3) of the Act, to "commercially exploit" a mask work is to distribute to the public a semiconductor chip product embodying the mask work, and to include an offer to sell or transfer the semiconductor chip product, provided the offer is in writing and occurs after the product embodying the mask work is made.

An application for a registration of a mask work must be made on a form prescribed by the Register of Copyrights and must be accompanied by the appropriate fee and the identifying material specified, in accordance with Section 908(c) of the Act. The effective date of registration is the date the Copyright Office receives a complete registration packet.

Under the Act, mask works have a very different term of protection and form of notice from other copyright protected works. The duration of protection for mask works, as set forth in Section 904 of the Act, is ten years from either (i) the date the mask work is registered or (ii) the date on which the mask work is first commercially exploited. In either case, all terms of protection for mask works run until the end of the calendar year during which they would otherwise expire.

Although notice on mask works is optional, it is nevertheless advisable because it is prima facie evidence that the work was protected. An appropriate notice would contain the letter "M" in a circle, followed by the owner's name.

As with other types of works, registration of the work is a prerequisite to bringing a lawsuit for infringement. There is a 3-year statute of limitations in which the owner may bring a lawsuit. The federal district courts have exclusive jurisdiction over such infringement claims.

The Audio Home Recording Act of 1992

The Audio Home Recording Act was enacted in 1992 in response to concerns by the recording industry over a newly developed digital audio recording technology ("DART") that permits consumers to make nearly flawless copies of prerecorded music. The recording industry was concerned that there would be a wave of home recording that would severely impact sales of recorded music.

The text of the Audio Home Recording Act sets forth a compromise reached between the recording industry and the electronics industry that would both promote the new technology and protect the recording industry from depressed sales resulting from home recording.

Under the Act, copyright infringement actions based on the manufacture, importation or distribution of a digital audio recording device for private non-commercial audio recording are barred. The Act also requires digital recording machines to be equipped with the Serial Copy Management System ("SCMS") which blocks the user from making copies from copies, although copying original works is unlimited.

The Act also sets forth a royalty payment provision for copyright owners and music creators. The manufacturers and importers of digital hardware and blank digital software are required to pay royalties according to sales of these items as set forth in the Act. The royalty system is administered by the Register of Copyright.

The Act also sets forth civil remedies limited to violations of the royalty provision or the SCMS provision, and permits injured parties to bring an action in Federal district court. Remedies for violations under the Act include injunctive relief, damages, and legal fees and costs, with increased damages to repeat offenders.

The text of the Audio Home Recording Act of 1992 is set forth at Appendix 16.

Digital Information Technology

Digital information technology refers to the storage, manipulation, and transmission of information by means of strings of binary code. The difference between the digitization of information and its predecessor, analog technology, is that analog technology embodies an image so that one is able to directly perceive it, e.g., a photograph. Digital technology encodes the same image, e.g. on a CD-ROM. Unlike analog, one cannot perceive the image on the CD-ROM, however, the encoded description of the image can be quickly reconstructed and manipulated by electronic means, e.g. by inserting the CD- ROM into a computer which "reads" the encoded description and displays the image.

The digital transmission of information has made it possible for data to be sent by anybody, to anyone, anywhere in the world. This unlimited transmission of data is accomplished through a series of networks which form what is commonly known as the internet.

Because it is so easy to transmit, receive and manipulate digital information, copyright owners are concerned that their works have little protection in this environment. Although there are so-called technological "safeguards" in place to deter infringement, such as encryption, scrambling, and secure servers, etc., such devices often fall prey to computer savvy individuals who are able to bypass them. Thus, Congress recently interceded and passed legislation to address these concerns.

The Digital Millennium Copyright Act of 1998

The Digital Millennium Copyright Act ("DMCA") was passed in 1998 in an attempt to address the concerns created by digital technology. Title I of the DMCA amends U.S. copyright law to comply with the World Intellectual Property Organization (WIPO) Copyright Treaty and the WIPO Performances and Phonograms Treaty, adopted at the WIPO Diplomatic Conference in December 1996.

Two major provisions in the WIPO treaties require contracting parties to provide legal remedies against circumventing technological protection measures and tampering with copyright management information. To comply with these provisions, Chapter 12 was added to Title 17 of the U.S. Code.

Section 1201 - Circumvention of Copyright Protection Systems

The DMCA prohibits gaining unauthorized access to a work by circumventing a technological protection measure put in place by the copyright owner where such protection measure otherwise effectively controls access to a copyrighted work. This prohibition is to take effect two years after the Act's enactment, during which time the Library of Congress is to conduct a rulemaking proceeding to determine appropriate exceptions to the prohibition.

The DMCA also prohibits manufacturing or making available technologies, products and services used to defeat technological measures that control access. The Act also prohibits the manufacture and distribution of the means of circumventing technological measures that protect an owner's copyright reproduction. However, this prohibition applies only to those devices that:

(1) are primarily designed or produced for the purpose of circumventing;

(2) have only a limited commercially significant purpose or use other than to circumvent; or

(3) are marketed for use in circumventing.

The prohibition on the manufacture and distribution of circumvention devices was effective immediately upon enactment of the DMCA, however, the Act does not require manufacturers of consumer electronics, telecommunications, and computing products to design their products to respond to any particular technological protection measure.

The DMCA does not affect rights, remedies, limitations, or defenses to copyright infringement, including fair use, nor does it alter the existing doctrines of vicarious and contributory liability. However, a defense to copyright infringement is not a defense to the Chapter 12 prohibitions.

Exceptions

In addition to the rulemaking procedure to be conducted by the Library of Congress, the DMCA provides for a number of exceptions to the prohibition on circumvention and circumvention devices:

Exception for Nonprofit Libraries, Archives, and Educational Institutions

Section 1201(d) provides an exception for nonprofit libraries, archives, and educational institutions to gain access to a commercially exploited copyrighted work solely to make a good faith determination of whether to acquire such work. A qualifying institution may gain access only when it cannot obtain a copy of an identical work by other means. The entity is not allowed to use this exemption for commercial advantage or financial gain and access may not last any longer than necessary.

Exception for Law Enforcement and Intelligence Activities

Section 1201(e) permits circumvention for any lawfully authorized investigative, protective, or intelligence activity by or at the direction of a federal, state, or local law enforcement agency, or of an intelligence agency of the United States.

Reverse Engineering Exception

Section 1201(f) allows software developers to circumvent technological protection measures of a lawfully obtained computer program in order to identify the elements necessary to achieve interoperability of an independently created computer program with other programs. However, a person may reverse engineer the lawfully acquired program only where the elements necessary to achieve interoperability are not readily available and reverse engineering is otherwise permitted under the copyright law. In addition, a person may develop and employ technological means to circumvent and make available to others the information or means for the purpose of achieving interoperability.

Encryption Research Exception

Section 1201(g) was enacted to improve the ability of copyright owners to prevent the theft of their copyrighted works by providing for an encryption research exception intended to advance the state of knowledge in the field of encryption technology and to assist in the development of encryption products. Thus, circumvention in the course of a good faith encryption research may be allowed under the following conditions:

(1) the researcher lawfully obtained the copyrighted work;

(2) circumvention is necessary for the encryption research;

(3) the researcher made a good faith effort to obtain authorization from the copyright owner before the circumvention; and

(4) circumvention is otherwise permissible under the applicable laws.

Further, the DMCA directs the court to consider three other factors:

(1) whether the information derived from the research was disseminated to advance the knowledge or development of encryption technology or to facilitate infringement;

(2) whether the researcher is engaged in a legitimate course of study, is employed, or is appropriately trained or experienced in the field of encryption technology; and

(3) whether the researcher timely notifies the copyright owner with the findings and documentation of the research.

Exception Regarding Minors

Section 1201(h) was enacted to alleviate concern that the DMCA might inadvertently make it unlawful for parents to protect their children from pornography and other harmful material available on the Internet, the DMCA permits the manufacture of a circumvention component whose sole purpose is to assist parents in preventing access of minors to objectionable material, provided that the component is included in a product which does not itself violate the provisions of the Act.

Exception for the Protection of Personally Identifying Information

Section 1201(i) addresses personal privacy concerns by permitting circumvention for the limited purpose of identifying and disabling the means to collect or disseminate personally identifying information reflecting the online activities of the user. This exception is only applicable if the user is not provided with adequate notice and the capability to prevent or restrict such collection or dissemination, and if the circumvention has no other effect on the ability of any person to gain access to any work.

Security Testing Exception

Section 1201(j) sets forth a security testing exception that permits circumvention conducted in the course of security testing if it is otherwise legal under applicable law. Security testing is defined as obtaining access, with proper authorization, to a computer, computer system, or computer network for the sole purpose of testing, investigating or correcting a potential or actual security flaw, or vulnerability or processing problem. In determining whether this exception is applicable, the DMCA requires the court to consider whether the information derived from the security testing was used solely to improve the security measures or whether it was used or maintained so as not to facilitate infringement. The DMCA also permits the development, production or distribution of technological means for the sole purpose of performing permitted acts of security testing.

Certain Analog Devices and Certain Technological Measures.

Section 1201(k) contains a provision which specifically addresses the protection of analog television programming and prerecorded movies in relation to recording capabilities of ordinary consumer analog video cassette recorders. The Act requires analog video cassette recorders to conform to the two forms of copy control technology that are in wide use in the market today and prohibits tampering with these analog copy control technologies to render them ineffective.

Section 1202 - Copyright Management Information

Section 1202 of the DMCA prohibits tampering with copyright management information (CMI). Specifically, the Act creates liability for any person who intentionally provides or distributes false CMI. The Act also prohibits the intentional removal or alteration of CMI, and the knowing distribution of illegally modified CMI.

Copyright management information may constitute any of the following:

(1) information that identifies the copyrighted work, including the title of a work, the author, and the copyright owner;

(2) information that identifies a performer whose performance is fixed in a work, with certain exceptions;

(3) in case of an audiovisual work, information that identifies the writer, performer, or director, with certain exceptions;

(4) terms and conditions for use of the work;

(5) identifying numbers or symbols that accompany the above information or links to such information, for example, embedded pointers and hypertext links; or

(6) other information as the Register of Copyrights may prescribe by regulation, with an exception to protect the privacy of users.

The Act recognizes special problems that certain broadcasting entities—e.g., radio, television and cable broadcasting systems—may have with transmission of CMI. Those entities which do not intend to induce, enable, facilitate or conceal infringement may limit their liability in certain circumstances. Thus, in the case of an analog transmission, a transmitting entity will not be held liable for violating the Act if it is not technically feasible to avoid the violation, or if avoiding the violation would "create an undue financial hardship. In the case of digital transmission, the Act contemplates voluntary digital transmission standards for the placement of CMI.

The Act creates civil remedies and criminal penalties for violations of Sections 1201 or 1202. The federal district court has jurisdiction over civil actions, and may grant injunctions, and award damages, attorney's fees and costs. The court may award treble damages to repeat offenders, and reduce damages against innocent violators. The court may also order that the violative device be impounded, modified or destroyed. There are also substantial criminal penalties for willful violations committed for commercial advantage or private financial gain but such criminal penalties are inapplicable to nonprofit libraries, archives, and educational institutions.

Online Service Provider Liability

Title II of the DMCA limits an online service provider's ("OSP") liability for copyright infringement and creates certain "safe harbors" for specified OSP activity. If an OSP's activity qualifies for one of the safe harbors set forth in the Act, the OSP is not liable for any monetary relief for claims of copyright infringement based on that activity and any possible injunctive relief against the OSP is limited. However, if the activity does not fall within a safe harbor, the existence of infringement and any defenses thereto are decided under traditional copyright law.

To be eligible for any of the exemptions, an OSP must adopt, reasonably implement, and inform its users of its policy providing for termination of repeat infringers. Nevertheless, an OSP does not need to monitor its service or affirmatively seek out information about copyright infringement on its service.

In addition, an OSP must accommodate "standard" technical measures used by copyright owners to identify and protect copyrighted works, including, e.g., digital watermarks. Further, an OSP does not have to access, remove, or block material in order to qualify for its exemptions if such action is prohibited by law.

Exemptions for OSP Activities

The two most important exemptions for OSP activities include:

(1) An exemption for storing material on an OSP's system at the request of a user; and

(2) Referring users to material at other online locations by means of, for example, a search engine or link.

The Act limits an OSPs liability for copyright infringement based on the material stored or referred to if the OSP meets the following conditions:

(1) The OSP doesn't actually know that the material is infringing;

(2) The OSP isn't aware of information from which the infringing nature of the material is apparent;

(3) If the OSP acquires such knowledge or awareness, the OSP acts expeditiously to remove or block access to the material;

(4) The OSP doesn't get a financial benefit directly attributable to the infringing material while having the right and ability to control the material; and

(5) The OSP complies with the "notice and take down" provisions of the Act which allow copyright owners to notify an OSP of allegedly infringing material on the OSP's system and require the OSP to remove or block access to such material after receiving such notice.

CHAPTER 8:

INTERNATIONAL COPYRIGHT LAW

Historical Background

As originally written, the United States Copyright Act did not provide any protection for foreigner's rights in their works. Gradually, momentum grew for the grant of some protection to such works. In 1891, limited copyright protection was finally granted to foreigners, provided that copies of the work distributed in the United States were first published in the United States.

Attempts were made repeatedly to bring the 1909 Act into conformance with an international system of copyright protection, enabling works to be protected as easily by foreigners as by U.S. citizens.

Presently, the United States has copyright relations with more than 100 countries throughout the world under which each other's citizens' copyrights are recognized and honored. Further, any work that is protected by U.S. Copyright law can be registered with the U.S. Copyright Office. This includes many works of foreign origin.

All works that are unpublished, regardless of the nationality of the author, are now protected in the United States. In addition, published works of foreign nationals are eligible for United States copyright protection on the date of first publication if:

1. One of the authors is a national or domiciliary of the United States or a national or domiciliary of a foreign nation that is a party to a copyright treaty to which the United States is a party; or

2. The work is first published in the United States, or in a foreign country that is a party to the Universal Copyright Convention; or

3. The work is published by the United Nations or any of its specialized agencies, or by the Organization of American States (OAS); or

4. The work comes within the scope of a presidential proclamation.

There is no such thing as a "worldwide" copyright that governs an author's works uniformly throughout the world. One must look to the laws of each individual country to determine the extent of protection provided. Nevertheless, two major conventions—The Universal Copyright Convention (UCC) and the Berne Convention—which are further discussed below, do provide an author some minimum rights in all countries which are members of those conventions. Nevertheless, the United States does not have copyright relationships with every country.

The Universal Copyright Convention

In 1954, the United States ratified the Universal Copyright Convention (UCC). At that time, the United States was precluded from entering the Berne Convention, the major international copyright convention, because U.S. Copyright law did not conform to the Berne requirements. The UCC was negotiated as a temporary alternative until the U.S. was able to amend its copyright law to conform to the Berne requirements.

The UCC requires all of its member countries to afford the same protection to eligible foreign works as it does to works authored by its own nationals. The key difference between the UCC and the Berne Convention is that the UCC allows its members to require formalities.

For example, under the UCC, published works may still be required to affix a copyright notice, a formality prohibited under Berne. In addition, a member nation may require additional formalities for published works. Unpublished works require no formalities under the UCC.

Under the UCC, a copyright term of 25 years from publication, or life of the author plus 25 years, is a minimum requirement for all member nations.

The UCC applies to all works created or published in the U.S. after it joined the UCC. However, insofar as the U.S. finally gained entry to the Berne Convention in 1989, the UCC only has relevance for works by U.S. nationals:

1. in countries that have signed the U.C.C. but not Berne; and

2. for works first published in the U.S. before March 1, 1989, but not published at the same time in a Berne Convention country.

The UCC further provides that a Berne Convention nation cannot denounce the provisions of Berne and instead rely on the UCC in its dealings with another member of the Berne Convention. Thus, because the U.S. subsequently joined the Berne Convention, it cannot rely on UCC provisions in its copyright relations with a Berne member nation, even if that nation is also a member of the UCC. It can, however, rely on UCC provisions in copyright relations with another UCC signatory, who is not a member of the Berne convention.

A list of Universal Copyright Convention Signatories who are not Berne signatories is set forth At Appendix 17.

The Berne Convention for the Protection of Literary and Artistic Works

The Berne Convention for the Protection of Literary and Artistic Works was ratified in 1886 in Berne, Switzerland, making it the oldest multilateral copyright convention. Berne was a diplomatic joinder of European nations seeking to establish a mutually satisfactory uniform copyright law to replace the need for separate registration in every country. Berne is administered by the World Intellectual Property Organization ("WIPO"), headquartered in Geneva, Switzerland.

The goals of the Berne Convention provide the basis for mutual recognition of copyright between sovereign nations in foreign works and promote development of international norms with regard to copyright protection.

The Berne Convention has been revised five times since 1886. The most significant amendments occurred in 1908 and 1928. In 1908, the Berlin Act set the duration of copyright at "life of the author plus 50 years," expanded the scope of the act to include newer technologies, and prohibited formalities as a prerequisite of copyright protection.

In 1928, the Rome Act first recognized the moral rights of authors and artists, and gave them the right to object to modifications or to the destruction of a work in a way that might prejudice or decrease the artist's reputation.

In 1988, the United States became a Berne signatory with the enactment of the Berne Convention Implementation Act. The Act did away with those provisions of U.S. Copyright Law that conflicted with the Berne Convention and prevented the United States from gaining entry. The major changes for the U.S. copyright system as a result of joining Berne were greater protection for proprietors, new copyright relations with 24 additional countries, and elimination of the requirement of a copyright notice on a copyrighted work.

Every Berne Convention member must afford citizens of other Berne Convention members at least the same copyright protection enjoyed by their citizens or permanent residents. This provision applies to both published and unpublished works.

At a minimum, every Berne signatory must provide copyright protection which includes the following three elements:

1. Copyright protection for at least the author's life plus 50 years;

2. Moral rights for authors; and

3. Some mechanism for free use of copyright protected works.

Of course, each member nation is free to grant even greater rights than those required under Berne.

Berne Convention Work

A "Berne Convention Work" is one which:

(1) in the case of an unpublished work, one or more of the authors is a national of a nation adhering to the Berne Convention, or in the case of a published work, one or more of the authors is a national of a nation adhering to the Berne Convention on the date of first publication;

(2) was first published in a nation adhering to the Berne Convention, or was simultaneously first published in a nation adhering to the Berne Convention and in a foreign nation that does not adhere to the Berne Convention; and

(3) in the case of an audiovisual work:

(A) if one or more of the authors is a legal entity, that author has its headquarters in a nation adhering to the Berne Convention; or

(B) if one or more of the authors is an individual, that author is domiciled, or has his or her habitual residence in, a nation adhering to the Berne Convention; and

(4) in the case of a pictorial, graphic, or sculptural work that is incorporated in a building or other structure, the building or structure is located in a nation adhering to the Berne Convention; or

(5) in the case of an architectural work embodied in a building, such building is erected in a country adhering to the Berne Convention.

For purposes of paragraph (1), an author who is domiciled in, or has his or her habitual residence in, a nation adhering to the Berne Convention is considered to be a national of that nation.

For purposes of paragraph (2), a work is considered to have been simultaneously published in two or more nations if its dates of publication are within 30 days of one another.

Country of Origin

The country of origin of a Berne Convention Work, for purposes of infringement actions under U.S. Copyright Law Section 411, is the United States if:

(1) in the case of a published work, the work is first published:

(A) in the United States;

(B) simultaneously in the United States and another nation or nations adhering to the Berne Convention, whose law grants a term of copyright protection that is the same as or longer than the term provided in the United States;

(C) simultaneously in the United States and a foreign nation that does not adhere to the Berne Convention; or

(D) in a foreign nation that does not adhere to the Berne Convention, and all of the authors of the work are nationals, domiciliaries, or habitual residents of, or in the case of an audiovisual work legal entities with headquarters in, the United States;

(2) in the case of an unpublished work, all the authors of the work are nationals, domiciliaries, or habitual residents of the United States, or, in the case of an unpublished audiovisual work, all the authors are legal entities with headquarters in the United States; or

(3) in the case of a pictorial, graphic, or sculptural work incorporated in a building or structure, the building or structure is located in the United States.

A list of Berne Convention signatories is set forth at Appendix 18.

The World Trade Organization and GATT

There has been growing concern that the international copyright conventions had significant shortcomings, e.g., they were slow to afford protection to new technologies and were unable to enforce copyright protection adequately in developing countries.

Member nations turned to the General Agreement on Tariffs and Trade (GATT) for a solution to this dilemma. The connection between trade and intellectual property protection relies on the proposition that inadequate protection of intellectual property undermines the goal of free trade.

Under GATT, there have been periodic multilateral negotiations called "Rounds." The "final round" was the Uruguay Round completed in 1993, which focused heavily on intellectual property protection. The Uruguay Round resulted in a broad world trade agreement. The World Trade Organization (WTO)—a reformulation and replacement for GATT—was established in 1995 to oversee the trade agreement and settle disputes which arise under its provisions.

Incorporated into the trade agreement were intellectual property provisions—known as the "TRIPS" Agreement—which provide both national treatment and minimum standards of protection for intellectual property rights. Under TRIPS, any advantage or privilege granted by a signatory to the nationals of one country must be accorded to the nationals of all other member nations. This is know as "most favored nation" treatment. In addition, TRIPS provides for a gradual implementation and enforcement of its standards according to a nation's level of development.

A list of GATT/WTO signatories is set forth at Appendix 19.

NAFTA

The North American Free Trade Agreement ("NAFTA") is an agreement concerning free trade in the North American market, including Canada, Mexico and the United States. NAFTA was entered into in December 1993 and took effect on January 1, 1994. NAFTA's goal is to promote free access to the markets of member states by eliminating barriers that obstruct trade among the member nations. Under NAFTA, the failure to provide adequate intellectual property protection is viewed as a trade barrier.

NAFTA provides that each party to the treaty must accord the nationals of the other party the same treatment as it accords its own nationals. As it pertains to copyright law, a significant provision under NAFTA requires signatories to effectively enforce intellectual property rights, including the granting of injunctive relief. Both Canada and Mexico had to make substantial changes to their copyright law to comply with NAFTA's intellectual property provisions.

The United States was required to restore the copyrights of certain Canadian and Mexican motion pictures that had previously fallen into the public domain. Mexican films from the 1950's and 1960's had entered the public domain because they did not include copyright notice or a renewal was not obtained in time.

In addition, it was negotiated that U.S. copyright protection will be restored to many other foreign motion pictures, articles, musical compositions, books, and works of fine art. In return, the U.S. negotiated to retrieve certain U.S. works from the public domain of other countries.

Selected provisions of the North American Free Trade Agreement ("NAFTA") on Trade-Related Aspects of Intellectual Property Rights are set forth at Appendix 20.

APPENDICES

APPENDIX 1:

SELECTED PROVISIONS OF THE UNITED STATES COPYRIGHT ACT OF 1976

SECTION 102. Subject Matter of Copyright: In General.

(a) Copyright protection subsists, in accordance with this title, in original works of authorship fixed in any tangible medium of expression, now known or later developed, from which they can be perceived, reproduced, or otherwise communicated, either directly or with the aid of a machine or device. Works of authorship include the following categories:

(1) literary works;

(2) musical works, including any accompanying words;

(3) dramatic works, including any accompanying music;

(4) pantomimes and choreographic works;

(5) pictorial, graphic, and sculptural works;

(6) motion pictures and other audiovisual works;

(7) sound recordings; and

(8) architectural works.

(b) In no case does copyright protection for an original work of authorship extend to any idea, procedure, process, system, method of operation, concept, principle or discovery, regardless of the form in which it is described, explained, illustrated, or embodied in such work.

SECTION 103. Subject Matter of Copyright: Compilations and Derivative Works.

(a) The subject matter of copyright as specified by section 102 includes compilations and derivative works, but protection for a work employing preexisting material in which copyright subsists does not extend to any part of the work in which such material has been used unlawfully.

(b) The copyright in a compilation or derivative work extends only to the material contributed by the author of such work, as distinguished from the preexisting material employed in the work, and does not imply any exclusive right in the preexisting material. The copyright in such work is independent of, and does not affect or enlarge the scope, duration, ownership, or subsistence of, any copyright protection in the preexisting material.

SECTION 104. Subject Matter of Copyright: National Origin.

(a) Unpublished Works.—The works specified by sections 102 and 103, while unpublished, are subject to protection under this title without regard to the nationality or domicile of the author.

(b) Published Works.—The works specified by sections 102 and 103, when published, are subject to protection under this title if—

(1) on the date of first publication, one or more of the authors is a national or domiciliary of the United States, or is a national, domiciliary, or sovereign authority of a foreign nation that is a party to a copyright treaty to which the United States is also a party, or is a stateless person, wherever that person may be domiciled; or

(2) the work is first published in the United States or in a foreign nation that, on the date of first publication, is a party to the Universal Copyright Convention; or

(3) the work is first published by the United Nations or any of its specialized agencies, or by the Organization of American States; or

(4) the work is a Berne Convention work; or

(5) the work comes within the scope of a Presidential proclamation. Whenever the President finds that a particular foreign nation extends, to works by authors who are nationals or domiciliaries of the United States or to works that are first published in the United States, copyright protection on substantially the same basis as that on which the foreign nation extends protection to works of its own nationals and domiciliaries and works first published in that nation, the President may by proclamation extend protection under this title to works of which one or more of the authors is, on the date of first publication, a national, domiciliary, or sovereign authority of that nation, or which was first published in that nation. The President may revise, suspend, or revoke any such proclamation or impose any conditions or limitations on protection under a proclamation.

(c) Effect of Berne Convention.—No right or interest in a work eligible for protection under this title may be claimed by virtue of, or in reliance upon, the provisions of the Berne Convention, or the adherence of the United States thereto. Any rights in a work eligible for protection under this title that derive from this title, other Federal or State statutes, or the common law, shall not be expanded or reduced by virtue of, or in reliance upon, the provisions of the Berne Convention, or the adherence of the United States thereto.

SECTION 104A. Copyright in Restored Works

(a) Automatic Protection and Term.—

(1) Term.—

(A) Copyright subsists, in accordance with this section, in restored works, and vests automatically on the date of restoration.

(B) Any work in which copyright is restored under this section shall subsist for the remainder of the term of copyright that the work would have otherwise been granted in the United States if the work never entered the public domain in the United States.

(2) Exception.—Any work in which the copyright was ever owned or administered by the Alien Property Custodian and in which the restored copyright would be owned by a government or instrumentality thereof, is not a restored work.

(b) Ownership of Restored Copyright.—A restored work vests initially in the author or initial rightholder of the work as determined by the law of the source country of the work.

(c) Filing of Notice of Intent to Enforce Restored Copyright Against Reliance Parties.—On or after the date of restoration, any person who owns a copyright in a restored work or an exclusive right therein may file with the Copyright Office a notice of intent to enforce that person's copyright or exclusive right or may serve such a notice directly on a reliance party. Acceptance of a notice by the Copyright Office is effective as to any reliance parties but shall not create a presumption of the validity of any of the facts stated therein. Service on a reliance party is effective as to that reliance party and any other reliance parties with actual knowledge of such service and of the contents of that notice.

(d) Remedies for Infringement of Restored Copyrights.

(1) Enforcement of copyright in restored works in the absence of a reliance party.—As against any party who is not a reliance party, the remedies provided in chapter 5 of this title shall be available on or after the date of restoration of a restored copyright with respect to an act of infringement of the restored copyright that is commenced on or after the date of restoration.

(2) Enforcement of copyright in restored works as against a reliance party.—As against a reliance party, except to the extent provided in paragraphs (3) and (4), the remedies provided in chapter 5 of this title shall be available, with respect to an act of infringement of a restored

copyright, on or after the date of restoration of the restored copyright if the requirements of either the following subparagraphs are met:

(A)(i) The owner of the restored copyright (or such owner's agent) or the owner of an exclusive right therein (or such owner's agent) files with the Copyright Office, during the 24-month period beginning on the date of restoration, a notice of intent to enforce the restored copyright; and

(ii)(I) the act of infringement commenced after the end of the 12-month period beginning on the date of publication of the notice in the Federal Register;

(II) the act of infringement commenced before the end of the 12-month period described in subclause (I) and continued after the end of that 12-month period, in which case remedies shall be available only for infringement occurring after the end of that 12-month period; or

(III) copies or phonorecords of a work in which copyright has been restored under this section are made after publication of the notice of intent in the Federal Register.

(B)(i) The owner of the restored copyright (or such owner's agent) or the owner of an exclusive right therein (or such owner's agent) serves upon a reliance party a notice of intent to enforce a restored copyright; and

(ii)(I) the act of infringement commenced after the end of the 12-month period beginning on the date the notice of intent is received;

(II) the act of infringement commenced before the end of the 12-month period described in subclause (I) and continued after the end of that 12-month period, in which case remedies shall be available only for the infringement occurring after the end of that 12-month period; or

(III) copies or phonorecords of a work in which copyright has been restored under this section are made after receipt of the notice of intent.

In the event that notice is provided under both subparagraphs (A) and (B), the 12-month period referred to in such subparagraphs shall run from the earlier of publication or service of notice.

(3) Existing derivative works. (A) In the case of a derivative work that is based upon a restored work and is created:

(i) before the date of the enactment of the Uruguay Round Agreements Act, if the source country of the derivative work is an eligible country on such date, or

(ii) before the date of adherence or proclamation, if the source country of the derivative work is not an eligible country on such date of enactment, a reliance party may continue to exploit that work for the duration of the restored copyright if the reliance party pays to the owner of the restored copyright reasonable compensation for conduct which would be subject to a remedy for infringement but for the provisions of this paragraph.

(B) In the absence of an agreement between the parties, the amount of such compensation shall be determined by an action in United States district court, and shall reflect any harm to the actual or potential market for or value of the restored work from the reliance party's continued exploitation of the work, as well as compensation for the relative contributions of expression of the author of the restored work and the reliance party to the derivative work.

(4) Commencement of infringement for reliance parties.—For purposes of section 412, in the case of reliance parties, infringement shall be deemed to have commenced before registration when acts which would have constituted infringement had the restored work been subject to copyright were commenced before the date of restoration.

(e) Notice of Intent To Enforce a Restored Copyright.—

(1) Notices of intent filed with the copyright office.—

(A)(i) A notice of intent filed with the Copyright Office to enforce a restored copyright shall be signed by the owner of the restored copyright or the owner of an exclusive right therein, who files the notice under subsection (d)(2)(A)(i) (hereafter in this paragraph referred to as the "owner"), or by the owner's agent, shall identify the title of the restored work, and shall include an English translation of the title and any other alternative titles known to the owner by which the restored work may be identified, and an address and telephone number at which the owner may be contacted. If the notice is signed by an agent, the agency relationship must have been constituted in a writing signed by the owner before the filing of the notice. The Copyright Office may specifically require in regulations other information to be included in the notice, but failure to provide such other information shall not invalidate the notice or be a basis for refusal to list the restored work in the Federal Register.

(ii) If a work in which copyright is restored has no formal title, it shall be described in the notice of intent in detail sufficient to identify it.

(iii) Minor errors or omissions may be corrected by further notice at any time after the notice of intent is filed. Notices of corrections for such minor errors or omissions shall be accepted after the period established in subsection (d)(2)(A)(i). Notices shall be published in the Federal Register pursuant to subparagraph (B).

(B)(i) The Register of Copyrights shall publish in the Federal Register, commencing not later than 4 months after the date of restoration for a particular nation and every 4 months thereafter for a period of 2 years, lists identifying restored works and the ownership thereof if a notice of intent to enforce a restored copyright has been filed.

(ii) Not less than 1 list containing all notices of intent to enforce shall be maintained in the Public Information Office of the Copyright Office and shall be available for public inspection and copying during regular business hours pursuant to sections 705 and 708. Such list shall also be published in the Federal Register on an annual basis for the first 2 years after the applicable date of restoration.

(C) The Register of Copyrights is authorized to fix reasonable fees based on the costs of receipt, processing, recording, and publication of notices of intent to enforce a restored copyright and corrections thereto.

(D)(i) Not later than 90 days before the date the Agreement on Trade-Related Aspects of Intellectual Property referred to in section 101(d)(15) of the Uruguay Round Agreements Act enters into force with respect to the United States, the Copyright Office shall issue and publish in the Federal Register regulations governing the filing under this subsection of notices of intent to enforce a restored copyright.

(ii) Such regulations shall permit owners of restored copyrights to file simultaneously for registration of the restored copyright.

(2) Notices of intent served on a reliance party.—

(A) Notices of intent to enforce a restored copyright may be served on a reliance party at any time after the date of restoration of the restored copyright.

(B) Notices of intent to enforce a restored copyright served on a reliance party shall be signed by the owner or the owner's agent, shall identify the restored work and the work in which the restored work is used, if any, in detail sufficient to identify them, and shall include an English translation of the title, any other alternative titles know to the owner by which the work may be identified, the use or uses to which the owner objects, and an address and telephone number at which the reliance party may contact the owner. If the notice is signed by an agent, the agency relationship must have been constituted in writing and signed by the owner before service of the notice.

(3) Effect of material false statements—Any material false statement knowingly made with respect to any restored copyright identified in any notice of intent shall make void all claims and assertions made with respect to such restored copyright.

(f) Immunity From Warranty and Related Liability.—

(1) In general, any person who warrants, promises, or guarantees that a work does not violate an exclusive right granted in section 106 shall not be liable for legal, equitable, arbitral, or administrative relief if the warranty, promise, or guarantee is breached by virtue of the restoration of copyright under this section, if such warranty, promise, or guarantee is made before January 1, 1995.

(2) Performances—No person shall be required to perform any act if such performance is made infringing by virtue of the restoration of copyright under the provisions of this section, if the obligation to perform was undertaken before January 1, 1995.

(g) Proclamation of Copyright Restoration—Whenever the President finds that a particular foreign nation extends, to works by authors who are nationals or domiciliaries of the United States, restored copyright protection on substantially the same basis as provided under this section, the President may be proclamation extend restored protection provided under this section to any work:

(1) of which one or more of the authors is, on the date of first publication, a national, domiciliary, or sovereign authority of that nation; or

(2) which was first published in that nation.

The President may revise, suspend, or revoke any such proclamation or impose any conditions or limitations on protection under such a proclamation.

(h) Definitions.—For purposes of this section and section 109(a):

(1) The term "date of adherence or proclamation" means the earlier of the date on which a foreign nation which, as of the date of the WTO Agreement enters into force with respect to the United States, is not a nation adhering to the Berne Convention or a WTO member country, becomes—

(A) a nation adhering to the Berne Convention or a WTO member country; or

(B) subject to a Presidential Proclamation under subsection (g).

(2) The "date of restoration" of a restored copyright is the later of—

(A) the date on which the Agreement on Trade-Related Aspects of Intellectual Property referred to in section 101(d)(15) of the Uruguay Round Agreements Act enters into force with respect to the United States, if the source country of the restored work is a nation adhering to the Berne Convention or a WTO member country on such date; or

(B) the date of adherence or proclamation, in the case of any other source country of the restored work.

(3) The term "eligible country" means a nation, other than the United States, that is a WTO member country, adheres to the Berne Convention, or is subject to a proclamation under section 104A(g).

(4) The term "reliance party" means any person who—

(A) with respect to a particular work, engages in acts, before the source country of that work becomes an eligible country, which would have violated section 106 if the restored work had been subject to copyright protection, and who, after the source country becomes an eligible country, continues to engage in such acts;

(B) before the source country of a particular work becomes an eligible country, makes or acquires 1 or more copies or phonorecords of that work; or

(C) as the result of the sale or other disposition of a derivative work covered under subsection (d)(3), or significant assets of a person described in subparagraph (A) or (B), is a successor, assignee, or licensee of that person.

(5) The term "restored copyright" means copyright in a restored work under this section.

(6) The term "restored work" means an original work of authorship that—

(A) is protected under subsection (a);

(B) is not in the public domain in its source country through expiration of term of protection;

(C) is in the public domain in the United States due to—

(i) noncompliance with formalities imposed at any time by United States copyright law, including failure or renewal, lack of proper notice, or failure to comply with any manufacturing requirements;

(ii) lack of subject matter protection in the case of sound recordings fixed before February 15, 1972; or

(iii) lack of national eligibility; and

(D) has at least one author or rightholder who was, at the time the work was created, a national or domiciliary or an eligible country, and if published, was first published in an eligible country and not published in the United States during the 30-day period following publication in such eligible country.

(7) The term "rightholder" means the person—

(A) who, with respect to a sound recording, first fixed a sound recording with authorization, or

(B) who was acquired rights from the person described in subparagraph (A) by means of any conveyance or by operation of low.

(8) The "source country" of a restored work is—

(A) a nation other than the United States.

(B) in the case of an unpublished work—

(i) the eligible country in which the author or rightholder is a national or domiciliary, or, if a restored work has more than 1 author or rightholder, the majority of foreign authors or rightholders are nationals or domiciliaries of eligible countries; or

(ii) if the majority of authors or rightholders are not foreign, the nation other than the United States which has the most significant contacts with the work; and

(C) in the case of a published work—

(i) the eligible country in which the work is first published, or

(ii) if the restored work is published on the same day in 2 or more eligible countries, the eligible country which has the most significant contacts with the work.

(9) The terms "WTO Agreement" and "WTO member country" have the meanings given those terms in paragraph (9) and (10), respectively, of section 2 of the Uruguay Round Agreements Act.

SECTION 106A. Rights of Certain Authors to Attribution and Integrity.

(a) Rights of Attribution and Integrity—Subject to section 107 and independent of the exclusive rights provided in section 106, the author of a work of visual art—

(1) shall have the right—

(A) to claim authorship of that work, and

(B) to prevent the use of his or her name as the author of any work of visual art which he or she did not create;

(2) shall have the right to prevent the use of his or her name as the author of the work of visual art in the event of a distortion, mutilation, or other modification of the work which would be prejudicial to his or her honor or reputation; and

(3) subject to the limitations set forth in section 113(d), shall have the right—

(A) to prevent any intentional distortion, mutilation, or other modification of that work which would be prejudicial to his or her honor or reputation, and any intentional distortion, mutilation, or modification of that work is a violation of that right, and

(B) to prevent any destruction of a work of recognized stature, and any intentional or grossly negligent destruction of that work is a violation of that right.

(b) Scope and Exercise of Rights.—Only the author of a work of visual art has the rights conferred by subsection (a) in that work, whether or not the author is the copyright owner. The authors of a joint work of visual art are co-owners of the rights conferred by subsection (a) in that work.

(c) Exceptions.—(1) The modification of a work of visual art which is a result of the passage of time or the inherent nature of the materials is not a distortion, mutilation, or other modification described in subsection (a)(3)(A).

(2) The modification of a work of visual art which is the result of conservation, or of the public presentation, including lighting and placement, of the work is not a destruction, distortion, mutilation, or other modification described in subsection (a)(3) unless the modification is caused by gross negligence.

(3) The rights described in paragraphs (1) and (2) of subsection (a) shall not apply to any reproduction, depiction, portrayal, or other use of a work in, upon, or in any connection with any item described in subparagraph (A) or (B) of the definition of "work of visual art" in section 101, and any such reproduction, depiction, portrayal, or other use of a work is not a destruction, distortion, mutilation, or other modification described in paragraph (3) of subsection (a).

(d) Duration of Rights.—(1) With respect to works of visual art created on or after the effective date set forth in section 610(a) of the Visual Artists Rights Act of 1990, the rights conferred by subsection (a) shall endure for a term consisting of the life of the author.

(2) With respect to works of visual art created before the effective date set forth in section 610(a) of the Visual Artists Rights Act of 1990, but title to which has not, as of such effective date, been transferred from the author, the rights conferred by subsection (a) shall be coextensive with, and shall expire at the same time as, the rights conferred by section 106.

(3) In the case of a joint work prepared by two or more authors, the rights conferred by subsection (a) shall endure for a term consisting of the life of the last surviving author.

(4) All terms of the rights conferred by subsection (a) run to the end of the calendar year in which they would otherwise expire.

(e) Transfer and Waiver.—(1) The rights conferred by subsection (a) may not be transferred, but those rights may be waived if the author expressly agrees to such waiver in a written instrument signed by the author. Such instrument shall specifically identify the work, and uses of that work, to which the waiver applies, and the waiver shall apply only to the work and uses so identified. In the case of a joint work prepared by two or more authors, a waiver of rights under this paragraph made by one such author waives such rights for all such authors.

(2) Ownership of the rights conferred by subsection (a) with respect to a work of visual art is distinct from ownership of any copy of that work, or of a copyright or any exclusive right under a copyright in that work. Transfer of ownership of any copy of a work of visual art, or of a copyright or any exclusive right under a copyright, shall not constitute a

waiver of the rights conferred by subsection (a). Except as may otherwise be agreed by the author in a written instrument signed by the author, a waiver of the rights conferred by subsection (a) with respect to a work of visual art shall not constitute a transfer of ownership of any copy of that work, or of ownership of a copyright or of any exclusive right under a copyright in that work.

SECTION 107. Limitations on Exclusive Rights: Fair Use.

Notwithstanding the provisions of sections 106 and 106A, the fair use of a copyrighted work, including such use by reproduction in copies or phonorecords or by any other means specified by that section, for purposes such as criticism, comment, news reporting, teaching (including multiple copies for classroom use), scholarship, or research, is not an infringement of copyright. In determining whether the use made of a work in any particular case is a fair use the factors to be considered shall include:

(1) the purpose and character of the use, including whether such use is of a commercial nature or is for nonprofit educational purposes;

(2) the nature of the copyrighted work;

(3) the amount and substantiality of the portion used in relation to the copyrighted work as a whole; and

(4) the effect of the use upon the potential market for or value of the copyrighted work.

The fact that a work is unpublished shall not itself bar a finding of fair use if such finding is made upon consideration of all the above factors.

SECTION 108. Limitations on Exclusive Rights: Reproduction by Libraries and Archives.

(a) Notwithstanding the provisions of section 106, it is not an infringement of copyright for a library or archives, or any of its employees acting within the scope of their employment, to reproduce no more than one copy or phonorecord of a work, or to distribute such copy or phonorecord, under the conditions specified by this section, if—

(1) the reproduction or distribution is made without any purpose of direct or indirect commercial advantage;

(2) the collections of the library or archives are (i) open to the public, or (ii) available not only to researchers affiliated with the library or archives or with the institution of which it is a part, but also to other persons doing research in a specialized field; and

(3) the reproduction or distribution of the work includes a notice of copyright.

(b) The rights of reproduction and distribution under this section apply to a copy or phonorecord of an unpublished work duplicated in facsimile form solely for purposes of preservation and security or for deposit for research use in another library or archives of the type described by clause (2) of subsection (a), if the copy or phonorecord reproduced is currently in the collections of the library or archives.

(c) The right of reproduction under this section applies to a copy or phonorecord of a published work duplicated in facsimile form solely for the purpose of replacement of a copy or phonorecord that is damaged, deteriorating, lost, or stolen, if the library or archives has, after a reasonable effort, determined that an unused replacement cannot be obtained at a fair price.

(d) The rights of reproduction and distribution under this section apply to a copy, made from the collection of a library or archives where the user makes his or her request or from that of another library or archives, of no more than one article or other contribution to a copyrighted collection or periodical issue, or to a copy or phonorecord of a small part of any other copyrighted work, if—

(1) the copy or phonorecord becomes the property of the user, and the library or archives has had no notice that the copy or phonorecord would be used for any purpose other than private study, scholarship, or research; and

(2) the library or archives displays prominently, at the place where orders are accepted, and includes on its order form, a warning of copyright in accordance with requirements that the Register of Copyrights shall prescribe by regulation.

(e) The rights of reproduction and distribution under this section apply to the entire work, or to a substantial part of it, made from the collection of a library or archives where the user makes his or her request or from that of another library or archives, if the library or archives has first determined, on the basis of a reasonable investigation, that a copy or phonorecord of the copyrighted work cannot be obtained at a fair price, if—

(1) the copy or phonorecord becomes the property of the user, and the library or archives has had no notice that the copy or phonorecord would be used for any purpose other than private study, scholarship, or research; and

(2) the library or archives displays prominently, at the place where orders are accepted, and includes on its order form, a warning of copyright in accordance with requirements that the Register of Copyrights shall prescribe by regulation.

(f) Nothing in this section—

(1) shall be construed to impose liability for copyright infringement upon a library or archives or its employees for the unsupervised use of reproducing equipment located on its premises: *Provided*, that such equipment displays a notice that the making of a copy may be subject to the copyright law;

(2) excuses a person who uses such reproducing equipment or who requests a copy or phonorecord under subsection (d) from liability for copyright infringement for any such act, or for any later use of such copy or phonorecord, if it exceeds fair use as provided by section 107;

(3) shall be construed to limit the reproduction and distribution by lending of a limited number of copies and excerpts by a library or archives of an audiovisual news program, subject to clauses (1), (2), and (3) of subsection (a); or

(4) in any way affects the right of fair use as provided by section 107, or any contractual obligations assumed at any time by the library or archives when it obtained a copy or phonorecord of a work in its collections.

(g) The rights of reproduction and distribution under this section extend to the isolated and unrelated reproduction or distribution of a single copy or phonorecord of the same material on separate occasions, but do not extend to cases where the library or archives, or its employee—

(1) is aware or has substantial reason to believe that it is engaging in the related or concerted reproduction or distribution of multiple copies or phonorecords of the same material, whether made on one occasion or over a period of time, and whether intended for aggregate use by one or more individuals or for separate use by the individual members of a group; or

(2) engages in the systematic reproduction or distribution of single or multiple copies or phonorecords of material described in subsection (d): *Provided*, That nothing in this cause prevents a library or archives from participating in interlibrary arrangements that do not have, as their purpose or effect, that the library or archives receiving such copies or phonorecords for distribution does so in such aggregate quantities as to substitute for a subscription to or purchase of such work.

(h) The rights of reproduction and distribution under this section do not apply to a musical work, a pictorial, graphic or sculptural work, or a motion picture or other audiovisual work other than an audiovisual work dealing with news, except that no such limitation shall apply with respect to rights granted by subsections (b) and (c), or with respect to pictorial or graphic works published as illustrations, diagrams, or similar adjuncts to works of which copies are reproduced or distributed in accordance with subsections (d) and (e).

SECTION 110. Limitations on Exclusive Rights: Exemption of Certain Performances and Displays.

Notwithstanding the provisions of section 106, the following are not infringements of copyright:

(1) performance or display of a work by instructors or pupils in the course of face-to-face teaching activities of a nonprofit educational institution, in a classroom or similar place devoted to instruction, unless, in the case of a motion picture or other audiovisual work, the performance, or the display of individual images, is given by means of a copy that was not lawfully made under this title, and that the person responsible for the performance knew or had reason to believe was not lawfully made;

(2) performance of a nondramatic literary or musical work or display of a work, by or in the course of a transmission, if—

(A) the performance or display is a regular part of the systematic instructional activities of a governmental body or a nonprofit educational institution; and

(B) the performance or display is directly related and of material assistance to the teaching content of the transmission; and

(C) the transmission is made primarily for—

(i) reception in classrooms or similar places normally devoted to instruction, or

(ii) reception by persons to whom the transmission is directed because their disabilities or other special circumstances prevent their attendance in classrooms or similar places normally devoted to instruction, or

(iii) reception by officers or employees of governmental bodies as a part of their official duties or employment;

(3) performance of a nondramatic literary or musical work or of a dramatic-musical work of a religious nature, or display of a work, in the course of services at a place of worship or other religious assembly;

(4) performance of a nondramatic literary or musical work otherwise than in a transmission to the public, without any purpose of direct or indirect commercial advantage and without payment of any fee or other compensation for the performance to any of its performers, promoters, or organizers, if—

(A) there is no direct or indirect admission charge; or

(B) the proceeds, after deducting the reasonable costs of producing the performance, are used exclusively for educational, religious, or charitable purposes and not for private financial gain, except where the copyright owner has served notice of objection to the performance under the following conditions;

(i) the notice shall be in writing and signed by the copyright owner or such owner's duly authorized agent; and

(ii) the notice shall be served on the person responsible for the performance at least seven days before the date of the performance, and shall state the reasons for the objection; and

(iii) the notice shall comply, in form, content, and manner of service, with requirements that the Register of Copyrights shall prescribe by regulation;

(5) communication of a transmission embodying a performance or display of a work by the public reception of the transmission on a single receiving apparatus of a kind commonly used in private homes, unless—

(A) a direct charge is made to see or hear the transmission; or

(B) the transmission thus received is further transmitted to the public;

(6) performance of a nondramatic musical work by a governmental body or a nonprofit agricultural or horticultural organization, in the course of an annual agricultural or horticultural fair or exhibition conducted by such body or organization; the exemption provided by this clause shall extend to any liability for copyright infringement that would otherwise be imposed on such body or organization, under doctrines of vicarious liability or related infringement, for a performance by a concessionaire, business establishment, or other person at such fair or exhibition, but shall not excuse any such person from liability for the performance;

(7) performance of a nondramatic musical work by a vending establishment open to the public at large without any direct or indirect admission charge, where the sole purpose of the performance is to promote the retail sale of copies or phonorecords of the work, and the performance is not transmitted beyond the place where the establishment is located and is within the immediate area where the sale is occurring;

(8) performance of a nondramatic literary work, by or in the course of a transmission specifically designed for and primarily directed to blind or other handicapped persons who are unable to read normal printed material as a result of their handicap, or deaf or other handicapped persons who are unable to hear the aural signals accompanying a transmission of visual signals, if the performance is made without any purpose of direct or indirect commercial advantage and its transmission is made through the facilities of: (i) a governmental body; or (ii) a noncommercial educational broadcast station (as defined in section 397 of title 47); or (iii) a radio subcarrier authorization (as defined in 47 CFR 73.293-73.295 and 73.593-595); or (iv) a cable system (as defined in section 111(f)).

(9) performance on a single occasion of a dramatic literary work published at least ten years before the date of the performance, by or in the course of a transmission specifically designed for and primarily directed to blind or other handicapped persons who are unable to read normal printed material as a result of their handicap, if the performance is made without any purpose of direct or indirect commercial advantage and its transmission is made through the facilities of a radio subcarrier authorization referred to in clause (8)(iii), *Provided,* That the provisions of this clause shall not be applicable to more than one performance of the same work by the same performers or under the auspices of the same organization.

(10) notwithstanding paragraph 4 above, the following is not an infringement of copyright: performance of a nondramatic literary or musical work in the course of a social function which is organized and promoted by a nonprofit veterans' organization or a nonprofit fraternal organization to which the general public is not invited, but not including the invitees of the organizations, if the proceeds from the performance, after deducting the reasonable costs of producing the performance, are used exclusively for charitable purposes and not for financial gain. For purposes of this section the social functions of any college or university fraternity or sorority shall not be included unless the social function is held solely to raise funds for a specific charitable purpose.

SECTION 116. Scope of Exclusive Rights in Nondramatic Musical Works: Compulsory Licenses for Public Performances by Means of Coin-Operated Phonorecord Players.

(a) Limitation on Exclusive Right—In the case of a nondramatic musical work embodied in a phonorecord, the performance of which is subject to this section as provided in section 116A, the exclusive right under clause (4) of section 106 to perform the work publicly by means of a coin-operated phonorecord player is limited as follows:

(1) The proprietor of the establishment in which the public performance takes place is not liable for infringement with respect to such public performance unless—

(A) such proprietor is the operator of the phonorecord player; or

(B) such proprietor refuses or fails, within one month after receipt by registered or certified mail of a request, at a time during which the certificate required by clause (1)(C) of subsection (b) is not affixed to the phonorecord player, by the copyright owner, to make full disclosure, by registered or certified mail, of the identity of the operator of the phonorecord player.

(2) The operator of the coin-operated phonorecord player may obtain a compulsory license to perform the work publicly on that phonorecord player by filing the application, affixing the certificate, and paying the royalties provided by subsection (b).

(b) Recordation of Coin-Operated Phonorecord Player, Affixation of Certificate, and Royalty Payable Under Compulsory License.—

(1) Any operator who wishes to obtain a compulsory license for the public performance of works on a coin-operated phonorecord player shall fulfill the following requirements:

(A) Before or within one month after such performances are made available on a particular phonorecord player, and during the month of January in each succeeding year that such performances are made available on that particular phonorecord player, the operator shall file in the Copyright Office, in accordance with requirements that the Register of Copyrights, after consultation with the Copyright Royalty Tribunal (if and when the Tribunal has been constituted), shall prescribe by regulation, an application containing the name and address of the operator of the phonorecord player and the manufacturer and serial number or other explicit identification of the phonorecord player, and deposit with the Register of Copyrights a royalty fee for the current calendar year of $8 for that particular phonorecord player. If such performances are made available on a particular phonorecord player for the first time after July 1 of any year, the royalty fee to be deposited for the remainder of that year shall be $4.

(B) Within twenty days of receipt of an application and a royalty fee pursuant to subclause (A), the Register of Copyrights shall issue to the applicant a certificate for the phonorecord player.

(C) On or before March 1 of the year in which the certificate prescribed by subclause (B) of this clause is issued, or within ten days after the date of issue of the certificate, the operator shall affix to the particular phonorecord player, in a position where it can be readily examined by the public, the certificate, issued by the Register of Copyrights under subclause (B), of the latest application made by such operator under subclause (A) of this clause with respect to that phonorecord player.

(2) Failure to file the application, to affix the certificate, or to pay the royalty required by clause (1) of this subsection renders the public performance actionable as an act of infringement under section 501 and fully subject to the remedies provided by sections 502 through 506 and 509.

(c) Distribution of Royalties.—

(1) The Register of Copyrights shall receive all fees deposited under this section and, after deducting the reasonable costs incurred by the Copyright Office under this section, shall deposit the balance in the Treasury of the United States, in such manner as the Secretary of the Treasury directs. All funds held by the Secretary of the Treasury shall be invested in interest-bearing United States securities for later distribution with interest by the Copyright Royalty Tribunal as provided by this title. The Register shall submit to the Copyright Royalty Tribunal, on an annual basis, a detailed statement of account covering all fees received for the relevant period provided by subsection (b).

(2) During the month of January in each year, every person claiming to be entitled to compulsory license fees under this section for performances during the preceding twelve-month period shall file a claim with the Copyright Royalty Tribunal, in accordance with requirements that the Tribunal shall prescribe by regulation. Such claim shall include an agreement to accept as final, except as provided in section 810 of this title, the determination of the Copyright Royalty Tribunal in any controversy concerning the distribution of royalty fees deposited under subclause (A) of subsection (b)(1) of this section to which the claimant

is a party. Notwithstanding any provisions of the antitrust laws, for purposes of this subsection any claimants may agree among themselves as to the proportionate division of compulsory licensing fees among them, may lump their claims together and file them jointly or as a single claim, or may designate a common agent to receive payment on their behalf.

(3) After the first day of October of each year, the Copyright Royalty Tribunal shall determine whether there exists a controversy concerning the distribution of royalty fees deposited under subclause (A) of subsection (b)(1). If the Tribunal determines that no such controversy exists, it shall, after deducting its reasonable administrative costs under this section, distribute such fees to the copyright owners entitled, or to their designated agents. If it finds that such a controversy exists, it shall, pursuant to chapter 8 of this title, conduct a proceeding to determine the distribution of royalty fees.

(4) The fees to be distributed shall be divided as follows:

(A) to every copyright owner not affiliated with a performing rights society, the pro rata share of the fees to be distributed to which such copyright owner proves entitlement.

(B) to the performing rights societies, the remainder of the fees to be distributed in such pro rata shares as they shall by agreement stipulate among themselves, or, if they fail to agree, the pro rata share to which such performing rights societies prove entitlement.

(C) during the pendency of any proceeding under this section, the Copyright Royalty Tribunal shall withhold from distribution an amount sufficient to satisfy all claims with respect to which a controversy exists, but shall have discretion to proceed to distribute any amounts that are not in controversy.

(5) The Copyright Royalty Tribunal shall promulgate regulations under which persons who can reasonably be expected to have claims may, during the year in which performances take place, without expense to or harassment of operators or proprietors of establishments in which phonorecord players are located, have such access to such establishments and to the phonorecord players located therein and such opportunity to obtain information with respect thereto as may be reasonably necessary to determine, by sampling procedures or otherwise, the proportion of contribution of the musical works of each such person to the earnings of the phonorecord players for which fees shall have been deposited. Any person who alleges that he or she has been denied the access permitted under the regulations prescribed by the Copyright Royalty Tribunal may bring an action in the United States District

Court for the District of Columbia for the cancellation of the compulsory license of the phonorecord player to which such access has been denied, and the court shall have the power to declare the compulsory license thereof invalid from the date of issue thereof.

(d) Criminal Penalties—Any person who knowingly makes a false representation of a material fact in an application filed under clause (1)(A) of subsection (b), or who knowingly alters a certificate issued under clause (1)(B) of subsection (b) or knowingly affixes such certificate to a phonorecord player other than the one it covers, shall be fined not more than $2,500.

(e) Definitions—As used in this section and section 116A, the following terms and their variant forms mean the following:

(1) A "coin-operated phonorecord player" is a machine or device that—

(A) is employed solely for the performance of non-dramatic musical works by means of phonorecords upon being activated by insertion of coins, currency, tokens, or other monetary units or their equivalent;

(B) is located in an establishment making no direct or indirect charge for admission;

(C) is accompanied by a list of the titles of all the musical works available for performance on it, which list is affixed to the phonorecord player or posted in the establishment in a prominent position where it can be readily examined by the public; and

(D) affords a choice of works available for performance and permits the choice to be made by the patrons of the establishment in which it is located.

(2) An "operator" is any person who, alone or jointly with others:

(A) owns a coin-operated phonorecord player, or

(B) has the power to make a coin-operated phonorecord player available for placement in an establishment for purpose of public performance; or

(C) has the power to exercise primary control over the selection of the musical works made available for public performance on a coin-operated phonorecord player.

(3) A "performing rights society" is an association or corporation that licenses the public performance of nondramatic musical works on behalf

of the copyright owners, such as the American Society of composers, Authors and Publishers, Broadcast Music, Inc., and SESAC, Inc.

CHAPTER 2. COPYRIGHT OWNERSHIP AND TRANSFER

SECTION 201. Ownership of Copyright.

(a) Works made for Hire—In the case of a work made for hire, the employer or other person for whom the work was prepared is considered the author for purposes of this title, and unless the parties have expressly agreed otherwise in a written instrument signed by them, owns all of the rights comprised in the copyright.

SECTION 203. Termination of Transfers and Licenses Granted by the Author.

(a) Conditions for Termination—In the case of any work other than a work made for hire, the exclusive or nonexclusive grant of a transfer or license of copyright or of any right under a copyright, executed by the author on or after January 1, 1978, otherwise than by will, is subject to termination under the following conditions:

(1) In the case of a grant executed by one author, termination of the grant may be effected by that author or, if the author is dead, by the person or persons who, under clause (2) of this subsection, own and are entitled to exercise a total of more than one-half of that author's termination interest. In the case of a grant executed by two or more authors of a joint work, termination of the grant may be effected by a majority of the authors who executed it; if any of such authors is dead, the termination interest of any such author may be exercised as a unit by the person or persons who, under clause (2) of this subsection, own and are entitled to exercise a total of more than one-half of that author's interest.

(2) Where an author is dead, his or her termination interest is owned, and may be exercised, by his widow or her widower and his or her children or grandchildren as follows:

(A) the widow or widower owns the author's entire termination interest unless there are any surviving children or grandchildren of the author, in which case the widow or widower owns one-half of the author's interest;

(B) the author's surviving children, and the surviving children of any dead child of the author, own the author's entire termination interest unless there is a widow or widower, in which case the owner-ship of one-half of the author's interest is divided among them;

(C) the rights of the author's children and grandchildren are in all cases divided among them and exercised on a per stirpes basis ac-cording to the number of such author's children represented; the share of the children of a dead child in a termination interest can be exercised only by the action of a majority of them.

(3) Termination of the grant may be effected at any time during a pe-riod of five years beginning at the end of thirty-five years from the date of execution of the grant; or, if the grant covers the right of publication of the work, the period begins at the end of thirty-five years from the date of publication of the work under the grant or at the end of forty years from the date of execution of the grant, whichever term ends earlier.

(4) The termination shall be effected by serving an advance notice in writing, signed by the number and proportion of owners of termina-tion interests required under clauses (1) and (2) of this subsection, or by their duly authorized agents, upon the grantee or the grantee's suc-cessor in title.

(A) The notice shall state the effective date of the termination, which shall fall within the five-year period specified by clause (3) of this subsection, and the notice shall be served not less than two or more than ten years before that date. A copy of the notice shall be re-corded in the Copyright Office before the effective date of termina-tion, as a condition to its taking effect.

(B) The notice shall comply, in form, content, and manner of serv-ice, with requirements that the Register of Copyrights shall prescribe by regulation.

(5) Termination of the grant may be effected notwithstanding any agreement to the contrary, including an agreement to make a will or to make any future grant.

(b) Effect of Termination—Upon the effective date of termination, all rights under this title that were covered by the terminated grants revert to the author, authors, and other persons owning termination interests under clauses (1) and (2) of subsection (a), including those owners who did not join in signing the notice of termination under clause (4) of subsection (a), but with the following limitations:

(1) A derivative work prepared under authority of the grant before its termination may continue to be utilized under the terms of the grant after its termination, but this privilege does not extend to the preparation after

the termination of other derivative works based upon the copyrighted work covered by the terminated grant.

(2) The future rights that will revert upon termination of the grant become vested on the date the notice of termination has been served as provided by clause (4) of subsection (a). The rights vest in the author, authors, and other persons named in, and in the proportionate shares provided by, clauses (1) and (2) of subsection (a).

(3) Subject to the provisions of clause (4) of this subsection, a further grant, or agreement to make a further grant, of any right covered by a terminated grant is valid only if it is signed by the same number and proportion of the owners, in whom the right has vested under clause (2) of this subsection, as are required to terminate the grant under clauses (1) and (2) of subsection (a). Such further grant or agreement is effective with respect to all of the persons in whom the right it covers has vested under clause (2) of this subsection, including those who did not join in signing it. If any person dies after rights under a terminated grant have vested in him or her, that person's legal representatives, legatees, or heirs at law represent him or her for purposes of this clause.

(4) A further grant, or agreement to make a further grant, of any right covered by a terminated grant is valid only if it is made after the effective date of the termination. As an exception, however, an agreement for such a further grant may be made between the persons provided by clause (3) of this subsection and the original grantee or such grantee's successor in title, after the notice of termination has been served as provided by clause (4) of subsection (a).

(5) Termination of a grant under this section affects only those rights covered by the grants that arise under this title, and in no way affects rights arising under any other Federal, State, or foreign laws.

(6) Unless and until termination is affected under this section, the grant, if it does not provide otherwise, continues in effect for the term of copyright provided by this title.

CHAPTER 3. DURATION OF COPYRIGHT

SECTION 301. Duration of Copyright: Preemption With Respect to Other Laws.

(a) On and after January 1, 1978, all legal or equitable rights that are equivalent to any of the exclusive rights within the general scope of copyright as specified by section 106 in works of authorship that are fixed in a tangible medium of expression and come within the subject matter of copyright as specified by sections 102 and 103, whether created before or after the date and whether published or unpublished, are governed exclusively by this title. Thereafter, no person is entitled to any such right or equivalent right in any such work under the common law or statutes of any State.

(b) Nothing in this title annuls or limits any rights or remedies under the common law or statutes of any State with respect to—

(1) subject matter that does not come within the subject matter of copyright as specified by sections 102 and 103, including works of authorship not fixed in any tangible medium of expression; or

(2) any cause of action arising from undertakings commenced before January 1, 1978;

(3) activities violating legal or equitable rights that are not equivalent to any of the exclusive rights within the general scope of copyright as specified by section 106; or

(4) State and local landmarks, historic preservation, zoning, or building codes, relating to architectural works protected under section 102(a)(8).

(c) With respect to sound recordings fixed before February 15, 1972, any rights or remedies under the common law or statutes of any State shall not be annulled or limited by this title until February 15, 2047. The preemptive provisions of subsection (a) shall apply to any such rights and remedies pertaining to any cause of action arising from undertakings commenced on and after February 15, 2047. Notwithstanding the provisions of section 303, no sound recording fixed before February 15, 1972, shall be subject to copyright under this title before, on, or after February 15, 2047.

(d) Nothing in this title annuls or limits any rights or remedies under any other Federal statute.

(e) The scope of Federal preemption under this section is not affected by the adherence of the United States to the Berne Convention or the satisfaction of obligations of the United States thereunder.

(f)(1) On or after the effective date set forth in section 610(a) of the Visual Artists Rights Act of 1990, all legal or equitable rights that are equivalent to any of the rights conferred by section 106A with respect to works of visual art to which the rights conferred by section 106A apply are governed exclusively by section 106A and section 113(d) and the provisions of this title relating to such sections. Thereafter, no person is entitled to any such right or equivalent right in any work of visual art under the common law or statutes of any State.

(2) Nothing in paragraph (1) annuls or limits any rights or remedies under the common law or statutes of any State with respect to—

(A) any cause of action from undertakings commenced before the effective date set forth in section 610(a) of the Visual Artists Rights Act of 1990;

(B) activities violating legal or equitable rights that are not equivalent to any of the rights conferred by section 106A with respect to works of visual art; or

(C) activities violating legal or equitable rights which extend beyond the life of the author.

SECTION 302. Duration of Copyright: Works Created on or After January 1, 1978.

(a) In General—Copyright in a work created on or after January 1, 1978, subsists from its creation and, except as provided by the following subsections, endures for a term consisting of the life of the author and fifty years after the author's death.

(b) Joint Works—In the case of a joint work prepared by two or more authors who did not work for hire, the copyright endures for a term consisting of the life of the last surviving author and fifty years after such last surviving author's death.

CHAPTER 4. COPYRIGHT NOTICE, DEPOSIT, AND REGISTRATION

SECTION 401. Notice of Copyright: Visually Perceptible Copies.

(a) General Provisions—Whenever a work protected under this title is published in the United States or elsewhere by authority of the copyright owner, a notice of copyright as provided by this section may be placed on publicly distributed copies from which the work can be visually perceived, either directly or with the aid of a machine or device.

(b) Form of Notice—If a notice appears on the copies, it shall consist of the following three elements:

(1) the symbol (c) (the letter C in a circle), or the word "Copyright", or the abbreviation "Copr."; and

(2) the year of first publication of the work; in the case of compilations or derivative works incorporating previously published material, the year date of first publication of the compilation or derivative work is sufficient. The year date may be omitted where a pictorial, graphic, or

sculptural work, with accompanying text matter, if any, is reproduced in or on greeting cards, postcards, stationary, jewelry, dolls, toys, or any useful articles; and

(3) the name of the owner of copyright in the work, or an abbreviation by which the name can be recognized, or a generally known alternative designation of the owner.

(c) Position of Notice—The notice shall be affixed to the copies in such manner and location as to give reasonable notice of the claim of copyright. The Register of Copyrights shall prescribe by regulation, as examples, specific methods of affixation and positions of the notice on various types of works that will satisfy this requirement, but these specifications shall not be considered exhaustive.

(d) Evidentiary Weight of Notice—If a notice of copyright in the form and position specified by this section appears on the published copy or copies to which a defendant in a copyright infringement suit had access, then no weight shall be given to such a defendant's interposition of a defense based on innocent infringement in mitigation of actual or statutory damages, except as provided in the last sentence of section 504(c)(2).

SECTION 402. Notice of Copyright: Phonorecords of Sound Recordings

(a) General Provisions—Whenever a sound recording protected under this title is published in the United States or elsewhere by authority of the copyright owner, a notice of copyright as provided by this section may be placed on publicly distributed phonorecords of the sound recording.

(b) Form of Notice—If a notice appears on the phonorecords, it shall consist of the following three elements:

(1) the symbol P (the letter P in a circle); and

(2) the year of first publication of the sound recording; and

(3) the name of the owner of copyright in the sound recording, or an abbreviation by which the name can be recognized, or a generally known alternative designation of the owner; if the producer of the sound recording is named on the phonorecord labels or containers, and if no other name appears in conjunction with the notice, the producer's name shall be considered a part of the notice.

(c) Position of Notice—The notice shall be placed on the surface of the phonorecord, or on the phonorecord label or container, in such manner and location as to give reasonable notice of the claim of copyright.

(d) Evidentiary Weight of Notice—If a notice of copyright in the form and position specified by this section appears on the published phonorecord or phonorecords to which a defendant in a copyright infringement suit had access, then no weight shall be given to such a defendant's interposition of a defense based on innocent infringement in mitigation of actual or statutory damages, except as provided in the last sentence of section 504(c)(2).

SECTION 403. Notice of Copyright: Publications Incorporating United States Government Works

Sections 401(d) and 402(d) shall not apply to a work published in copies or phonorecords consisting predominantly of one or more works of the United States Government unless the notice of copyright appearing on the published copies or phonorecords to which a defendant in the copyright infringement suit had access includes a statement identifying, either affirmatively or negatively, those portions of the copies or phonorecords embodying any work or works protected under this title.

SECTION 404. Notice of Copyright: Contributions to Collective Works

(a) A separate contribution to a collective work may bear its own notice of copyright, as provided by sections 401 through 403. However, a single notice applicable to the collective work as a whole is sufficient to invoke the provisions of section 401(d) or 402(d) as applicable with respect to the separate contributions it contains (not including advertisements inserted on behalf of persons other than the owner of copyright in the collective work), regardless of the ownership of copyright in the contributions and whether or not they have been previously published.

(b) With respect to copies and phonorecords publicly distributed by authority of the copyright owner before the effective date of the Berne Convention Implementation Act of 1988, where the person named in a single notice applicable to a collective work as a whole is not the owner of copyright in a separate contribution that does not bear its own notice, the case is governed by the provisions of section 406(a).

SECTION 405. Notice of Copyright: Omission of Notice on Certain Copies and Phonorecords

(a) Effect of Omission on Copyright—With respect to copies and phonorecords publicly distributed by authority of the copyright owner before the effective date of the Berne Convention Implementation Act of 1988, the omission of the copyright notice described in sections 401 through 403 from copies or phonorecords publicly distributed by authority of the copyright owner does not invalidate the copyright in a work if—

(1) the notice has been omitted from no more than a relatively small number of copies or phonorecords distributed to the public; or

(2) registration for the work has been made before or is made within five years after the publication without notice, and a reasonable effort is made to add notice to all copies or phonorecords that are distributed to the public in the United States after the omission has been discovered; or

(3) the notice has been omitted in violation of an express requirement in writing that, as a condition of the copyright owner's authorization of the public distribution of copies or phonorecords, they bear the prescribed notice.

(b) Effect of Omission on Innocent Infringers—Any person who innocently infringes a copyright, in reliance upon an authorized copy or phonorecord from which the copyright notice has been omitted and which was publicly distributed by authority of the copyright owner before the effective date of the Berne Convention Implementation Act of 1988, incurs no liability for actual or statutory damages under section 504 for any infringing acts committed before receiving actual notice that registration for the work has been made under section 408, if such person proves that he or she was misled by the omission of notice. In a suit for infringement in such a case the court may allow or disallow recovery of any of the infringer's profits attributable to the infringement, and may enjoin the continuation of the infringing undertaking or may require, as a condition or permitting the continuation of the infringing undertaking, that the infringer pay the copyright owner a reasonable license fee in an amount and on terms fixed by the court.

(c) Removal of Notice—Protection under this title is not affected by the removal, destruction, or obliteration of the notice, without the authorization of the copyright owner, from any publicly distributed copies or phonorecords.

SECTION 406. Notice of Copyright: Error in Name or Date on Certain Copies and Phonorecords

(a) Error in Name—With respect to copies and phonorecords publicly distributed by authority of the copyright owner before the effective date of the Berne Convention Implementation Act of 1988, where the person named in the copyright notice on copies or phonorecords publicly distributed by authority of the copyright owner is not the owner of copyright, the validity and ownership of the copyright are not affected. In such a case, however, any person who innocently begins an undertaking that infringes the copyright has a complete defense to any action for such infringement if such person proves that he or she was misled by the notice and began the undertaking in good faith under a purported transfer or license from the person named therein, unless before the undertaking was begun—

(1) registration for the work had been made in the name of the owner of copyright; or

(2) a document executed by the person named in the notice and showing the ownership of the copyright had been recorded.

The person named in the notice is liable to account to the copyright owner for all receipts from transfers or licenses purportedly made under the copyright by the person named in the notice.

(b) Error in Date—When the year date in the notice on copies or phonorecords distributed before the effective date of the Berne Convention Implementation Act of 1988, by authority of the copyright owner is earlier than the year in which publication first occurred, any period computed from the year of first publication under section 302 is to be computed from the year in the notice. Where the year date is more than one year later than the year in which publication first occurred, the work is considered to have been published without any notice and is governed by the provisions of section 405.

(c) Omission of Name or Date—Where copies or phonorecords publicly distributed before the effective date of the Berne Convention Implementation Act of 1988 by authority of the copyright owner contain no name or no date that could reasonably be considered a part of the notice, the work is considered to have been published without any notice and is governed by the provisions of section 405 as in effect on the day before the effective date of the Berne Convention Implementation Act of 1988.

SECTION 407. Deposit of Copies or Phonorecords for Library of Congress

(a) Except as provided by subsection (c), and subject to the provisions of subsection (e), the owner of copyright or of the exclusive right of publication in a work published in the United States shall deposit, within three months after the date of such publication—

(1) two complete copies of the best edition; or

(2) if the work is a sound recording, two complete phonorecords of the best edition, together with any printed or other visually perceptible material published with such phonorecords.

Neither the deposit requirements of this subsection nor the acquisition provisions of subsection (e) are conditions of copyright protection.

(b) The required copies or phonorecords shall be deposited in the Copyright Office for the use or disposition of the Library of Congress. The Register of Copyrights shall, when requested by the depositor and upon payment of the fee prescribed by section 708, issue a receipt for the deposit.

(c) The Register of Copyrights may be regulation exempt any categories of material from the deposit requirements of this section, or require deposit of only one copy or phonorecord with respect to any categories. Such regulations shall provide either for complete exemption from the deposit requirements of this section, or for alternative forms of deposit aimed at providing a satisfactory archival record of a work without imposing practical or financial hardships on the depositor, where the individual author is the owner of copyright in a pictorial, graphic, or sculptural work and (i) less than five copies of the work have been published, or (ii) the work has been published in a limited edition consisting of numbered copies, the monetary value of which would make the mandatory deposit of two copies of the best edition of the work burdensome, unfair, or unreasonable.

(d) At any time after publication of a work as provided by subsection (a), the Register of Copyrights may make written demand for the required deposit on any of the persons obligated to make the deposit under subsection (a). Unless deposit is made within three months after the demand is received, the person or persons on whom the demand was made are liable—

(1) to a fine of not more than $250 for each work; and

(2) to pay into a specially designated fund in the Library of Congress the total retail price of the copies or phonorecords demanded, or, if no retail price has been fixed, the reasonable cost of the Library of Congress of acquiring them; and

(3) to pay a fine of $2,500, in addition to any fine or liability imposed under clauses (1) and (2), if such person willfully or repeatedly fails or refuses to comply with such a demand.

(e) With respect to transmission programs that have been fixed and transmitted to the public in the United States but have not been published, the Register of Copyrights shall, after consulting with the Librarian of Congress and other interested organizations and officials, establish regulations governing the acquisition, through deposit or otherwise, of copies or phonorecords of such programs for the collections of the Library of Congress.

(1) The Librarian of Congress shall be permitted, under the standards and conditions set forth in such regulations, to make a fixation of a transmission program directly from a transmission to the public, and to reproduce one copy or phonorecord from such fixation for archival purposes.

(2) Such regulations shall also provide standards and procedures by which the Register of Copyrights may make written demand, upon the owner of the right of transmission in the United States, for the deposit of a copy or phonorecord of a specific transmission program. Such deposit may, at the option of the owner of the right of transmission in the United States, be accomplished by gift, by loan for purposes of reproduction, or by sale at a price not to exceed the cost of reproducing and supplying the copy or phonorecord. The regulations established under this clause shall provide reasonable periods of not less than three months for compliance with a demand, and shall allow for extensions of such periods and adjustments in the scope of the demand or the methods for fulfilling it, as reasonably warranted by the circumstances. Willful failure or refusal to comply with the conditions prescribed by such regulations shall subject the owner of the right of transmission in the United States to liability for an amount, not to exceed the cost of reproducing and supplying the copy or phonorecord in question, to be paid into a specially designated fund in the Library of Congress.

(3) Nothing in this subsection shall be construed to require the making or retention, for purposes of deposit, of any copy or phonorecord of an unpublished transmission program, the transmission of which occurs before the receipt of a specific written demand as provided by clause (2).

(4) No activity undertaken in compliance with regulations prescribed under clauses (1) or (2) of this subsection shall result in liability if intended solely to assist in the acquisition of copies or phonorecords under this subsection.

SECTION 408. Copyright Registration in General

(a) Registration Permissive—At any time during the subsistence of the first term of copyright in any published or unpublished work in which the copyright was secured before January 1, 1978, and during the subsistence of any copyright secured on or after that date, the owner of copyright or of any exclusive right in the work may obtain registration of the copyright claim by delivering to the Copyright Office the deposit specified by this section, together with the application and fee specified by sections 409 and 708. Such registration is not a condition of copyright protection.

(b) Deposits for Registration—Except as provided by subsection (c), the material deposited for registration shall include—

(1) in the case of an unpublished work, one complete copy or phonorecord;

(2) in the case of the published work, two complete copies or phonorecords of the best edition;

(3) in the case of a work first published outside the United States, one complete copy or phonorecord as so published.

(4) in the case of a contribution to a collective work, one complete copy or phonorecord of the best edition of the collective work.

Copies or phonorecords deposited for the Library of Congress under section 407 may be used to satisfy the deposit provisions of this section, if they are accompanied by the prescribed application and fee, and by any additional identifying material that the Register may, by regulation, require. The Register shall also prescribe regulations establishing requirements under which copies or phonorecords acquired for the Library of Congress under subsection (e) of section 407, otherwise than by deposit, may be used to satisfy the deposit provisions of this section.

(c) Administrative Classification and Optional Deposit.—

(1) The Register of Copyrights is authorized to specify by regulation the administrative classes into which works are to be placed for purposes of deposit and registration, and the nature of the copies or phonorecords to be deposited in the various classes specified. The regulations may require or permit, for particular classes, the deposit of identifying material instead of copies or phonorecords, the deposit of only one copy or phonorecord where two would normally be required, or a single registration for a group of related works. This administrative classification of works has no significance with respect to the subject matter of copyright of the exclusive rights provided by this title.

(2) Without prejudice to the general authority provided under clause (1), the Register of Copyrights shall establish regulations specifically permitting a single registration for a group of works by the same individual author, all first published as contributions to periodicals, including newspapers, within a twelve-month period, on the basis of a single deposit, application, and registration fee, under the following conditions:

(A) if the deposit consists of one copy of the entire issue of the periodical, or of the entire section in the case of a newspaper, in which each contribution was first published; and

(B) if the application identifies each work separately, including the periodical containing it and its date of first publication.

(3) As an alternative to separate renewal registrations under subsection (a) of section 304, a single renewal registration may be made for a group of works by the same individual author, all first published as contributions to periodicals, including newspapers, upon the filing of a single application and fee, under all of the following conditions:

(A) the renewal claimant or claimants, and the basis of claim or claims under section 304(a), is the same for each of the works; and

(B) the works were all copyrighted upon their first publication, either through separate copyright notice and registration or by virtue of a general copyright notice in the periodical issue as a whole; and

the renewal application and fee are received not more than twenty-eight or less than twenty-seven years after the thirty-first day of December of the calendar year in which all of the works were first published; and

(D) the renewal application identifies each work separately, including the periodical containing it and its date of first publication.

(d) Corrections and Amplifications—The Register may also establish, by regulation, formal procedures for the filing of an application for supplementary registration, to correct an error in a copyright registration or to amplify the information given in a registration. Such application shall be accompanied by the fee provided by section 708, and shall clearly identify the registration to be corrected or amplified. The information contained in a supplementary registration augments but does not supersede that contained in the earlier registration.

(e) Published Edition of Previously Registered Work—Registration for the first published edition of a work previously registered in unpublished form may be made even though the work as published is substantially the same as the unpublished version.

SECTION 409. Application for Copyright Registration

The application for copyright registration shall be made on a form prescribed by the Register of Copyrights and shall include—

(1) the name and address of the copyright claimant;

(2) in the case of a work other than an anonymous or pseudonymous work, the name and nationality or domicile of the author or authors, and, if one or more of the authors is dead, the dates of their deaths;

(3) if the work is anonymous or pseudonymous, the nationality or domicile of the author or authors;

(4) in the case of a work made for hire, a statement to this effect;

(5) if the copyright claimant is not the author, a brief statement of how the claimant obtained ownership of the copyright;

(6) the title of the work, together with any previous or alternative titles under which the work can be identified;

(7) the year in which creation of the work was completed;

(8) if the work has been published, the date and nation of its first publication;

(9) in the case of a compilation or derivative work, an identification of any preexisting work or works that it is based on or incorporates, and a brief, general statement of the additional material covered by the copyright claim being registered;

(10) in the case of a published work containing material of which copies are required by section 601 to be manufactured in the United States, the names of the persons or organizations who performed the processes specified by subsection (c) of section 601 with respect to that material, and the places where those processes were performed; and

(11) any other information regarded by the Register of Copyrights as bearing upon the preparation or identification of the work or the existence, ownership, or duration of the copyright.

If an application is submitted for the renewed and extended term provided for in section 304(a)(3)(A) and an original term registration has not been made, the Register may request information with respect to the existence, ownership, or duration of the copyright for the original term.

SECTION 410. Registration of Claim and Issuance of Certificate

(a) When, after examination, the Register of Copyrights determines that, in accordance with the provisions of this title, the material deposited constitutes copyrightable subject matter and that the other legal and formal requirements of this title have been met, the Register shall register the claim and issue to the applicant a certificate of registration under the seal of the Copyright Office. The certificate shall contain the information given in the application, together with the number and effective date of the registration.

(b) In any case in which the Register of Copyrights determines that, in accordance with the provisions of this title, the material deposited does not constitute copyrightable subject matter or that the claim is invalid for any other reason, the Register shall refuse registration and shall notify the applicant in writing of the reasons for such refusal.

(c) In any judicial proceedings the certificate of a registration made before or within five years after first publication of the work shall constitute prima facie evidence of the validity of the copyright and of the facts stated in the certificate. The evidentiary weight to be accorded the certificate of a registration made thereafter shall be within the discretion of the court.

(d) The effective date of a copyright registration is the day on which an application, deposit, and fee, which are later determined by the Register of Copyrights or by a court of competent jurisdiction to be acceptable for registration, have all been received in the Copyright Office.

SECTION 411. Registration and Infringement Actions

(a) Except for actions for infringement of copyright in Berne Convention works whose country of origin is not the United States and an action brought for a violation of the rights of the author under section 106A(a), and subject to the provisions of subsection (b), no action for infringement of the copyright in any work shall be instituted until registration of the copyright claim has been made in accordance with this title. In any case, however, where the deposit, application, and fee required for registration have been delivered to the Copyright Office in proper form and registration has been refused, the applicant is entitled to institute an action for infringement if notice thereof, with a copy of the complaint, is served on the Register of Copyrights. The Register may, at his or her option, become a party to the action with respect to the issue of registrability of the copyright claim by entering an appearance within sixty days after such service, but the Register's failure to become a party shall not deprive the court of jurisdiction to determine that issue.

(b) In the case of a work consisting of sounds, images, or both, the first fixation of which is made simultaneously with its transmission, the copyright owner may, either before or after such fixation takes place, institute an action for infringement under section 501, fully subject to the remedies provided by sections 502 through 506 and sections 509 and 510, if, in accordance with requirements that the Register of Copyrights shall prescribe by regulation, the copyright owner—

(1) serves notice upon the infringer, not less than ten or more than thirty days before such fixation; identifying the work and the specific time and source of its first transmission, and declaring an intention to secure copyright in the work; and

(2) makes registration for the work, if required by subsection (a), within three months after its first transmission.

SECTION 412. Registration as Prerequisite to Certain Remedies for Infringement

In any action under this title, other than an action brought for a violation of the rights of the author under section 106A(a) or an action instituted under section 411(b), no award of statutory damages or of attorney's fees, as provided by sections 504 and 505, shall be made for—

(1) any infringement of copyright in an unpublished work commenced before the effective date of its registration; or

(2) any infringement of copyright commenced after first publication of the work and before the effective date of its registration, unless such registration is made within three months after the first publication of the work.

SECTION 504. Remedies for Infringement: Damages and Profits

(a) In General.—Except as otherwise provided by this title, an infringer of copyright is liable for either—

(1) the copyright owner's actual damages and any additional profits of the infringer, as provided by subsection (b); or

(2) statutory damages, as provided by subsection (c).

(b) Actual Damages and Profits.—The copyright owner is entitled to recover the actual damages suffered by him or her as a result of the infringement, and any profits of the infringer that are attributable to the infringement and are not taken into account in computing the actual damages. In establishing the infringer's profits, the copyright owner is required to present proof only of the infringer's gross revenue, and the infringer is required to prove his or her deductible expenses and the elements of profit attributable to factors other than the copyrighted work.

(c) Statutory Damages.—

(1) Except as provided by clause (2) of this subsection, the copyright owner may elect, at any time before final judgment is rendered, to recover, instead of actual damages and profits, an award of statutory damages for all infringements involved in the action, with respect to any one work, for which any one infringer is liable individually, or for which any two or more infringers are liable jointly and severally, in a sum of not less than $500 or more than $20,000 as the court considers just. For the purposes of this subsection, all the parts of a compilation or derivative work constitute one work.

(2) In a case where the copyright owner sustains the burden of proving, and the court finds, that infringement was committed willfully, the court in its discretion may increase the award of statutory damages to a sum of not more than $100,000. In a case where the infringer sustains the burden of proving, and the court finds, that such infringer was not aware and had no reason to believe that his or her acts constituted an infringement of copyright, the court in its discretion may reduce the award of statutory damages to a sum of not less than $200. The court shall remit statutory damages in any case where an infringer believed and had reasonable grounds for believing that his or her use of the copyrighted work was a fair use under section 107, if the infringer was: (i) an employee or agent of a nonprofit educational institution, library, or archives acting within the scope of his or her employment who, or such institution, library, or archives itself, which infringed by reproducing the work in copies or phonorecords; or (ii) a public broadcasting entity which or a person who, as a regular part of the nonprofit activities of a public broadcasting entity (as defined in subsection (g) of section 118) infringed by performing a published nondramatic literary work or by reproducing a transmission program embodying a performance of such a work.

SECTION 505. Remedies for Infringement: Costs and Attorney's Fees

In any civil action under this title, the court in its discretion may allow the recovery of full costs by or against any party other than the United States or an officer thereof. Except as otherwise provided by this title, the court may also award a reasonable attorney's fee to the prevailing party as part of the costs.

SECTION 601. Manufacture, Importation, and Public Distribution of Certain Copies

(a) Prior to July 1, 1986, and except as provided by subsection (b), the importation into or public distribution in the United States of copies of a work consisting preponderantly of nondramatic literary material that is in the English language and is protected under this title is prohibited unless the portions consisting of such material have been manufactured in the United States or Canada.

(b) The provisions of subsection (a) do not apply—

(1) where, on the date when importation is sought or public distribution in the United States is made, the author of any substantial part of such material is neither a national nor a domiciliary of the United States or, if such author is a national of the United States, he or she has been domiciled outside the United States for a continuous period of at least one year immediately preceding that date; in the case of a work made for hire, the exemption provided by this clause does not apply unless a substantial part of the work was prepared for an employer or other person who is not a national or domiciliary of the United States or a domestic corporation or enterprise;

(2) where the United States Customs Service is presented with an import statement issued under the seal of the Copyright Office, in which case a total of no more than two thousand copies of any one such work shall be allowed entry; the import statement shall be issued upon request to the copyright owner or to a person designated by such owner at the time of registration for the work under section 408 or at any time thereafter;

(3) where importation is sought under the authority or for the use, other than in schools, of the Government of the United States or of any State or political subdivision of a State;

(4) where importation, for use and not for sale, is sought—

(A) by any person with respect to no more than one copy of any work at any one time;

(B) by any person arriving from outside the United States, with respect to copies forming part of such person's personal baggage; or

(C) by an organization operated for scholarly, educational, or religious purposes and not for private gain, with respect to copies intended to form a part of its library;

(5) where the copies are reproduced in raised characters for the use of the blind; or

(6) where, in addition to copies imported under clauses (3) and (4) of this subsection, no more than two thousand copies of any one such work, which have not been manufactured in the United States or Canada, are publicly distributed in the United States; or

(7) where, on the date when importation is sought or public distribution in the United States is made—

(A) the author of any substantial part of such material is an individual and receives compensation for the transfer or license of the right to distribute the work in the United States; and

(B) the first publication of the work has previously taken place outside the United States under a transfer or license granted by such author to a transferee or licensee who was not a national or domiciliary of the United States or a domestic corporation or enterprise; and

(C) there has been no publication of an authorized edition of the work of which the copies were manufactured in the United States; and

(D) the copies were reproduced under a transfer or license granted by such author or by the transferee or licensee of the right of first publication as mentioned in subclause (B), and the transferee or the licensee of the right of reproduction was not a national or domiciliary of the United States or a domestic corporation or enterprise.

(c) The requirement of this section that copies be manufactured in the United States or Canada is satisfied if—

(1) in the case where the copies are printed directly from type that has been set, or directly from plates made from such type, the setting of the type and the making of the plates have been performed in the United States or Canada; or

(2) in the case where the making of plates by a lithographic or photoengraving process is a final or intermediate step preceding the printing of the copies, the making of the plates has been performed in the United States or Canada; and

(3) in any case, the printing or other final process of producing multiple copies and any binding of the copies have been performed in the United States or Canada.

(d) Importation or public distribution of copies in violation of this section does not invalidate protection for a work under this title. However, in any civil action or criminal proceeding for infringement of the exclusive rights to reproduce and distribute copies of the work, the infringer has a complete defense with respect to all of the nondramatic literary material comprised in the work and any other parts of the work in which the exclusive rights to reproduce and distribute copies are owned by the same person who owns such exclusive rights in the nondramatic literary material, if the infringer proves—

(1) that copies of the work have been imported into or publicly distributed in the United States in violation of this section by or with the authority of the owner of such exclusive rights; and

(2) that the infringing copies were manufactured in the United States or Canada in accordance with the provisions of subsection (c); and

(3) that the infringement was commenced before the effective date of registration for an authorized edition of the work, the copies of which have been manufactured in the United States or Canada in accordance with the provisions of subsection (c).

(e) In any action for infringement of the exclusive rights to reproduce and distribute copies of a work containing material required by this section to be manufactured in the United States or Canada, the copyright owner shall set forth in the complaint the names of the persons or organizations who performed the processes specified by subsection (c) with respect to that material, and the places where those processes were performed.

SECTION 602. Infringing Importation of Copies or Phonorecord

(a) Importation into the United States, without the authority of the owner of copyright under this title, of copies or phonorecords of a work that have been acquired outside the United States is an infringement of the exclusive right to distribute copies or phonorecords under section 106, actionable under section 501. This subsection does not apply to—

(1) importation of copies or phonorecords under the authority or for the use of the Government of the United States or of any State or political subdivision of a State, but not including copies or phonorecords for use in schools, or copies of any audiovisual work imported for purposes other than archival use;

(2) importation, for the private use of the importer and not for distribution, by any person with respect to no more than one copy or phonorecord of any one work at any one time, or by any person arriving from outside the United States with respect to copies or phonorecords forming part of such person's personal baggage; or

(3) importation by or for an organization operated for scholarly, educational, or religious purposes and not for private gain, with respect to no more than one copy of an audiovisual work solely for its archival purposes, and no more than five copies or phonorecords of any other work for its library lending or archival purposes, unless the importation of such copies or phonorecords is part of an activity consisting of systematic reproduction or distribution, engaged in by such organization in violation of the provisions of section 108(g)(2).

(b) In a case where the making of the copies or phonorecords would have constituted an infringement of copyright if this title had been applicable, their importation is prohibited. In a case where the copies or phonorecords were lawfully made, the United States Customs Service has no authority to prevent their importation unless the provisions of section 601 are applicable. In either case, the Secretary of the Treasury is authorized to prescribe, by regulation, a procedure under which any person claiming an interest in the copyright in a particular work may, upon payment of a specified fee, be entitled to notification by the Customs Service of the importation of articles that appear to be copies or phonorecords of the work.

SECTION 603. Importation Prohibitions: Enforcement and Disposition of Excluded Articles

(a) The Secretary of the Treasury and the United States Postal Service shall separately or jointly make regulations for the enforcement of the provisions of this title prohibiting importation.

(b) These regulations may require, as a condition for the exclusion of articles under section 602—

(1) that the person seeking exclusion obtain a court order enjoining importation of the articles; or

(2) that the person seeking exclusion furnish proof, of a specified nature and in accordance with prescribed procedures, that the copyright in which such person claims an interest is valid and that the importation would violate the prohibition in section 602; the person seeking exclusion may also be required to post a surety bond for any injury that may result if the detention or exclusion of the articles proves to be unjustified.

(c) Articles imported in violation of the importation prohibitions of this title are subject to seizure and forfeiture in the same manner as property imported in violation of the customs revenue laws. Forfeited articles shall be destroyed as directed by the Secretary of the Treasury or the court, as the case may be; however, the articles may be returned to the country of export whenever it is shown to the satisfaction of the Secretary of the Treasury that the importer had no reasonable grounds for believing that his or her acts constituted a violation of law.

SECTION 701.The Copyright Office: General Responsibilities and Organization

(a) All administrative functions and duties under this title, except as otherwise specified, are the responsibility of the Register of Copyrights as director of the Copyright Office of the Library of Congress. The Register of Copyrights, together with the subordinate officers and employees of the Copyright Office, shall be appointed by the Librarian of Congress, and shall act under the Librarian's general direction and supervision.

(b) The Register of Copyrights shall adopt a seal to be used on and after January 1, 1978, to authenticate all certified documents issued by the Copyright Office.

(c) The Register of Copyrights shall make an annual report to the Librarian of Congress of the work and accomplishments of the Copyright Office during the previous fiscal year. The annual report of the Register of Copyrights shall be published separately and as a part of the annual report of the Librarian of Congress.

(d) Except as provided by section 706(b) and the regulations issued thereunder, all actions taken by the Register of Copyrights under this title are subject to the provisions of the Administrative Procedure Act of June 11, 1946, as amended (c. 324, 60 Stat. 237, title 5, United States Code, Chapter 5, Subchapter II and Chapter 7).

(e) The Register of Copyrights shall be compensated at the rate of pay in effect for level IV of the Executive Schedule under section 5315 of title 5. The Librarian of Congress shall establish not more than four positions for Associate Registers of Copyrights, in accordance with the recommendations of the Register of Copyrights. The Librarian shall make appointments to such positions after consultation with the Register of Copyrights. Each Associate Register of Copyrights shall be paid at a rate not to exceed the maximum annual rate of basic pay payable for GS-18 of the General Schedule under section 5332 of title 5.

SECTION 702. Copyright Office Regulations

The Register of Copyrights is authorized to establish regulations not inconsistent with law for the administration of the functions and duties made the responsibility of the Register under this title. All regulations established by the Register under this title are subject to the approval of the Librarian of Congress.

SECTION 801. Copyright Arbitration Royalty Panels: Establishment and Purpose

(a) Establishment—The Librarian of Congress, upon the recommendation of the Register of Copyrights, is authorized to appoint and convene copyright arbitration royalty panels.

(b) Subject to the provisions of this chapter, the purposes of the copyright arbitration royalty panels shall be—

(1) to make determinations concerning the adjustment of reasonable copyright royalty rates as provided in sections 115 and 116, and to make determinations as to reasonable terms and rates of royalty payments as provided in section 118. The rates applicable under sections 115 and 116 shall be calculated to achieve the following objectives:

(A) To maximize the availability of creative works to the public;

(B) To afford the copyright owner a fair return for his creative work and the copyright user a fair income under existing economic conditions;

(C) To reflect the relative roles of the copyright owner and the copyright user in the product made available to the public with respect to relative creative contribution, technological contribution, capital investment, cost, risk, and contribution to the opening of new markets for creative expression and media for their communication;

(D) To minimize any disruptive impact on the structure of the industries involved and on generally prevailing industry practices.

(2) to make determinations concerning the adjustment of the copyright royalty rates in section 111 solely in accordance with the following provisions:

(A) The rates established by section 111(d)(1)(B) may be adjusted to reflect (i) national monetary inflation or deflation or (ii) changes in the average rates charged cable subscribers for the basic service of providing secondary transmissions to maintain the real constant dollar level of the royalty fee per subscriber which existed as of the date of enactment of this Act: Provided, That if the average rates charged cable system subscribers for the basic service of providing secondary transmissions are changed so that the average rates exceed national monetary inflation, no change in the rates established by section 111(d)(1)(B) shall be permitted: *And provided further,* That no increase in the royalty fee shall be permitted based on any reduction in the average number of distant signal equivalents per subscriber. The copyright arbitration royalty panels may consider all factors relating to the maintenance of such level of payments including, as an extenuating factor, whether the cable industry has been restrained by subscriber rate regulating authorities from increasing the rates for the basic service of providing secondary transmissions.

(B) In the event that the rules and regulations of the Federal Communications Commission are amended at any time after April 15, 1976, to permit the carriage by cable systems of additional television broadcast signals beyond the local service area of the primary transmitters of such signals, the royalty rates established by section 111(d)(1)(B) may be adjusted to insure that the rates for the additional distant signal equivalents resulting from such carriage are reasonable in the light of the changes effected by the amendment to such rules and regulations. In determining the reasonableness of rates proposed following an amendment of Federal Communications Commission rules and regulations, the copyright arbitration royalty panels shall consider, among other factors, the economic impact on copyright owners and users: *Provided,* That no adjustment in royalty rates shall be made under this subclause with respect to any distant signal equivalent or fraction thereof represented by (i) carriage of any signal permitted under the rules and regulations of the Federal Communications Commission in effect on April 15, 1976, or the carriage of a signal of the same type (that is, independent, network, or noncommercial educational) substituted for such permitted signal, or (ii) a television broadcast signal first carried after April 15, 1976, pursuant to an individual waiver of the rules and regulations of the Federal Communications Commission, as such rules and regulations were in effect on April 15, 1976.

(C) In the event of any change in the rules and regulations of the Federal Communications Commission with respect to syndicated and sports program exclusively after April 15, 1976, the rates established by section 111(d)(1)(B) may be adjusted to assure that such rates are reasonable in light of the changes to such rules and regulations, but any such adjustment shall apply only to the affected television broadcast signals carried on those systems affected by the change.

(D) The gross receipts limitations established by section 111(d)(1)(C) and (D) shall be adjusted to reflect national monetary inflation or deflation or changes in the average rates charged cable system subscribers for the basic service of providing secondary transmissions to maintain the real constant dollar value of the exemption provided by such section; and the royalty rate specified therein shall not be subject to adjustment; and

(3) to distribute royalty fees deposited with the Register of Copyrights under Sections 111 and 116, 119(b) and 1003, and to determine, in cases where controversy exists, the distribution of such fees.

(4) to distribute royalty payments deposited with the Register of Copyrights under section 1003, to determine the distribution of such payments, and to carry out its other responsibilities under chapter 10.

(c) Rulings—The Librarian of Congress, upon the recommendation of the Register of Copyrights, may, before a copyright arbitration royalty panel is convened, make any necessary procedural or evidentiary rulings that would apply to the proceedings conducted by such panel; and

(d) Administrative Support of Copyright Arbitration Royalty Panels—The Library of Congress, upon the recommendation of the Register of Copyrights, shall provide the copyright arbitration royalty panels with the necessary administrative services related to proceedings under this chapter.

SECTION 802. Membership and Proceedings of Copyright Arbitration Royalty Panels

(a) Composition of Copyright Arbitration Royalty Panels—A copyright arbitration royalty panel shall consist of 3 arbitrators selected by the Librarian of Congress pursuant to subsection (b).

(b) Selection of Arbitration Panel—Not later than 10 days after publication of a notice in the Federal Register initiating an arbitration proceeding under section 803, and in accordance with procedures specified by the Register of Copyrights, the Librarian of Congress shall, upon the recommendation of the Register of Copyrights, select 2 arbitrators from lists provided by professional arbitration associations. Qualifications of the arbitrators shall include experience in conducting arbitration proceedings and facilitating the resolution and settlement of disputes, and any qualifications which the Librarian of Congress, upon the recommendation of the Register of Copyrights, shall adopt by regulation. The 2 arbitrators so selected shall, within 10 days after their selection, choose a third arbitrator from the same lists, who shall serve as the chairperson of the arbitrators. If such 2 arbitrators fail to agree upon the selection of a third arbitrator, the Librarian of Congress shall promptly select the third arbitrator. The Librarian of Congress, upon the recommendation of the Register of Copyrights, shall adopt regulations regarding standards of conduct which shall govern arbitrators and the proceedings under this chapter.

(c) Arbitration Proceedings—Copyright arbitration royalty panels shall conduct arbitration proceedings, subject to subchapter II of chapter 5 of title 5, for the purpose of making their determinations in carrying out the purposes set forth in section 801. The arbitration panels shall act on the basis of a fully documented written record, prior decisions of the Copyright Royalty Tribunal, prior copyright arbitration panel determinations, and rulings by the Librarian of Congress under section 801(c). Any copyright owner who claims to be entitled to royalties under section 111, 116, or 119, or any interested copyright party who claims to be entitled to royalties under section 1006, may submit relevant information and proposals to the arbitration panels in proceedings applicable to such copyright owner or interested copyright party, and any other person participating in arbitration proceedings may submit such relevant information and proposals to the arbitration panel conducting the proceedings. In ratemaking proceedings, the parties to the proceedings shall bear the entire cost thereof in such manner and proportion as the arbitration panels shall direct. In distribution proceedings, the parties shall bear the cost in direct proportion to their share of the distribution.

(d) Procedures—Effective on the date of the enactment of the Copyright Royalty Tribunal Reform Act of 1993, the Librarian of Congress shall adopt the rules and regulations set forth in chapter 3 of title 37 of the Code of Federal Regulations to govern proceedings under this chapter. Such rules and regulations shall remain in effect unless and until the Librarian, upon the recommendation of the Register of Copyrights, adopts supplemental or superseding regulations under subchapter II of chapter 5 of title 5.

(e) Report to the Librarian of Congress—Not later than 180 days after publication of the notice in the Federal Register initiating an arbitration proceeding, the copyright arbitration royalty panel conducting the proceeding shall report the Librarian of Congress its determination concerning the royalty fee or distribution of royalty fees, as the case may be. Such report shall be accompanied by the written record, and shall set forth the facts that the arbitration panel found relevant to its determination.

(f) Action by Librarian of Congress—Within 60 days after receiving the report of a copyright arbitration royalty panel under subsection (e), the Librarian of Congress, upon the recommendation of the Register of Copyrights, shall adopt or reject the determination of the arbitration panel. The Librarian shall adopt the determination of the arbitration panel unless the Librarian finds that the determination is arbitrary or contrary to the applicable provisions of this title. If the Librarian rejects the determination of the arbitration panel, the Librarian shall, before the end of that 60-day period, and after full examination of the record created in the arbitration proceeding, issue an order setting the royalty fee or distribution of fees, as the case may be. The Librarian shall cause to be published in the Federal Register the determination of the arbitration panel, and the decision of the Librarian (including an order issued under the proceeding sentence). The Librarian shall also publicize such determination and decision in such other manner as the Librarian considers appropriate. The Librarian shall also make the report of the arbitration panel and the accompanying record available for public inspection and copying.

(g) Judicial Review—Any decision of the Librarian of Congress under subsection (f) with respect to a determination of an arbitration panel may be appealed, by any aggrieved party who would be bound by the determination, to the United States Court of Appeals for the District of Columbia Circuit, within 30 days after the publication of the decision in the Federal Register. If no appeal is brought within such 30-day period, the decision of the Librarian is final, and the royalty fee or determination with respect to the distribution of fees, as the case may be, shall take effect as set forth in the decision. The pendency of an appeal under this paragraph shall not relieve persons obligated to make royalty payments under sections 111, 115, 116, 118, 119, or 1003 who would be affected by the determination on appeal to deposit the statement of account and royalty fees specified in those sections. The court shall have jurisdiction to modify or vacate a decision of the Librarian only if it finds, on the basis of the record before the Librarian, that the Librarian acted in an arbitrary manner. If the court modifies the decision of the Librarian, the court shall have jurisdiction to enter its own determination with respect to the amount or distribution of royalty fees and costs, to order the repayment of any excess fees, and to order the payment of any underpaid fees, and the interest pertaining respectively thereto, in accordance with its final judgment. The court may further vacate the decision of the arbitration panel and remand the case to the Librarian for arbitration proceedings in accordance with subsection (c).

(h) Administrative Matters.—

(1) Deduction of costs from Royalty Fees.—The Librarian of Congress and the Register of Copyrights may, to the extent not otherwise provided under this title, deduct from royalty fees deposited or collected

under this title the reasonable costs incurred by the Library of Congress and the Copyright Office under this chapter. Such deduction may be made before the fees are distributed to any copyright claimants. If no royalty pool exists from which their costs can be deducted, the Librarian of Congress and the Copyright Office may assess their reasonable costs directly to the parties to the most recent relevant arbitration proceedings.

(2) Positions Required for Administration of Compulsory Licensing.—Section 307 of the Legislative Branch Appropriations Act, 1994, shall not apply to employee positions in the Library of Congress that are required to be filled in order to carry out section 111, 115, 116, 118, or 119 or chapter 10.

(c) Procedures of the Tribunal—Section 803 of title 17, United States Code, and the item relating to such section in the table of sections at the beginning of chapter 8 of such title, are repealed.

SECTION 803. Institution and Conclusion of Proceedings

(a)(1) With respect to proceedings under section 801(b)(1) concerning the adjustment of royalty rates as provided in sections 115 and 116, and with respect to proceedings under subparagraphs (A) and (D) of section 801(b)(2), during the calendar years specified in the schedule set forth in paragraphs (2), (3), and (4), any owner or user of a copyrighted work whose royalty rates are specified by this title, established by the Copyright Royalty Tribunal before the date of the enactment of the Copyright Royalty Tribunal Reform Act of 1993, or established by a copyright arbitration royalty panel after such date of enactment, may file a petition with the Librarian of Congress declaring that the petitioner requests an adjustment of the rate. The Librarian of Congress shall, upon the recommendation of the Register of Copyrights, make a determination as to whether the petitioner has such a significant interest in the royalty rate in which an adjustment is requested. If the Librarian determines that the petitioner has such a significant interest, the Librarian shall cause notice of this determination, with the reasons therefor, to be published in the Federal Register, together with the notice of commencement of proceedings under this chapter.

(2) In proceedings under section 801(b)(2)(A) and (D), a petition described in paragraph (1) may be filed during 1995 and in each subsequent fifth calendar year.

(3) In proceedings under section 801(b)(1) concerning the adjustment of royalty rates as provided in section 115, a petition described in para-

graph (1) may be filed in 1997 and in each subsequent tenth calendar year.

(4)(A) In proceedings under section 801(b)(1) concerning the adjustment of royalty rates as provided in section 116, a petition described in paragraph (1) may be filed at any time within 1 year after negotiated licenses authorized by section 116 are terminated or expire and are not replaced by subsequent agreements.

(B) If a negotiated license authorized by section 116 is terminated or expires and is not replaced by another such license agreement which provides permission to use a quantity of musical works not substantially smaller than the quantity of such works performed on coin-operated phonorecords players during the 1-year period ending March 1, 1989, the Librarian of Congress shall, upon petition filed under paragraph (1) within 1 year after such termination or expiration, convene a copyright arbitration royalty panel. The arbitration panel shall promptly establish an interim royalty rate or rates for the public performance by means of a coin-operated phonorecord player of non-dramatic musical works embodied in phonorecords which had been subject to the terminated or expired negotiated license agreement. Such rate or rates shall be the same as the last such rate or rates and shall remain in force until the conclusion of proceedings by the arbitration panel, in accordance with section 802, to adjust the royalty rates applicable to such works, or until superseded by a new negotiated license agreement, as provided in section 116(b).

(b) With respect to proceedings under subparagraph (B) or (C) of section 801(b)(2), following an event described in either of those subsections, any owner or user of a copyrighted work whose royalty rates are specified by section 111, or by a rate established by the Copyright Royalty Tribunal or the Librarian of Congress, may, within twelve months, file a petition with the Librarian declaring that the petitioner requests an adjustment of the rate. In this event the Librarian shall proceed as in subsection (a) of this section. Any change in royalty rates made by the Copyright Royalty Tribunal or the Librarian of Congress pursuant to this subsection may be reconsidered in 1980, 1985, and each fifth calendar year thereafter, in accordance with the provisions in section 801(b)(2) (B) or (C), as the case may be.

(c) With respect to proceedings under section 801(b)(1), concerning the determination of reasonable terms and rates of royalty payments as provided in section 118, the Librarian of Congress shall proceed when and as provided by that section.

(d) With respect to proceedings under section 801(b)(3), concerning the distribution of royalty fees in certain circumstances under section 111, 116, or 119, the Librarian of Congress shall, upon a determination that a controversy exists concerning such distribution, cause to be published in the Federal Register notice of commencement of proceedings under this chapter.

SECTION 1101. Unauthorized Fixation and Trafficking in Sound Recordings and Music Videos

(a) Unauthorized Acts—Anyone who, without the consent of the performer or performers involved—

(1) fixes the sounds or sounds and images of a live musical performance in a copy of phonorecord, or reproduces copies or phonorecords of such a performance from an unauthorized fixation,

(2) transmits or otherwise communicates, to the public the sound or sounds and images of a live music performance, or

(3) distributes or offers to distribute, sells or offers to sell, rents or offers to rent, or traffics in any copy or phonorecord fixed as described in paragraph (1), regardless or whether the fixations occurred in the United States, shall be subject to the remedies provided in section 502 through 505, to the same extent as an infringer of copyright.

(b) Definition—As used in this section, the term "traffic in" means transport, transfer, or otherwise dispose of, to another, as consideration for anything of value, or make or obtain control of with intent to transcript, transfer, or dispose of.

(c) Applicability—This section shall apply to any act or acts that occur on or after the date of the enactment of the Uruguay Round Agreements Act.

(d) State Law Not Preempted—Nothing in this section may be construed to annual or limit any rights or remedies under the common law or statutes or any States.

APPENDIX 2:

SELECTED PROVISIONS OF THE BERNE CONVENTION FOR THE PROTECTION OF LITERARY AND ARTISTIC WORKS
(Paris, July 24, 1971)

ARTICLE 1

The countries to which this Convention applies constitute a Union for the protection of the rights of authors in their literary and artistic works.

ARTICLE 2

(1) The expression "literary and artistic works" shall include every production in the literary, scientific and artistic domain, whatever may be the mode or form of its expression, such as books, pamphlets and other writings; lectures, addresses, sermons and other works of the same nature; dramatic or dramatico-musical works; choreographic works and entertainments in dumb show; musical compositions with or without words; cinematographic works to which are assimilated works expressed by a process analogous to cinematography; works of drawing, painting, architecture, sculpture, engraving and lithography; photographic works to which are assimilated works expressed by a process analogous to photography; works of applied art; illustrations, maps, plans, sketches and three-dimensional works relative to geography, topography, architecture or science.

(2) It shall, however, be a matter for legislation in the countries of the Union to prescribe that works in general or any specified categories of works shall not be protected unless they have been fixed in some material form.

(3) Translations, adaptations, arrangements of music and other alterations of a literary or artistic work shall be protected as original works without prejudice to the copyright in the original work.

(4) It shall be a matter for legislation in the countries of the Union to determine the protection to be granted to official texts of a legislative, administrative and legal nature, and to official translations of such texts.

(5) Collections of literary or artistic works such as encyclopedias and anthologies which, by reason of the selection and arrangement of their contents, constitute intellectual creations shall be protected as such, without prejudice to the copyright in each of the works forming part of such collections.

(6) The works mentioned in this article shall enjoy protection in all countries of the Union. This protection shall operate for the benefit of the author and his successors in title.

(7) Subject to the provisions of Article 7(4) of this Convention, it shall be a matter for legislation in the countries of the Union to determine the extent of the application of their laws to works of applied art and industrial designs and models, as well as the conditions under which such works, designs and models shall be protected. Works protected in the country of origin solely as designs and models shall be entitled in another country of the Union only to such special protection as is granted in that country to designs and models; however, if no such special protection is granted in that country, such works shall be protected as artistic works.

(8) The protection of this Convention shall not apply to news of the day or to miscellaneous facts having the character of mere items of press information.

ARTICLE 2 *bis*

(1) It shall be a matter for legislation in the countries of the Union to exclude, wholly or in part, from the protection provided by the preceding Article political speeches and speeches delivered in the course of legal proceedings.

(2) It shall also be a matter for legislation in the countries of the Union to determine the conditions under which lectures, addresses and other works of the same nature which are delivered in public may be reproduced by the press, broadcast, communicated to the public by wire and made the subject of public communication as envisaged in Article 11 *bis* (1) of this Convention, when such use is justified by the informatory purpose.

(3) Nevertheless, the author shall enjoy the exclusive right of making a collection of his works mentioned in the preceding paragraphs.

ARTICLE 3

(1) The protection of this Convention shall apply to:

(a) authors who are nationals of one of the countries of the Union, for their works, whether published or not;

(b) authors who are not nationals of one of the countries of the Union, for their works first published in one of those countries, or simultaneously in a country outside the Union and in a country of the Union.

(2) Authors who are not nationals of one of the countries of the Union but who have their habitual residence in one of them shall, for the purposes of this Convention, be assimilated to nationals of that country.

(3) The expression *published works* means works published with the consent of their authors, whatever may be the means of manufacture of the copies, provided that the availability of such copies has been such as to satisfy the reasonable requirements of the public, having regard to the nature of the work. The performance of a dramatic, dramatico-musical, cinematographic or musical work, the public recitation of a literary work, the communication by wire or the broadcasting of literary or artistic works, the exhibition of a work of art and the construction of a work of architecture shall not constitute publication.

(4) A work shall be considered as having been published simultaneously in several countries if it has been published in two or more countries within thirty days of its first publication.

ARTICLE 4

The protection of this Convention shall apply, even if the conditions of Article 3 are not fulfilled, to:

(a) authors of cinematographic works the maker of which has his headquarters or habitual residence in one of the countries of the Union;

(b) authors of works of architecture, erected in a country of the Union or of other artistic works incorporated in a building or other structure located in a country of the Union.

ARTICLE 5

(1) Authors shall enjoy, in respect of works for which they are protected under this Convention, in countries of the Union other than the country of origin, the rights which their respective laws do now or may hereafter grant to their nationals, as well as the rights specially granted by this Convention.

(2) The enjoyment and the exercise of these rights shall not be subject to any formality; such enjoyment and such exercise shall be independent of the existence of protection in the country of origin of the work. Consequently, apart from the provisions of this Convention, the extent of protection, as well as the means of redress afforded to the author to protect his rights, shall be governed exclusively by the laws of the country where protection is claimed.

(3) Protection in the country of origin is governed by domestic law. However, when the author is not a national of the country of origin of the work for which he is protected under this Convention, he shall enjoy in that country the same rights as national authors.

(4) The country of origin shall be considered to be

(a) in the case of works first published in a country of the Union, that country; in the case of works published simultaneously in several countries of the Union which grant different terms of protection, the country whose legislation grants the shortest term of protection;

(b) in the case of works published simultaneously in a country outside the Union and in a country of the Union, the latter country;

(c) in the case of unpublished works or of works first published in a country outside the Union, without simultaneous publication in a country of the Union, the country of the Union of which the author is a national, provided that:

(i) when these are cinematographic works the maker of which has his headquarters or his habitual residence in a country of the Union, the country of origin shall be that country, and

(ii) when these are works of architecture erected in a country of the Union or other artistic works incorporated in a building or other structure located in a country of the Union, the country of origin shall be that country.

ARTICLE 6

(1) Where any country outside the Union fails to protect in an adequate manner the works of authors who are nationals of one of the countries of the Union, the latter country may restrict the protection given to the works of authors who are, at the date of the first publication thereof, nationals of the other country and are not habitually resident in one of the countries of the Union. If the country of first publication avails itself of this right, the other countries of the Union shall not be required to grant to works thus subjected to special treatment a wider protection than that granted to them in the country of first publication.

(2) No restrictions introduced by virtue of the preceding paragraph shall affect the rights which an author may have acquired in respect of a work published in a country of the Union before such restrictions were put into force.

(3) The countries of the Union which restrict the grant of copyright in accordance with this Article shall give notice thereof to the Director General of the World Intellectual Property Organization (hereinafter designated as "the Director General") by a written declaration specifying the countries in regard to which protection is restricted, and the restrictions to which rights of authors who are nationals of those countries are subjected. The Director General shall immediately communicate this declaration to all the countries of the Union.

ARTICLE 6 *bis*

(1) Independently of the author's economic rights, and even after the transfer of the said rights, the author shall have the right to claim authorship of the work and to object to any distortion, mutilation or other modification of, or other derogatory action in relation to, the said work, which would be prejudicial to his honor or reputation.

(2) The rights granted to the author in accordance with the preceding paragraph shall, after his death, be maintained, at least until the expiry of the economic rights, and shall be exercisable by the persons or institutions authorized by the legislation of the country where protection is claimed. However, those countries whose legislation, at the moment of their ratification of or accession to this Act, does not provide for the protection after the death of the author of all the rights set out in the preceding paragraph may provide that some of these rights may, after his death, cease to be maintained.

(3) The means of redress for safeguarding the rights granted by this Article shall be governed by the legislation of the country where protection is claimed.

ARTICLE 7

(1) The term of protection granted by this Convention shall be the life of the author and fifty years after his death.

(2) However, in the case of cinematographic works, the countries of the Union may provide that the term of protection shall expire fifty years after the work has been made available to the public with the consent of the author, or, failing such an event within fifty years from the making of such a work, fifty years after the making.

(3) In the case of anonymous or pseudonymous works, the term of protection granted by this Convention shall expire fifty years after the work has been lawfully made available to the public. However, when the pseudonym

adopted by the author leaves no doubt as to his identity, the term of protection shall be that provided in paragraph (1). If the author of an anonymous or pseudonymous work discloses his identity during the above-mentioned period, the term of protection applicable shall be that provided in paragraph (1). The countries of the Union shall not be required to protect anonymous or pseudonymous works in respect of which it is reasonable to presume that their author has been dead for fifty years.

(4) It shall be a matter for legislation in the countries of the Union to determine the term of protection of photographic works and that of works of applied art in so far as they are protected as artistic works; however, this term shall last at least until the end of a period of twenty-five years from the making of such a work.

(5) The term of protection subsequent to the death of the author and the terms provided by paragraphs (2), (3) and (4), shall run from the date of death or of the event referred to in those paragraphs, but such terms shall always be deemed to begin on the 1 st of January of the year following the death or such event.

(6) The countries of the Union may grant a term of protection in excess of those provided by the preceding paragraphs.

(7) Those countries of the Union bound by the Rome Act of this Convention, which grant, in their national legislation in force at the time of signature of the present Act, shorter terms of protection than those provided for in the preceding paragraphs, shall have the right to maintain such terms when ratifying or acceding to the present Act.

(8) In any case, the term shall be governed by the legislation of the country where protection is claimed; however, unless the legislation of that country otherwise provides, the term shall not exceed the term fixed in the country of origin of the work.

ARTICLE 7 *bis*

The provisions of the preceding Article shall also apply in the case of a work of joint authorship, provided that the terms measured from the death of the author shall be calculated from the death of the last surviving author.

ARTICLE 8

Authors of literary and artistic works protected by this Convention shall enjoy the exclusive right of making and of authorizing the translation of their works throughout the term of protection of their rights in the original works.

ARTICLE 9

(1) Authors of literary and artistic works protected by this Convention shall have the exclusive right of authorizing the reproduction of these works, in any manner or form.

(2) It shall be a matter for legislation in the countries of the Union to permit the reproduction of such works in certain special cases, provided that such reproduction does not conflict with a normal exploitation of the work and does not unreasonably prejudice the legitimate interests of the author.

(3) Any sound or visual recording shall be considered as a reproduction for the purposes of this Convention.

ARTICLE 10

(1) It shall be permissible to make quotations from a work which has already been lawfully made available to the public, provided that their making is compatible with fair practice, and their extent does not exceed that justified by the purpose, including quotations from newspaper articles and periodicals in the form of press summaries.

(2) It shall be a matter for legislation in the countries of the Union, and for special agreements existing or to be concluded between them, to permit the utilization, to the extent justified by the purpose, of literary or artistic works by way of illustration in publications, broadcasts or sound or visual recordings for teaching, provided such utilization is compatible with fair practice.

(3) Where use is made of works in accordance with the preceding paragraphs of this Article, mention shall be made of the source, and of the name of the author, if it appears thereon.

ARTICLE 10 *bis*

(1) It shall be a matter for legislation in the countries of the Union to permit the reproduction by the press, the broadcasting or the communication to the public by wire, of articles published in newspapers or periodicals on current economic, political or religious topics, and of broadcast works of the same character, in cases in which the reproduction, broadcasting or such communication thereof is not expressly reserved. Nevertheless, the source must always be clearly indicated; the legal consequences of a breach of this

obligation shall be determined by the legislation of the country where protection is claimed.

(2) It shall also be a matter for legislation in the countries of the Union to determine the conditions under which, for the purpose of reporting current events by means of photography, cinematography, broadcasting or communication to the public by wire, literary or artistic works seen or heard in the course of the event may, to the extent justified by the informatory purpose, be reproduced and made available to the public.

ARTICLE 11

(1) Authors of dramatic, dramatico-musical and musical works shall enjoy the exclusive right of authorizing:

(i) the public performance of their works, including such public performance by any means or process;

(ii) any communication to the public of the performance of their works.

(2) Authors of dramatic or dramatico-musical works shall enjoy, during the full term of their rights in the original works, the same rights with respect to translations thereof.

ARTICLE 11 *bis*

(1) Authors of literary and artistic works shall enjoy the exclusive right of authorizing:

(i) the broadcasting of their works or the communication thereof to the public by any other means of wireless diffusion of signs, sounds or images;

(ii) any communication to the public by wire or by rebroadcasting of the broadcast of the work, when this communication is made by an organization other than the original one;

(iii) the public communication by loudspeaker or any other analogous instrument transmitting, by signs, sounds or images, the broadcast of the work.

(2) It shall be a matter for legislation in the countries of the Union to determine the conditions under which the rights mentioned in the preceding paragraph may be exercised, but these conditions shall apply only in the countries where they have been prescribed. They shall not in any circumstances be prejudicial to the moral rights of the author, nor to his right to ob-

tain equitable remuneration which, in the absence of agreement, shall be fixed by competent authority.

(3) In the absence of any contrary stipulation, permission granted in accordance with paragraph (1) of this Article shall not imply permission to record, by means of instruments recording sounds or images, the work broadcast. It shall, however, be a matter for legislation in the countries of the Union to determine the regulations for ephemeral recordings made by a broadcasting organization by means of its own facilities and used for its own broadcasts. The preservation of these recordings in official archives may, on the ground of their exceptional documentary character, be authorized by such legislation.

Article 11 *ter*

(1) Authors of literary works shall enjoy the exclusive right of authorizing:

(i) the public recitation of their works, including such public recitation by any means or process;

(ii) any communication to the public of the recitation of their works.

(2) Authors of literary works shall enjoy, during the full term of their rights in the original works, the same rights with respect to translations thereof.

ARTICLE 12

Authors of literary or artistic works shall enjoy the exclusive right of authorizing adaptations, arrangements and other alterations of their works.

ARTICLE 13

(1) Each country of the Union may impose for itself reservations and conditions on the exclusive right granted to the author of a musical work and to the author of any words, the recording of which together with the musical work has already been authorized by the latter, to authorize the sound recording of that musical work, together with such words, if any; but all such reservations and conditions shall apply only in the countries which have imposed them and shall not, in any circumstances, be prejudicial to the rights of these authors to obtain equitable remuneration which, in the absence of agreement, shall be fixed by competent authority.

(2) Recordings of musical works made in a country of the Union in accordance with Article 13 (3) of the Convention signed at Rome on June 2,

1928, and at Brussels on June 26, 1948, may be reproduced in that country without the permission of the author of the musical work until a date two years after that country becomes bound by this Act.

(3) Recordings made in accordance with paragraphs (1) and (2) of this Article and imported without permission from the parties concerned into a country where they are treated as infringing recordings shall be liable to seizure.

ARTICLE 14

(1) Authors of literary or artistic works shall have the exclusive right of authorizing:

(i) the cinematographic adaptation and reproduction of these works, and the distribution of the works thus adapted or reproduced;

(ii) the public performance and communication to the public by wire of the works thus adapted or reproduced.

(2) The adaptation into any other artistic form of a cinematographic production derived from literary or artistic works shall, without prejudice to the authorization of the author of the cinematographic production, remain subject to the authorization of the authors of the original works. (3) The provisions of Article 13 (1) shall not apply.

ARTICLE 14 *bis*

(1) Without prejudice to the copyright in any work which may have been adapted or reproduced, a cinematographic work shall be protected as an original work. The owner of copyright in a cinematographic work shall enjoy the same rights as the author of an original work, including the rights referred to in the preceding Article.

(2) (a) Ownership of copyright in a cinematographic work shall be a matter for legislation in the country where protection is claimed.

(b) However, in the countries of the Union which, by legislation include among the owners of copyright in a cinematographic work authors who have brought contributions to the making of the work, such authors, if they have undertaken to bring such contributions, may not, in the absence of any contrary or special stipulation, object to the reproduction, distribution, public performance, communication to the public by wire, broadcasting or any other communication to the public, or to the subtitling or dubbing of texts, of the work.

(c) The question whether or not the form of the undertaking referred to above should, for the application of the preceding subparagraph (b), be in a written agreement or a written act of the same effect shall be a matter for the legislation of the country where the maker of the cinematographic work has his headquarters or habitual residence. However, it shall be a matter for the legislation of the country of the Union where protection is claimed to provide that the said undertaking shall be in a written agreement or a written act of the same effect. The countries whose legislation so provides shall notify the Director General by means of a written declaration, which will be immediately communicated by him to all the other countries of the Union.

(d) By "contrary or special stipulation" is meant any restrictive condition which is relevant to the aforesaid undertaking.

(3) Unless the national legislation provides to the contrary, the provisions of paragraph (2) (b) above shall not be applicable to authors of scenarios, dialogues and musical works created for the making of the cinematographic work, nor to the principal director thereof. However, those countries of the Union whose legislation does not contain rules providing for the application of the said paragraph (2) (b) to such director shall notify the Director General by means of a written declaration, which will be immediately communicated by him to all the other countries of the Union.

ARTICLE 14 *ter*

(1) The author, or after his death the persons or institutions authorized by national legislation, shall, with respect to original works of art and original manuscripts of writers and composers, enjoy the inalienable right to an interest in any sale of the work subsequent to the first transfer by the author of the work.

(2) The protection provided by the preceding paragraph may be claimed in a country of the Union only if legislation in the country to which the author belongs so permits, and to the extent permitted by the country where this protection is claimed.

(3) The procedure for collection and the amounts shall be matters for determination by national legislation.

ARTICLE 15

(1) In order that the author of a literary or artistic work protected by this Convention shall, in the absence of proof to the contrary, be regarded as such, and consequently be entitled to institute infringement proceedings in

the countries of the Union, it shall be sufficient for his name to appear on the work in the usual manner. This paragraph shall be applicable even if this name is a pseudonym, where the pseudonym adopted by the author leaves no doubt as to his identity.

(2) The person or body corporate whose name appears on a cinematographic work in the usual manner shall, in the absence of proof to the contrary, be presumed to be the maker of the said work.

(3) In the case of anonymous and pseudonymous works, other than those referred to in paragraph (1) above, the publisher whose name appears on the work shall, in the absence of proof to the contrary, be deemed to represent the author, and in this capacity be shall be entitled to protect and enforce the author's rights. The provisions of this paragraph shall cease to apply when the author reveals his identity and establishes his claim to authorship of the work.

(4)(a) In the case of unpublished works where the identity of the author is unknown, but where there is every ground to presume that he is a national of a country of the Union, it shall be a matter for legislation in that country to designate the competent authority who shall represent the author and shall be entitled to protect and enforce his rights in the countries of the Union.

(b) Countries of the Union which make such designation under the terms of this provision shall notify the Director General by means of a written declaration giving full information concerning the authority thus designated. The Director General shall at once communicate this declaration to all other countries of the Union.

ARTICLE 16

(1) Infringing copies of a work shall be liable to seizure in any country of the Union where the work enjoys legal protection.

(2) The provisions of the preceding paragraph shall also apply to reproductions coming from a country where the work is not protected, or has ceased to be protected.

(3) The seizure shall take place in accordance with the legislation of each country.

ARTICLE 17

The provisions of this Convention cannot in any way affect the right of the Government of each country of the Union to permit, to control, or to prohibit by legislation or regulation, the circulation, presentation, or exhibition of any work or production in regard to which the competent authority may find it necessary to exercise that right.

ARTICLE 18

(1) This Convention shall apply to all works which, at the moment of its coming into force, have not yet fallen into the public domain in the country of origin through the expiry of the term of protection.

(2) If, however, through the expiry of the term of protection which was previously granted, a work has fallen into the public domain of the country where protection is claimed, that work shall not be protected anew.

(3) The application of this principle shall be subject to any provisions contained in special conventions to that effect existing or to be concluded between countries of the Union. In the absence of such provisions, the respective countries shall determine, each in so far as it is concerned, the conditions of application of this principle.

(4) The preceding provisions shall also apply in the case of new accessions to the Union and to cases in which protection is extended by the application of Article 7 or by the abandonment of reservations.

ARTICLE 19

The provisions of this Convention shall not preclude the making of a claim to the benefit of any greater protection which may be granted by legislation in a country of the Union.

ARTICLE 20

The Governments of the countries of the Union reserve the right to enter into special agreements among themselves, in so far as such agreements grant to authors more extensive rights than those granted by the Convention, or contain other provisions not contrary to this Convention. The provisions of existing agreements which satisfy these conditions shall remain applicable.

APPENDIX 3:

COPYRIGHT FORM PA

FORM PA
For a Work of the Performing Arts
UNITED STATES COPYRIGHT OFFICE

REGISTRATION NUMBER

PA   PAU

EFFECTIVE DATE OF REGISTRATION

Month   Day   Year

DO NOT WRITE ABOVE THIS LINE. IF YOU NEED MORE SPACE, USE A SEPARATE CONTINUATION SHEET.

1

TITLE OF THIS WORK ▼

PREVIOUS OR ALTERNATIVE TITLES ▼

NATURE OF THIS WORK ▼ See instructions

---

2 a

NAME OF AUTHOR ▼

DATES OF BIRTH AND DEATH
Year Born ▼   Year Died ▼

Was this contribution to the work a "work made for hire"?
☐ Yes
☐ No

AUTHOR'S NATIONALITY OR DOMICILE
Name of Country
OR { Citizen of ▶_____
{ Domiciled in_____

WAS THIS AUTHOR'S CONTRIBUTION TO THE WORK
Anonymous? ☐ Yes ☐ No
Pseudonymous? ☐ Yes ☐ No
If the answer to either of these questions is "Yes," see detailed instructions.

NATURE OF AUTHORSHIP Briefly describe nature of material created by this author in which copyright is claimed. ▼

NOTE

Under the law, the "author" of a "work made for hire" is generally the employer, not the employee (see instructions). For any part of this work that was "made for hire" check "Yes" in the space provided, give the employer (or other person for whom the work was prepared) as "Author" of that part, and leave the space for dates of birth and death blank.

b

NAME OF AUTHOR ▼

DATES OF BIRTH AND DEATH
Year Born ▼   Year Died ▼

Was this contribution to the work a "work made for hire"?
☐ Yes
☐ No

AUTHOR'S NATIONALITY OR DOMICILE
Name of Country
OR { Citizen of ▶_____
{ Domiciled in▶_____

WAS THIS AUTHOR'S CONTRIBUTION TO THE WORK
Anonymous? ☐ Yes ☐ No
Pseudonymous? ☐ Yes ☐ No
If the answer to either of these questions is "Yes," see detailed instructions.

NATURE OF AUTHORSHIP Briefly describe nature of material created by this author in which copyright is claimed. ▼

c

NAME OF AUTHOR ▼

DATES OF BIRTH AND DEATH
Year Born ▼   Year Died ▼

Was this contribution to the work a "work made for hire"?
☐ Yes
☐ No

AUTHOR'S NATIONALITY OR DOMICILE
Name of Country
OR { Citizen of ▶_____
{ Domiciled in▶_____

WAS THIS AUTHOR'S CONTRIBUTION TO THE WORK
Anonymous? ☐ Yes ☐ No
Pseudonymous? ☐ Yes ☐ No
If the answer to either of these questions is "Yes," see detailed instructions.

NATURE OF AUTHORSHIP Briefly describe nature of material created by this author in which copyright is claimed. ▼

---

3 a

YEAR IN WHICH CREATION OF THIS WORK WAS COMPLETED This information must be given ◀ Year In all cases.

b DATE AND NATION OF FIRST PUBLICATION OF THIS PARTICULAR WORK Complete this information ONLY if this work has been published. Month ▶_____ Day ▶_____ Year ▶_____ ◀ Nation

4

COPYRIGHT CLAIMANT(S) Name and address must be given even if the claimant is the same as the author given in space 2. ▼

APPLICATION RECEIVED

ONE DEPOSIT RECEIVED

TWO DEPOSITS RECEIVED

FUNDS RECEIVED

DO NOT WRITE HERE OFFICE USE ONLY

See instructions before completing this space.

TRANSFER If the claimant(s) named here in space 4 is (are) different from the author(s) named in space 2, give a brief statement of how the claimant(s) obtained ownership of the copyright. ▼

MORE ON BACK ▶ • Complete all applicable spaces (numbers 5-9) on the reverse side of this page.
• See detailed instructions. • Sign the form at line 8.

DO NOT WRITE HERE

Page 1 of _____ pages

EXAMINED BY

CHECKED BY

☐ CORRESPONDENCE
Yes

FORM PA

FOR
COPYRIGHT
OFFICE
USE
ONLY

DO NOT WRITE ABOVE THIS LINE. IF YOU NEED MORE SPACE, USE A SEPARATE CONTINUATION SHEET.

PREVIOUS REGISTRATION Has registration for this work, or for an earlier version of this work, already been made in the Copyright Office?
☐ Yes ☐ No If your answer is "Yes," why is another registration being sought? (Check appropriate box.) ▼ If your answer is "no," go to space 7.
a. ☐ This is the first published edition of a work previously registered in unpublished form.
b. ☐ This is the first application submitted by this author as copyright claimant.
c. ☐ This is a changed version of the work, as shown by space 6 on this application.
If your answer is "Yes," give: Previous Registration Number ▼   Year of Registration ▼

5

DERIVATIVE WORK OR COMPILATION Complete both space 6a and 6b for a derivative work; complete only 6b for a compilation.
Preexisting Material Identify any preexisting work or works that this work is based on or incorporates. ▼

a

6

See instructions
before completing
this space.

Material Added to This Work Give a brief, general statement of the material that has been added to this work and in which copyright is claimed. ▼

b

DEPOSIT ACCOUNT If the registration fee is to be charged to a Deposit Account established in the Copyright Office, give name and number of Account.
Name ▼   **Account Number ▼**

a

7

CORRESPONDENCE Give name and address to which correspondence about this application should be sent.   Name/Address/Apt/City/State/ZIP ▼

b

Area code and daytime telephone number ▶ (   )   Fax number ▶ (   )

Email ▶

CERTIFICATION* I, the undersigned, hereby certify that I am the
Check only one ▶
☐ author
☐ other copyright claimant
☐ owner of exclusive right(s)
☐ authorized agent of _____
Name of author or other copyright claimant, or owner of exclusive right(s) ▲
of the work identified in this application and that the statements made by me in this application are correct to the best of my knowledge.

8

Typed or printed name and date ▼ If this application gives a date of publication in space 3, do not sign and submit it before that date.

Date ▶ _____

Handwritten signature (X) ▼

x _____

Certificate
will be
mailed in
window
envelope
to this
address:

Name ▼

Number/Street/Apt ▼

City/State/ZIP ▼

YOU MUST:
• Complete all necessary spaces
• Sign your application in space 8
SEND ALL 3 ELEMENTS
IN THE SAME PACKAGE:
1. Application form
2. Nonrefundable filing fee in check or money
order payable to Register of Copyrights
3. Deposit material
MAIL TO:
Library of Congress
Copyright Office
101 Independence Avenue, S.E.
Washington, D.C. 20559-6000

As of July 1, 1999,
the filing fee for
Form PA is $30.

9

APPENDIX 4:

COPYRIGHT FORM SE

FORM SE
For a Serial
UNITED STATES COPYRIGHT OFFICE

REGISTRATION NUMBER

_____

U
_____
EFFECTIVE DATE OF REGISTRATION

_____
Month _____ Day _____ Year _____

DO NOT WRITE ABOVE THIS LINE. IF YOU NEED MORE SPACE, USE A SEPARATE CONTINUATION SHEET.

1

TITLE OF THIS SERIAL ▼

Volume ▼   Number ▼   Date on Copies ▼   Frequency of Publication ▼

PREVIOUS OR ALTERNATIVE TITLES ▼

2 a

NAME OF AUTHOR ▼

DATES OF BIRTH AND DEATH
Year Born ▼   Year Died ▼

Was this contribution to the work a "work made for hire"?
☐ Yes
☐ No

AUTHOR'S NATIONALITY OR DOMICILE
Name of Country
OR { Citizen of ▶_____
{ Domiciled in▶_____

WAS THIS AUTHOR'S CONTRIBUTION TO THE WORK
Anonymous? ☐ Yes ☐ No
Pseudonymous? ☐ Yes ☐ No
If the answer to either of these questions is "Yes," see detailed instructions.

NATURE OF AUTHORSHIP Briefly describe nature of material created by this author in which copyright is claimed. ▼
☐ Collective Work   Other:

NOTE

Under the law, the "author" of a "work made for hire" is generally the employer, not the employee (see instructions). For any part of this work that was "made for hire" check "Yes" in the space provided, give the employer (or other person for whom the work was prepared) as "Author" of that part, and leave the space for dates of birth and death blank.

b

NAME OF AUTHOR ▼

DATES OF BIRTH AND DEATH
Year Born ▼   Year Died ▼

Was this contribution to the work a "work made for hire"?
☐ Yes
☐ No

AUTHOR'S NATIONALITY OR DOMICILE
Name of Country
OR { Citizen of ▶_____
{ Domiciled in▶_____

WAS THIS AUTHOR'S CONTRIBUTION TO THE WORK
Anonymous? ☐ Yes ☐ No
Pseudonymous? ☐ Yes ☐ No
If the answer to either of these questions is "Yes," see detailed instructions.

NATURE OF AUTHORSHIP Briefly describe nature of material created by this author in which copyright is claimed. ▼
☐ Collective Work   Other:

c

NAME OF AUTHOR ▼

DATES OF BIRTH AND DEATH
Year Born ▼   Year Died ▼

Was this contribution to the work a "work made for hire"?
☐ Yes
☐No

AUTHOR'S NATIONALITY OR DOMICILE
Name of Country
OR { Citizen of ▶_____
{ Domiciled in▶_____

WAS THIS AUTHOR'S CONTRIBUTION TO THE WORK
Anonymous? ☐ Yes ☐ No
Pseudonymous? ☐ Yes ☐ No
If the answer to either of these questions is "Yes," see detailed instructions.

NATURE OF AUTHORSHIP Briefly describe nature of material created by this author in which copyright is claimed. ▼
☐ Collective Work   Other:

3 a

YEAR IN WHICH CREATION OF THIS ISSUE WAS COMPLETED
This information must be given
◀Year in all cases.

b

DATE AND NATION OF FIRST PUBLICATION OF THIS PARTICULAR ISSUE
Complete this information Month▶ _____ Day▶ _____ Year▶ _____
ONLY if this work
has been published. ◀ Nation

4

See instructions before completing this space.

COPYRIGHT CLAIMANT(S) Name and address must be given even if the claimant is the same as the author given in space 2. ▼

TRANSFER If the claimant(s) named here in space 4 is (are) different from the author(s) named in space 2, give a brief statement of how the claimant(s) obtained ownership of the copyright. ▼

DO NOT WRITE HERE OFFICE USE ONLY

APPLICATION RECEIVED

ONE DEPOSIT RECEIVED

TWO DEPOSITS RECEIVED

REMITTANCE NUMBER AND DATE

MORE ON BACK ▶   • Complete all applicable spaces (numbers 5-9) on the reverse side of this page.
• See detailed instructions.   • Sign the form at line 8.

DO NOT WRITE HERE

Page 1 of _____ pages

DO NOT WRITE ABOVE THIS LINE. IF YOU NEED MORE SPACE, USE A SEPARATE CONTINUATION SHEET.

PREVIOUS REGISTRATION Has registration for this work, or for an earlier version of this work, already been made in the Copyright Office?

☐ Yes ☐ No If your answer is "Yes," why is another registration being sought? (Check appropriate box.) ▼

a. ☐ This is the first published edition of a work previously registered in unpublished form.

b. ☐ This is the first application submitted by this author as copyright claimant.

c. ☐ This is a changed version of the work, as shown by space 6 on this application.

If your answer is "Yes," give: Previous Registration Number ▼   Year of Registration ▼

5

DERIVATIVE WORK OR COMPILATION Complete both space 6a and 6b for a derivative work; complete only 6b for a compilation.

Preexisting Material Identify any preexisting work or works that this work is based on or incorporates. ▼

a

6

See instructions before completing this space.

Material Added to This Work Give a brief, general statement of the material that has been added to this work and in which copyright is claimed. ▼

b

DEPOSIT ACCOUNT If the registration fee is to be charged to a Deposit Account established in the Copyright Office, give name and number of Account.

Name ▼   Account Number ▼

a

7

CORRESPONDENCE Give name and address to which correspondence about this application should be sent.   Name/Address/Apt/City/State/ZIP ▼

b

▶   ▶

▶

CERTIFICATION* I, the undersigned, hereby certify that I am the

Check only one ▶
{ ☐ author
☐ other copyright claimant
☐ owner of exclusive right(s)
☐ authorized agent of _____

of the work identified in this application and that the statements made by me in this application are correct to the best of my knowledge.

Name of author or other copyright claimant, or owner of exclusive right(s) ▲

8

Typed or printed name and date ▼ If this application gives a date of publication in space 3, do not sign and submit it before that date.

_____ Date ▶ _____

☞   Handwritten signature (X) ▼

X _

9

*17 U.S.C. § 506(e): Any person who knowingly makes a false representation of a material fact in the application for copyright registration provided for by section 409, or in any written statement filed in connection with the application, shall be fined not more than $2,500.

June 1999—50,000   ♻ PRINTED ON RECYCLED PAPER   ☆U.S. GOVERNMENT PRINTING OFFICE: 1999-454-879/59

WEB REV: June 1999

APPENDIX 5:

COPYRIGHT FORM SR

FORM SR
For a Sound Recording
UNITED STATES COPYRIGHT OFFICE

REGISTRATION NUMBER

SR	SRU

EFFECTIVE DATE OF REGISTRATION

Month	Day	Year

DO NOT WRITE ABOVE THIS LINE. IF YOU NEED MORE SPACE, USE A SEPARATE CONTINUATION SHEET.

1

TITLE OF THIS WORK ▼

PREVIOUS, ALTERNATIVE, OR CONTENTS TITLES (CIRCLE ONE) ▼

2 a

NAME OF AUTHOR ▼

DATES OF BIRTH AND DEATH
Year Born ▼   Year Died ▼

Was this contribution to the work a "work made for hire"?
☐ Yes
☐ No

AUTHOR'S NATIONALITY OR DOMICILE
Name of Country
OR { Citizen of ▶_____
     { Domiciled in ▶_____

WAS THIS AUTHOR'S CONTRIBUTION TO THE WORK
Anonymous? ☐ Yes ☐ No
Pseudonymous? ☐ Yes ☐ No
If the answer to either of these questions is "Yes," see detailed instructions.

NATURE OF AUTHORSHIP Briefly describe nature of material created by this author in which copyright is claimed. ▼

NOTE
Under the law, the "author" of a "work made for hire" is generally the employer, not the employee (see instructions). For any part of this work that was "made for hire," check "Yes" in the space provided, give the employer (or other person for whom the work was prepared) as "Author" of that part, and leave the space for dates of birth and death blank.

b

NAME OF AUTHOR ▼

DATES OF BIRTH AND DEATH
Year Born ▼   Year Died ▼

Was this contribution to the work a "work made for hire"?
☐ Yes
☐ No

AUTHOR'S NATIONALITY OR DOMICILE
Name of Country
OR { Citizen of ▶_____
     { Domiciled in ▶_____

WAS THIS AUTHOR'S CONTRIBUTION TO THE WORK
Anonymous? ☐ Yes ☐ No
Pseudonymous? ☐ Yes ☐ No
If the answer to either of these questions is "Yes," see detailed instructions.

NATURE OF AUTHORSHIP Briefly describe nature of material created by this author in which copyright is claimed. ▼

c

NAME OF AUTHOR ▼

DATES OF BIRTH AND DEATH
Year Born ▼   Year Died ▼

Was this contribution to the work a "work made for hire"?
☐ Yes
☐ No

AUTHOR'S NATIONALITY OR DOMICILE
Name of Country
OR { Citizen of ▶_____
     { Domiciled in ▶_____

WAS THIS AUTHOR'S CONTRIBUTION TO THE WORK
Anonymous? ☐ Yes ☐ No
Pseudonymous? ☐ Yes ☐ No
If the answer to either of these questions is "Yes," see detailed instructions.

NATURE OF AUTHORSHIP Briefly describe nature of material created by this author in which copyright is claimed. ▼

3 a

YEAR IN WHICH CREATION OF THIS WORK WAS COMPLETED
This information must be given
◀ Year in all cases.

b

DATE AND NATION OF FIRST PUBLICATION OF THIS PARTICULAR WORK
Complete this information Month ▶_____ Day ▶_____ Year ▶_____
ONLY if this work
has been published.
◀ Nation

4 a

COPYRIGHT CLAIMANT(S) Name and address must be given even if the claimant is the same as the author given in space 2. ▼

b

TRANSFER If the claimant(s) named here in space 4 is (are) different from the author(s) named in space 2, give a brief statement of how the claimant(s) obtained ownership of the copyright. ▼

See instructions before completing this space.

APPLICATION RECEIVED

ONE DEPOSIT RECEIVED

TWO DEPOSITS RECEIVED

FUNDS RECEIVED

DO NOT WRITE HERE
OFFICE USE ONLY

MORE ON BACK ▶ • Complete all applicable spaces (numbers 5-9) on the reverse side of this page.
• See detailed instructions.   • Sign the form at line 8.

DO NOT WRITE HERE

Page 1 of _____ pages

EXAMINED BY	FORM SR
CHECKED BY	
CORRESPONDENCE □ Yes	FOR COPYRIGHT OFFICE USE ONLY

DO NOT WRITE ABOVE THIS LINE. IF YOU NEED MORE SPACE, USE A SEPARATE CONTINUATION SHEET.

PREVIOUS REGISTRATION Has registration for this work, or for an earlier version of this work, already been made in the Copyright Office?

□ Yes   □ No   If your answer is "Yes," why is another registration being sought? (Check appropriate box) ▼

a. □ This work was previously registered in unpublished form and now has been published for the first time.

b. □ This is the first application submitted by this author as copyright claimant.

c. □ This is a changed version of the work, as shown by space 6 on this application.

If your answer is "Yes," give: Previous Registration Number ▼   Year of Registration ▼

5

DERIVATIVE WORK OR COMPILATION

a Preexisting Material Identify any preexisting work or works that this work is based on or incorporates. ▼

6

See instructions before completing this space.

b Material Added to This Work Give a brief, general statement of the material that has been added to this work and in which copyright is claimed. ▼

a **DEPOSIT ACCOUNT** If the registration fee is to be charged to a Deposit Account established in the Copyright Office, give name and number of Account.

Name ▼   Account Number ▼

7

b **CORRESPONDENCE** Give name and address to which correspondence about this application should be sent. Name/Address/Apt/City/State/ZIP ▼

Area code and daytime telephone number ▶   Fax number ▶

Email ▶

CERTIFICATION* I, the undersigned, hereby certify that I am the

Check only one ▼

□ author

□ other copyright claimant

□ owner of exclusive right(s)

□ authorized agent of _____

Name of author or other copyright claimant, or owner of exclusive right(s) ▲

8

of the work identified in this application and that the statements made by me in this application are correct to the best of my knowledge.

Typed or printed name and date ▼ If this application gives a date of publication in space 3, do not sign and submit it before that date.

Date ▶ _____

Handwritten signature (x) ▼

X _

Certificate will be mailed in window envelope to this address	Name ▼	**YOU MUST:** • Complete all necessary spaces • Sign your application in space 8	**9**
	Number/Street/Apt ▼	**SEND ALL 3 ELEMENTS IN THE SAME PACKAGE:** 1. Application form 2. Nonrefundable filing fee in check or money order payable to *Register of Copyrights* 3. Deposit material	As of July 1, 1999, the filing fee for Form SR is $30.
	City/State/ZIP ▼	**MAIL TO:** Library of Congress Copyright Office 101 Independence Avenue, S.E. Washington, D.C. 20559-6000	

*17 U.S.C. § 506(e): Any person who knowingly makes a false representation of a material fact in the application for copyright registration provided for by section 409, or in any written statement filed in connection with the application, shall be fined not more than $2,500.

June 1999—50,000   ♺ PRINTED ON RECYCLED PAPER   ☆U.S. GOVERNMENT PRINTING OFFICE: 1999-454-879/48

WEB REV: June 1999

APPENDIX 6:

COPYRIGHT FORM TX

FORM TX
For a Nondramatic Literary Work
UNITED STATES COPYRIGHT OFFICE

REGISTRATION NUMBER

_____

TX _____ TXU

EFFECTIVE DATE OF REGISTRATION

_____

Month   Day   Year

DO NOT WRITE ABOVE THIS LINE. IF YOU NEED MORE SPACE, USE A SEPARATE CONTINUATION SHEET.

1

TITLE OF THIS WORK ▼

PREVIOUS OR ALTERNATIVE TITLES ▼

PUBLICATION AS A CONTRIBUTION If this work was published as a contribution to a periodical, serial, or collection, give information about the collective work in which the contribution appeared.   **Title of Collective Work ▼**

If published in a periodical or serial give: Volume ▼   Number ▼   Issue Date ▼   On Pages ▼

2 **a**

NAME OF AUTHOR ▼

DATES OF BIRTH AND DEATH
Year Born ▼   Year Died ▼

Was this contribution to the work a "work made for hire"?
☐ Yes
☐ No

AUTHOR'S NATIONALITY OR DOMICILE
Name of Country
OR { Citizen of ▶_____
Domiciled in▶_____

WAS THIS AUTHOR'S CONTRIBUTION TO THE WORK
Anonymous?   ☐ Yes ☐ No
Pseudonymous? ☐ Yes ☐ No
If the answer to either of these questions is "Yes," see detailed instructions.

NATURE OF AUTHORSHIP Briefly describe nature of material created by this author in which copyright is claimed. ▼

NOTE

Under the law, the "author" of a "work made for hire" is generally the employer, not the employee (see instructions). For any part of this work that was "made for hire" check "Yes" in the space provided, give the employer (or other person for whom the work was prepared) as "Author" of that part, and leave the space for dates of birth and death blank.

b

NAME OF AUTHOR ▼

DATES OF BIRTH AND DEATH
Year Born ▼   Year Died ▼

Was this contribution to the work a "work made for hire"?
☐ Yes
☐ No

AUTHOR'S NATIONALITY OR DOMICILE
Name of Country
OR { Citizen of ▶_____
Domiciled in▶_____

WAS THIS AUTHOR'S CONTRIBUTION TO THE WORK
Anonymous?   ☐ Yes ☐ No
Pseudonymous? ☐ Yes ☐ No
If the answer to either of these questions is "Yes," see detailed instructions.

NATURE OF AUTHORSHIP Briefly describe nature of material created by this author in which copyright is claimed. ▼

c

NAME OF AUTHOR ▼

DATES OF BIRTH AND DEATH
Year Born ▼   Year Died ▼

Was this contribution to the work a "work made for hire"?
☐ Yes
☐ No

AUTHOR'S NATIONALITY OR DOMICILE
Name of Country
OR { Citizen of ▶_____
Domiciled in▶_____

WAS THIS AUTHOR'S CONTRIBUTION TO THE WORK
Anonymous?   ☐ Yes ☐ No
Pseudonymous? ☐ Yes ☐ No
If the answer to either of these questions is "Yes," see detailed instructions.

NATURE OF AUTHORSHIP Briefly describe nature of material created by this author in which copyright is claimed. ▼

3 **a**

YEAR IN WHICH CREATION OF THIS WORK WAS COMPLETED This information must be given ◄ Year in all cases.

b DATE AND NATION OF FIRST PUBLICATION OF THIS PARTICULAR WORK
Complete this information Month ▶_____ Day ▶_____ Year ▶_____
ONLY if this work has been published.
◄ Nation

4

COPYRIGHT CLAIMANT(S) Name and address must be given even if the claimant is the same as the author given in space 2. ▼

See instructions before completing this space.

TRANSFER If the claimant(s) named here in space 4 is (are) different from the author(s) named in space 2, give a brief statement of how the claimant(s) obtained ownership of the copyright. ▼

APPLICATION RECEIVED

ONE DEPOSIT RECEIVED

TWO DEPOSITS RECEIVED

FUNDS RECEIVED

DO NOT WRITE HERE OFFICE USE ONLY

MORE ON BACK ▶ • Complete all applicable spaces (numbers 5-9) on the reverse side of this page.
• See detailed instructions.   • Sign the form at line 8.

DO NOT WRITE HERE
Page 1 of _____ pages

EXAMINED BY	FORM TX
CHECKED BY	
☐ CORRESPONDENCE Yes	FOR COPYRIGHT OFFICE USE ONLY

DO NOT WRITE ABOVE THIS LINE. IF YOU NEED MORE SPACE, USE A SEPARATE CONTINUATION SHEET.

PREVIOUS REGISTRATION Has registration for this work, or for an earlier version of this work, already been made in the Copyright Office?

☐ Yes   ☐ No   If your answer is "Yes," why is another registration being sought? (Check appropriate box.) ▼

a. ☐ This is the first published edition of a work previously registered in unpublished form.

b. ☐ This is the first application submitted by this author as copyright claimant.

c. ☐ This is a changed version of the work, as shown by space 6 on this application.

If your answer is "Yes," give: **Previous Registration Number** ▶   **Year of Registration** ▶

5

DERIVATIVE WORK OR COMPILATION

Preexisting Material Identify any preexisting work or works that this work is based on or incorporates. ▼

a   **6**

See instructions before completing this space.

Material Added to This Work Give a brief, general statement of the material that has been added to this work and in which copyright is claimed. ▼

b

DEPOSIT ACCOUNT If the registration fee is to be charged to a Deposit Account established in the Copyright Office, give name and number of Account.

Name ▼   **Account Number** ▼

a   **7**

CORRESPONDENCE Give name and address to which correspondence about this application should be sent.   Name/Address/Apt/City/State/ZIP ▼

b

Area code and daytime telephone number ▶   Fax number ▶

Email ▶

CERTIFICATION* I, the undersigned, hereby certify that I am the

Check only one ▶

☐ author

☐ other copyright claimant

☐ owner of exclusive right(s)

☐ authorized agent of _____

Name of author or other copyright claimant, or owner of exclusive right(s) ▲

of the work identified in this application and that the statements made by me in this application are correct to the best of my knowledge.

8

Typed or printed name and date ▼ If this application gives a date of publication in space 3, do not sign and submit it before that date.

_____ Date ▶ _____

Handwritten signature (X) ▼

X _____

Certificate will be mailed in window envelope to this address:	Name ▼	YOU MUST: • Complete all necessary spaces • Sign your application in space 8
		SEND ALL 3 ELEMENTS IN THE SAME PACKAGE: 1. Application form 2. Nonrefundable filing fee in check or money order payable to Register of Copyrights 3. Deposit material
	Number/Street/Apt ▼	MAIL TO: Library of Congress Copyright Office 101 Independence Avenue, S.E. Washington, D.C. 20559-6000
	City/State/ZIP ▼	As of July 1, 1999, the filing fee for Form TX is $30.

9

*17 U.S.C. § 506(e): Any person who knowingly makes a false representation of a material fact in the application for copyright registration provided for by section 409, or in any written statement filed in connection with the application, shall be fined not more than $2,500.

June 1999—200,000   ⟳ PRINTED ON RECYCLED PAPER   ☆U.S. GOVERNMENT PRINTING OFFICE: 1999-454-879/49

WEB REV: June 1999

APPENDIX 7:

COPYRIGHT FORM VA

FORM VA ⊘
For a Work of the Visual Arts
UNITED STATES COPYRIGHT OFFICE

REGISTRATION NUMBER

_____
VA   VAU
EFFECTIVE DATE OF REGISTRATION

_____
Month   Day   Year

DO NOT WRITE ABOVE THIS LINE. IF YOU NEED MORE SPACE, USE A SEPARATE CONTINUATION SHEET.

1

TITLE OF THIS WORK ▼   NATURE OF THIS WORK ▼ See instructions

PREVIOUS OR ALTERNATIVE TITLES ▼

Publication as a Contribution If this work was published as a contribution to a periodical, serial, or collection, give information about the collective work in which the contribution appeared.   **Title of Collective Work ▼**

If published in a periodical or serial give: Volume ▼   Number ▼   Issue Date ▼   On Pages ▼

2

NAME OF AUTHOR ▼   DATES OF BIRTH AND DEATH
                                               Year Born ▼   Year Died ▼

NOTE

Under the law, the "author" of a "work made for hire" is generally the employer, not the employee (see instructions). For any part of this work that was "made for hire" check "Yes" in the space provided, give the employer (or other person for whom the work was prepared) as "Author" of that part, and leave the space for dates of birth and death blank.

Was this contribution to the work a "work made for hire"?
☐ Yes
☐ No

Author's Nationality or Domicile
Name of Country
OR { Citizen of ▶_____
     Domiciled in ▶_____

Was This Author's Contribution to the Work
Anonymous?   ☐ Yes ☐ No
Pseudonymous? ☐ Yes ☐ No
If the answer to either of these questions is "Yes," see detailed instructions.

NATURE OF AUTHORSHIP Check appropriate box(es). **See instructions**
☐ 3-Dimensional sculpture   ☐ Map   ☐ Technical drawing
☐ 2-Dimensional artwork   ☐ Photograph   ☐ Text
☐ Reproduction of work of art ☐ Jewelry design   ☐ Architectural work

NAME OF AUTHOR ▼   DATES OF BIRTH AND DEATH
                                               Year Born ▼   Year Died ▼

Was this contribution to the work a "work made for hire"?
☐ Yes
☐ No

Author's Nationality or Domicile
Name of Country
OR { Citizen of ▶_____
     Domiciled in ▶_____

Was This Author's Contribution to the Work
Anonymous?   ☐ Yes ☐ No
Pseudonymous? ☐ Yes ☐ No
If the answer to either of these questions is "Yes," see detailed instructions.

NATURE OF AUTHORSHIP Check appropriate box(es). **See instructions**
☐ 3-Dimensional sculpture   ☐ Map   ☐ Technical drawing
☐ 2-Dimensional artwork   ☐ Photograph   ☐ Text
☐ Reproduction of work of art ☐ Jewelry design   ☐ Architectural work

3

Year in Which Creation of This Work Was Completed
This information must be given ◀ Year in all cases.

Date and Nation of First Publication of This Particular Work
Complete this information   Month ▶ _____ Day ▶ _____ Year ▶ _____
ONLY if this work has been published.   ◀ Nation

4

COPYRIGHT CLAIMANT(S) Name and address must be given even if the claimant is the same as the author given in space 2. ▼

See instructions before completing this space.

Transfer If the claimant(s) named here in space 4 is (are) different from the author(s) named in space 2, give a brief statement of how the claimant(s) obtained ownership of the copyright. ▼

APPLICATION RECEIVED

ONE DEPOSIT RECEIVED

TWO DEPOSITS RECEIVED

FUNDS RECEIVED

DO NOT WRITE HERE
OFFICE USE ONLY

MORE ON BACK ▶ • Complete all applicable spaces (numbers 5-9) on the reverse side of this page.
                  • See detailed instructions.   • Sign the form at line 8.

DO NOT WRITE HERE
Page 1 of _____ pages

EXAMINED BY   FORM VA

CHECKED BY

☐ CORRESPONDENCE Yes

FOR COPYRIGHT OFFICE USE ONLY

DO NOT WRITE ABOVE THIS LINE. IF YOU NEED MORE SPACE, USE A SEPARATE CONTINUATION SHEET.

PREVIOUS REGISTRATION Has registration for this work, or for an earlier version of this work, already been made in the Copyright Office?

☐ Yes ☐ No If your answer is "Yes," why is another registration being sought? (Check appropriate box.) ▼

a. ☐ This is the first published edition of a work previously registered in unpublished form.

b. ☐ This is the first application submitted by this author as copyright claimant.

c. ☐ This is a changed version of the work, as shown by space 6 on this application.

If your answer is "Yes," give: **Previous Registration Number ▼**   **Year of Registration ▼**

DERIVATIVE WORK OR COMPILATION Complete both space 6a and 6b for a derivative work; complete only 6b for a compilation.

a. **Preexisting Material** Identify any preexisting work or works that this work is based on or incorporates. ▼

See instructions before completing this space.

b. **Material Added to This Work** Give a brief, general statement of the material that has been added to this work and in which copyright is claimed. ▼

DEPOSIT ACCOUNT If the registration fee is to be charged to a Deposit Account established in the Copyright Office, give name and number of Account.

Name ▼   **Account Number ▼**

CORRESPONDENCE Give name and address to which correspondence about this application should be sent. Name/Address/Apt/City/State/ZIP ▼

Area code and daytime telephone number ▶ ( )   Fax number ▶ ( )

Email ▶

CERTIFICATION* I, the undersigned, hereby certify that I am the

check only one ▶
☐ author
☐ other copyright claimant
☐ owner of exclusive right(s)
☐ authorized agent of

Name of author or other copyright claimant, or owner of exclusive right(s) ▲

of the work identified in this application and that the statements made by me in this application are correct to the best of my knowledge.

Typed or printed name and date ▼ If this application gives a date of publication in space 3, do not sign and submit it before that date.

Date ▶

Handwritten signature (X) ▼

X

Certificate will be mailed in window envelope to this address:

Name ▼

Number/Street/Apt ▼

City/State/ZIP ▼

YOU MUST:
• Complete all necessary spaces
• Sign your application in space 8

SEND ALL 3 ELEMENTS IN THE SAME PACKAGE:
1. Application form
2. Nonrefundable filing fee in check or money order payable to Register of Copyrights
3. Deposit material

As of July 1, 1999, the filing fee for Form VA is $30.

MAIL TO:
Library of Congress Copyright Office 101 Independence Avenue, S.E. Washington, D.C. 20559-6000

*17 U.S.C. § 506(e): Any person who knowingly makes a false representation of a material fact in the application for copyright registration provided for by section 409, or in any written statement filed in connection with the application, shall be fined not more than $2,500.

June 1999—100,000 WEB REV: June 1999   ♻ PRINTED ON RECYCLED PAPER   ☆U.S. GOVERNMENT PRINTING OFFICE: 1999-454-879/71

APPENDIX 8:

COPYRIGHT FORM GR/CP

ADJUNCT APPLICATION
for Copyright Registration for a
Group of Contributions to Periodicals

- Use this adjunct form only if you are making a single registration for a group of contributions to periodicals, and you are also filing a basic application on Form TX, Form PA, or Form VA. Follow the instructions, attached.
- Number each line in Part B consecutively. Use additional Forms GR/CP if you need more space.
- Submit this adjunct form with the basic application form. Clip (do not tape or staple) and fold all sheets together before submitting them.
- Fees are effective through June 30, 2002. After that date, check the Copyright Office Website at www.loc.gov/copyright or call (202) 707-3000 for current fee information.

FORM GR/CP
For a Group of Contributions to Periodicals
UNITED STATES COPYRIGHT OFFICE
REGISTRATION NUMBER

_____

TX _____ PA _____ VA _____
EFFECTIVE DATE OF REGISTRATION

Month _____ Day _____ Year _____
FORM GR/CP RECEIVED

Page _____ of _____ pages

DO NOT WRITE ABOVE THIS LINE. FOR COPYRIGHT OFFICE USE ONLY

A
Identification of Application

IDENTIFICATION OF BASIC APPLICATION:
• This application for copyright registration for a group of contributions to periodicals is submitted as an adjunct to an application filed on: (Check which)

☐ Form TX   ☐ Form PA   ☐ Form VA

IDENTIFICATION OF AUTHOR AND CLAIMANT: (Give the name of the author and the name of the copyright claimant in all of the contributions listed in Part B of this form. The names should be the same as the names given in spaces 2 and 4 of the basic application.)

Name of Author _____

Name of Copyright Claimant _____

B
Registration for Group of Contributions

COPYRIGHT REGISTRATION FOR A GROUP OF CONTRIBUTIONS TO PERIODICALS: (To make a single registration for a group of works by the same individual author, all first published as contributions to periodicals within a 12-month period (see instructions), give full information about each contribution. If more space is needed, use additional Forms GR/CP.)

☐ Title of Contribution _____
Title of Periodical _____ Vol.____ No._____ Issue Date _____ Pages _____
Date of First Publication _____ Nation of First Publication _____
(Month)   (Day)   (Year)   (Country)

☐ Title of Contribution _____
Title of Periodical _____ Vol.____ No._____ Issue Date _____ Pages _____
Date of First Publication _____ Nation of First Publication _____
(Month)   (Day)   (Year)   (Country)

☐ Title of Contribution _____
Title of Periodical _____ Vol.____ No._____ Issue Date _____ Pages _____
Date of First Publication _____ Nation of First Publication _____
(Month)   (Day)   (Year)   (Country)

☐ Title of Contribution _____
Title of Periodical _____ Vol.____ No._____ Issue Date _____ Pages _____
Date of First Publication _____ Nation of First Publication _____
(Month)   (Day)   (Year)   (Country)

☐ Title of Contribution _____
Title of Periodical _____ Vol.____ No._____ Issue Date _____ Pages _____
Date of First Publication _____ Nation of First Publication _____
(Month)   (Day)   (Year)   (Country)

☐ Title of Contribution _____
Title of Periodical _____ Vol.____ No._____ Issue Date _____ Pages _____
Date of First Publication _____ Nation of First Publication _____
(Month)   (Day)   (Year)   (Country)

☐ Title of Contribution _____
Title of Periodical _____ Vol.____ No._____ Issue Date _____ Pages _____
Date of First Publication _____ Nation of First Publication _____
(Month)   (Day)   (Year)   (Country)

FORM GR/CP

DO NOT WRITE ABOVE THIS LINE. FOR COPYRIGHT OFFICE USE ONLY.

Title of Contribution _____
Title of Periodical _____ Vol.____ No.____ Issue Date _____ Pages _____   **B**
Date of First Publication _____ Nation of First Publication _____   Continued
                          (Month)   (Day)   (Year)   (Country)

Title of Contribution _____
Title of Periodical _____ Vol.____ No.____ Issue Date _____ Pages _____
Date of First Publication _____ Nation of First Publication _____
                          (Month)   (Day)   (Year)   (Country)

Title of Contribution _____
Title of Periodical _____ Vol.____ No.____ Issue Date _____ Pages _____
Date of First Publication _____ Nation of First Publication _____
                          (Month)   (Day)   (Year)   (Country)

Title of Contribution _____
Title of Periodical _____ Vol.____ No.____ Issue Date _____ Pages _____
Date of First Publication _____ Nation of First Publication _____
                          (Month)   (Day)   (Year)   (Country)

Title of Contribution _____
Title of Periodical _____ Vol.____ No.____ Issue Date _____ Pages _____
Date of First Publication _____ Nation of First Publication _____
                          (Month)   (Day)   (Year)   (Country)

Title of Contribution _____
Title of Periodical _____ Vol.____ No.____ Issue Date _____ Pages _____
Date of First Publication _____ Nation of First Publication _____
                          (Month)   (Day)   (Year)   (Country)

Title of Contribution _____
Title of Periodical _____ Vol.____ No.____ Issue Date _____ Pages _____
Date of First Publication _____ Nation of First Publication _____
                          (Month)   (Day)   (Year)   (Country)

Title of Contribution _____
Title of Periodical _____ Vol.____ No.____ Issue Date _____ Pages _____
Date of First Publication _____ Nation of First Publication _____
                          (Month)   (Day)   (Year)   (Country)

Title of Contribution _____
Title of Periodical _____ Vol.____ No.____ Issue Date _____ Pages _____
Date of First Publication _____ Nation of First Publication _____
                          (Month)   (Day)   (Year)   (Country)

Title of Contribution _____
Title of Periodical _____ Vol.____ No.____ Issue Date _____ Pages _____
Date of First Publication _____ Nation of First Publication _____
                          (Month)   (Day)   (Year)   (Country)

Title of Contribution _____
Title of Periodical _____ Vol.____ No.____ Issue Date _____ Pages _____
Date of First Publication _____ Nation of First Publication _____
                          (Month)   (Day)   (Year)   (Country)

Title of Contribution _____
Title of Periodical _____ Vol.____ No.____ Issue Date _____ Pages _____
Date of First Publication _____ Nation of First Publication _____
                          (Month)   (Day)   (Year)   (Country)

June 1999—20,000
WEB REV: June 1999   ⊕ PRINTED ON RECYCLED PAPER   ☆U.S. GOVERNMENT PRINTING OFFICE: 1999-454-879/58

COPYRIGHT FEES AND INCREASES

Copyright Office Fees
Effective through June 30, 2001[1]

Copyright Registration Fees

Basic Registrations: (Fee to accompany an application and deposit for registration of a claim to copyright)
Form TX .... $ 30
    Short Form TX .... $ 30
Form VA .... $ 30
    Short Form VA .... $ 30
Form PA .... $ 30
    Short Form PA. .... $ 30
Form SE .... $ 30
    Short Form SE .... $ 30
Form SR .... $ 30
Form GATT .... $ 30
Form GR/CP (This Form is an adjunct to Forms VA, PA, and TX. There is no additional charge.)

Renewal Registrations: (For works published or registered before January 1, 1978)
Form RE .... $ 45
Addendum to Form RE .... $ 15

Group Registrations: (Fee to register a group of related claims, where appropriate)
Form SE/Group (minimum fee $30) (serials) .... $ 10 /serial issue
Form G/DN (daily newspapers and newsletters) .... $ 55
Form GATT/Grp (minimum fee $30) (restored works) .... $ 10 /restored work

Supplementary Registrations: (Fee to register a correction or amplification to a completed registration)
Form CA .... $ 65

Miscellaneous Registrations:
Form D-VH (vessel hulls) $75**
Form MW (mask works) $75

Special Services Related to Registration (Optional Services)

Special Handling for Registration of Qualified Copyright Claims:
(Fee to expedite processing of qualified claims)
Special handling fee (per claim) .... $ 500
Additional fee for each (non-special handling) claim using the same deposit ..... $ 50

Other Fees Associated with Registration:
Full-term retention of published copyright deposit .... $ 365
Secure test processing .... $ 60 /hour
Appeal fees (for claims previously refused registration)
    First appeal .... $ 200
        Additional claim in related group (each) .... $ 20
    Second appeal .... $ 500
        Additional claim in related group (each) .... $ 20

[1]Some of these fees went into effect on July 1, 1999; they will be considered again in 2002. Others went into effect on July 1, 1998; they will be considered again in 2001.

Continued on back ▶

Other Copyright Service Fees

Recordation of Documents Relating to Copyrighted Works
(Fee to make a public record of an assignment of rights or other document)
Recordation of a document containing no more than one title .... $ 50
Additional titles (per group of 10 titles) .... $ 15
Recordation of NIE containing no more than one title .... $ 30
Additional titles (each) .... $ 1

Special Handling of Recordation of Documents .... $ 330

Reference and Bibliography Reports on Copyrighted Works
(Fee for searching copyright records and preparing an official report)
Preparation of a report from official records .... $ 65 /hour

Surcharge for Expedited Reference and Bibliography Reports .... $ 125 / 1ˢᵗ hour
$ 95 /each add'l hour

Certification and Documents Services: Preparing Copies of Copyright Office Records
(Fees for locating, retrieving, and reproducing Copyright Office records)
Search fee for locating and/or retrieving records .... $ 65 /hour
Additional certificate of registration .... $ 25
Certification of Copyright Office records .... $65 /hour
Inspection of Copyright Office records .... $ 65
Copying fee (minimum $15) .... variable fee depending on format & size

Surcharge for Expedited Certification and Documents Services
Locating and/or retrieving in-process records .... $ 75 /hour
Additional certificate of registration .... $ 75 /hour
Certification of Copyright Office records .... $ 75 /hour
Copy of assignment or other recorded document .... $ 75 /hour
Copy of any other Copyright Office record .... $ 95 /1ˢᵗ hour
$75 / each add'l hour

Miscellaneous Fees
Receipt for deposit without registration (Section 407 deposit) .... $ 4
Online Service Provider Designation .... $20★
Notice to Libraries and Archives .... $50★★
$ 20 /each add'l title

Notice of Intention to obtain compulsory license to make and distribute phonorecords $12

★It is anticipated that the fee will increase when final regulations are announced later in 1999.
★★ This fee may change when final regulations are announced later in 1999.
Please check the Copyright Office Website at **www.loc.gov/copyright** or call (202) 707-3000 for the latest fee information.

Library of Congress • Copyright Office • 101 Independence Avenue, S.E. • Washington, D.C. 20559-6000
www.loc.gov/copyright
REV: June 1999—20,000 ⊕ PRINTED ON RECYCLED PAPER   ☼U.S. GOVERNMENT PRINTING OFFICE: 1999-454-879/63
WEB REV: June 1999

Effective on and after July 1, 1999

Basic registrations: (Fee to accompany an application and deposit for registration of a claim to copyright)

Form TX or Short Form TX .... $ 30
Form VA or Short Form VA .... $ 30
Form PA or Short Form PA. .... $ 30
Form SE or Short Form SE .... $ 30
Form SR .... $ 30
Form GATT .... $ 30

Renewal registrations: (For works published or registered before January 1, 1978)

Form RE .... $ 45
Addendum to Form RE .... $ 15

Group registrations: (Fee to register a group of related claims, where appropriate)

Form SE/Group (minimum fee $30) (serials) .... $ 10 /serial issue
Form G/DN (daily newspapers and newsletters) .... $ 55
Form GATT/Grp (minimum fee $30) (restored works) .... $ 10 /restored work

Supplementary registrations: (Fee to register a correction or amplification to a completed registration)

Form CA .... $ 65

Miscellaneous Registrations:

Form D-VH (vessel hulls) $75

Recordation of Documents Relating to Copyrighted Works (Public record of an assignment of rights or other document)

Recordation of a document containing no more than one title .... $ 50
Additional titles (per group of 10 titles) .... $ 15

Reference and Bibliographic Reports on Copyrighted Works (Fee for searching copyright records and preparing an official report)

Preparation of a report from official records .... $ 65 /hour

Preparation of Copies or Certifications of Copyright Office Records
(Fees for locating, retrieving, and reproducing Copyright Office records)

Search fee for locating and retrieving records .... $ 65 /hour
Additional certificate of registration .... $ 25
Copying fee (minimum $15) .... variable fee depending on format & size
Certifications .... $ 65 /hour

Current Fees that Will NOT Change on July 1, 1999

Special services related to registration (optional services)
Special handling for registration of qualified copyright claims: (Fee to expedite processing of qualified claims)

Special handling fee (per claim) .... $ 500
Additional fee for each (non-special handling) claim using the same deposit .... $ 50

Other fees associated with registration:

Full-term retention of published copyright deposit .... $ 365
Secure test processing .... $ 60 /hour
Appeal fees (for claims previously refused registration)
　　First appeal .... $ 200
　　　　Additional claim in related group (each) .... $ 20
　　Second appeal .... $ 500
　　　　Additional claim in related group (each) .... $ 20

Other Recordations

Recordation of NIE containing no more than one title .... $ 30
　　Additional titles (each) .... $ 1
Recordation of Notice of Intention to Make and Distribute Phonorecords .... $ 12

Special handling of Recordation of Documents .... $ 330

Surcharge **for Expedited Reference and Bibliographic Reports** .... $ 125
　　　$ 95 /each add'l hour

Surcharge **for Expediting Certification and Documents services**

Locating and retrieving Copyright Office records .... $ 95 /hour
　　　$ 75 /each add'l hour
Additional certificate of registration .... $ 75 /hour
Certifications .... $ 75 /hour
Copy of assignment or other recorded document .... $ 75 /hour

Miscellaneous fees

Receipt for deposit without registration (Section 407 deposit) .... $ 4
Form MW (mask works) $75
Licensing and related fees .... Please call 202-707-8150

APPENDIX 10:

LETTER REQUESTING PERMISSION TO USE COPYRIGHTED MATERIALS

TO: [Publisher Name and Address]

Dear [Insert Name]:

I am writing to ask your permission to incorporate into a printed publication the following material:

[Describe material, e.g., name of book/article; name of author; page number(s), etc.].

The material will be distributed/published as follows:

[Describe intended use of material, e.g., name of publication; publisher; publication date, etc.].

If you do not solely control the copyright in the requested material, please provide me with co-publisher information so that I can obtain the necessary joint approvals.

Thank you.

APPENDIX 11:

NON-EXCLUSIVE COPYRIGHT LICENSE

COPYRIGHT LICENSE

This Agreement (the "Agreement") is made by and between [Name of Copyright Owner] ("Owner"), and [Name of Licensee] ("Licensee") with its principal place of business at [Insert Address].

RECITALS

1. Licensee is [describe entity], engaged in [describe business activity relevant to copyrighted material].

2. Owner owns the copyright to certain copyrighted materials and is willing to allow Licensee to copy and utilize such materials under the terms herein set forth.

NOW THEREFORE, in consideration of the mutual covenants and promises herein contained, the Owner and Licensee agree as follows:

1. This Agreement shall be effective as of (the "Effective Date").

2. Owner hereby grants Licensee a non-exclusive right to copy certain copyrighted materials described in Exhibit A (the "Copyrighted Material"), in whole or in part, and to incorporate the Copyrighted Material, in whole or in part, into other works (the "Derivative Works") for Licensee's use only.

3. All right, title and interest in the Copyrighted Material, including without limitation, any copyright, shall remain with Owner.

4. Owner shall also own the copyright in the Derivative Works.

5. This Agreement may be terminated by the written agreement of both parties. In the event that either party shall be in default of its material obligations under this Agreement and shall fail to remedy such default within sixty (60) days after receipt of written notice thereof, this Agreement shall terminate upon expiration of the sixty (60) day period.

6. Exhibit A is incorporated herein and made a part hereof for all purposes.

7. This Agreement constitutes the entire and only agreement between the parties and all other prior negotiations, agreements, representations and understandings are superseded hereby.

8. This Agreement shall be construed and enforced in accordance with the laws of the United States of America and of the State of New York.

IN WITNESS WHEREOF, the parties have executed this Agreement, effective this _____ day of _____, 19___ .

_____   _____

OWNER/LICENSOR   LICENSEE

APPENDIX 12:

ASSIGNMENT OF COPYRIGHT

This Agreement is made between XYZ CORPORATION ("Assignee") and JOHN SMITH ("Author), whose address is [Insert Address]. Author represents and warrants that he/she is the sole creator and owner of [describe work] (the "Work"), designed and created for the Assignee's Public Relation's Department, and holds the complete and undivided copyright interest to the Work.

For valuable consideration, receipt and sufficiency of which are hereby acknowledged, Author and Assignee agree as follows:

Author does hereby sell, assign, and transfer to Assignee, its successors and assigns, the entire right, title and interest in and to the copyright in the Work and any registrations and copyright applications relating thereto and any renewals and extensions thereof, and in and to all works based upon, derived from, or incorporating the Work, and in an to all income, royalties, damages, claims and payments now or hereafter due or payable with respect thereto, and in and to all causes of action, either in law or in equity for past, present, or future infringement based on the copyrights, and in and to all rights corresponding to the foregoing throughout the world.

2. Author agrees to execute all papers and to perform such other proper acts as Assignee may deem necessary to secure for Assignee or its designee the rights herein assigned.

IN WITNESS WHEREOF, the parties have executed this Agreement, effective this _____ day of _____, 19___ .

XYZ CORPORATION, ASSIGNEE: AUTHOR:

_____   _____

Name/Title   Name/SSN

WORK MADE FOR HIRE AGREEMENT

This Agreement made the ____day of _____ 1999, by and between JOHN SMITH ("Author") and XYZ CORPORATION ("Employer").

THE AUTHOR AND THE EMPLOYER AGREE THAT:

1. Title and Copyright Assignment

(a) Author and Employer intend this to be a contract for services and each considers the products and results of the services to be rendered by Author hereunder to be a work made for hire (the "Work").

(b) Author acknowledges and agrees that the Work, and all rights therein including, without limitation, copyright, belongs to and shall be the sole and exclusive property of Employer.

(c) If for any reason the Work would not be considered a work made for hire under applicable law, Author does hereby sell, assign, and transfer to Employer, its successors and assigns, the entire right, title and interest in and to the copyright in the Work and any registrations and copyright applications relating thereto and any renewals and extensions thereof, and in and to all works based upon, derived from, or incorporating the Work, and in an to all income, royalties, damages, claims and payments now or hereafter due or payable with respect thereto, and in and to all causes of action, either in law or in equity for past, present, or future infringement based on the copyrights, and in and to all rights corresponding to the foregoing throughout the world.

(d) If the Work is one to which the provisions of 17 U.S.C. 106A apply, the Author hereby waives and appoints Employer to assert on the Author's behalf the Author's moral rights or any equivalent rights regarding the form or extent of any alteration to the Work including, without limitation, removal or destruction, or the making of any derivative works based on the Work, including, without limitation, photographs, drawings or other visual reproductions or the Work, in any medium, for Employer purposes.

(e) Author agrees to execute all papers and to perform such other proper acts as Employer may deem necessary to secure for Employer or its designee the rights herein assigned.

2. Delivery

(a) The Author will deliver to the Employer on or before [Insert Date] the completed Work in form and content satisfactory to the Employer.

(b) If the Author fails to deliver the Work on time, the Employer will have the right to terminate this agreement and to recover from the Author any sums advanced in connection with the Work. Upon such termination, the Author may not have the Work published elsewhere until such advances have been repaid.

3. Permission to Use Copyrighted Material

With the exception works in the public domain or works which constitute fair use, the Work will contain no material from other copyrighted works without a written consent of the copyright holder. Any obligations associated with obtaining such permissions will be the responsibility of the Author.

4. Warranty and Indemnification

The Author warrants that he or she is the sole owner of the Work and has full power and authority to make this agreement; that the Work does not infringe any copyright, violate any property rights, or contain any scandalous, libelous, or unlawful matter. The Author will defend, indemnify, and hold harmless the Employer and/or its licensees against all claims, suits, costs, damages, and expenses that the Employer and/or its licensees may sustain by reason of any scandalous, libelous, or unlawful matter contained or alleged to be contained in the Work or any infringement or violation by the Work of any copyright or property right; and until such claim or suit has been settled or withdrawn, the Employer may withhold any sums due the Author under this agreement.

5. Consideration

In consideration for delivery of the Work in accordance with the provisions of this Agreement, Employer shall pay Author [Insert Dollar Amount] within 30 days of receipt and acceptance of the Work.

6. Term

This agreement shall remain in effect for one (1) year from its effective date.

7. Default

In the event that either party shall be in default of its material obligations under this agreement and shall fail to remedy such default within sixty (60) days after receipt of written notice thereof, this agreement shall terminate upon expiration of the sixty (60) day period.

8. Miscellaneous

(a) The written provisions contained in this agreement constitute the sole and entire agreement made between the Author and the Employer concerning this Work, and any amendments to this agreement shall not be valid unless made in writing and signed by both parties.

(b) This agreement shall be construed and interpreted according to the laws of the State of New York and shall be binding upon the parties hereto, their heirs, successors, assigns, and personal representatives; and references to the Author and to the Employer shall include their heirs, successors, assigns, and personal representatives.

IN WITNESS WHEREOF, the parties have executed this Agreement, effective this _____ day of _____, 19___ .

XYZ CORPORATION, EMPLOYER: AUTHOR:

_____   _____

Name/Title   Name/SSN

APPENDIX 14:

PUBLIC DOMAIN RULES

DATE OF WORK	PROTECTED FROM	TERM
Created 1-1-78 or after	When work is fixed in tangible, medium of expression	Life + 70 years or if work of corporate authorship, the shorter of 95 years from publication or 120 years from creation[1,2]
Published before 1923	In public domain	None
Published from 1923 - 63	When published with notice	28 years plus could be renewed for 47 years; now extended by 20 years for a total renewal of 67 years. If not so renewed, now in public domain[3]
Published from 1964 - 77	When published with notice	28 years for first term; now automatic extension of 67 years for second term
Created before 1-1-78 but not published	1-1-78, the effective date of the 1976 Act which eliminated common law copyright	Life + 70 years or 12-31-2002, whichever is greater
Created before 1-1-78 but published between then and 12-31-2002	1-1-78, the effective date of the 1976 Act which eliminated common law copyright	Life + 70 years or 12-31-2047 whichever is greater

1. Term of joint works is measured by life of the longest-lived author.

2. Works for hire, anonymous and pseudonymous works also have this term. 17 U.S.C. § 302(c).

3. Under the 1909 Act, works published without notice went into the public domain upon publication. Works published without notice between 1-1-78 and 3-1-89, effective date of the Berne Convention Implementation Act, retained copyright only if, e.g., registration was made within five years. 17 U.S.C. § 405.

APPENDIX 15:

THE SEMICONDUCTOR CHIP PROTECTION ACT OF 1984

SECTION 901. Definitions.

(a) As used in this chapter—

(1) a "semiconductor chip product" is the final or intermediate form of any product—

(A) having two or more layers of metallic, insulating, or semiconductor material, deposited or otherwise placed on, or etched away or otherwise removed from, a piece of semiconductor material in accordance with a predetermined pattern; and

(B) intended to perform electronic circuitry functions;

(2) a "mask work" is a series of related images, however fixed or encoded—

(A) having or representing the predetermined three-dimensional pattern of metallic, insulating, or semiconductor material present or removed from the layers of a semiconductor chip product; and

(B) in which series the relation of the images to one another is that each image has the pattern of the surface of one form of the semiconductor chip product;

(3) a mask work is "fixed" in a semiconductor chip product when its embodiment in the product is sufficiently permanent or stable to permit the mask work to be perceived or reproduced from the product for a period of more than transitory duration;

(4) to "distribute" means to sell, or to lease, bail, or otherwise transfer, or to offer to sell, lease, bail, or otherwise transfer;

(5) to "commercially exploit" a mask work is to distribute to the public for commercial purposes a semiconductor chip product embodying the mask work; except that such term includes an offer to sell or transfer a semiconductor chip product only when the offer is in writing and occurs after the mask work is fixed in the semiconductor chip product;

(6) the "owner" of a mask work is the person who created the mask work, the legal representative of that person if that person is decreased or under a legal incapacity, or a party to whom all the rights under this chapter of such person or representative are transferred in accordance with section 903(b); except that, in the case of a work made within the scope of a person's employment, the owner is the employer for whom the per-

son created the mask work or a party to whom all the rights under this chapter of the employer are transferred in accordance with section 903(b);

(7) an "innocent purchaser" is a person who purchases a semiconductor chip product in good faith and without having notice of protection with respect to the semiconductor chip product;

(8) having "notice of protection" means having actual knowledge that, or reasonable grounds to believe that, a mask work is protected under this chapter; and

(9) an "infringing semiconductor chip product" is a semiconductor chip product which is made, imported, or distributed in violation of the exclusive rights of the owner of a mask work under this chapter.

(b) For purposes of this chapter, the distribution or importation of a product incorporating a semiconductor chip product as a part thereof is a distribution or importation of that semiconductor chip product.

SECTION 902. Subject Matter of Protection.

(a)(1) Subject to the provisions of subsection (b), a mask work fixed in a semiconductor chip product, by or under the authority of the owner of the mask work, is eligible for protection under this chapter if—

(A) on the date on which the mask work is registered under section 908, or is first commercially exploited anywhere in the world, whichever occurs first, the owner of the mask work is (i) a national or domiciliary of the United States, (ii) a national, domiciliary, or sovereign authority of a foreign nation that is a party to a treaty affording protection to mask works to which the United States is also a party, or (iii) a stateless person, wherever that person may be domiciled;

(B) the mask work is first commercially exploited in the United States; or

(C) the mask work comes within the scope of a Presidential proclamation issued under paragraph (2).

(2) Whenever the President finds that a foreign nation extends, to mask works of owners who are nationals or domiciliaries of the United States protection (A) on substantially the same basis as that on which the foreign nation extends protection to mask works of its own nationals and domiciliaries and mask works first commercially exploited in that nation, or (B) on substantially the same basis as provided in this chapter, the President may by proclamation extend protection under this chapter

to mask works (i) of owners who are, on the date on which the mask works are registered under section 908, or the date on which the mask works are first commercially exploited anywhere in the world, whichever occurs first, nationals, domiciliaries, or sovereign authorities of that nation, or (ii) which are first commercially exploited in that nation. The President may revise, suspend, or revoke any such proclamation or impose any conditions or limitations on protection extended under any such proclamation.

(b) Protection under this chapter shall not be available for a mask work that—

(1) is not original; or

(2) consists of designs that are staple, commonplace, or familiar in the semiconductor industry, or variations of such designs, combined in a way that, considered as a whole, is not original.

(c) In no case does protection under this chapter for a mask work extend to any idea, procedure, process, system, method of operation, concept, principle, or discovery, regardless of the form in which it is described, explained, illustrated, or embodied in such work.

SECTION 903. Ownership, Transfer, Licensing, and Recordation.

(a) The exclusive rights in a mask work subject to protection under this chapter belong to the owner of the mask work.

(b) The owner of the exclusive rights in a mask work may transfer all of those rights, or license all or less than all of those rights, by any written instrument signed by such owner or a duly authorized agent of the owner. Such rights may be transferred or licensed by operation of law, may be bequeathed by will, and may pass as personal property by the applicable laws of intestate succession.

(c)(1) Any document pertaining to a mask work may be recorded in the Copyright Office if the document filed for recordation bears the actual signature of the person who executed it, or if it is accompanied by a sworn or official certification that it is a true copy of the original, signed document. The Register of Copyrights shall, upon receipt of the document and the fee specified pursuant to section 908(d), record the document and return it with a certificate of recordation. The recordation of any transfer or license under this paragraph gives all persons constructive notice of the facts stated in the recorded document concerning the transfer or license.

(2) In any case in which conflicting transfers of the exclusive rights in a mask work are made, the transfer first executed shall be void as against a subsequent transfer which is made for a valuable consideration and without notice of the first transfer, unless the first transfer is recorded in accordance with paragraph (1) within three months after the date on which it is executed, but in no case later than the day before the date of such subsequent transfer.

(d) Mask works prepared by an officer or employee of the United States Government as part of that person's official duties are not protected under this chapter, but the United States Government is not precluded from receiving and holding exclusive rights in mask works transferred to the Government under subsection (b).

SECTION 904. Duration of Protection.

(a) The protection provided for a mask work under this chapter shall commence on the date on which the mask work is registered under section 908, or the date on which the mask work is first commercially exploited anywhere in the world, whichever occurs first.

(b) Subject to subsection (c) and the provisions of this chapter, the protection provided under this chapter to a mask work shall end ten years after the date on which such protection commences under subsection (a). @P = (c) All terms of protection provided in this section shall run to the end of the calendar year in which they would otherwise expire.

SECTION 905. Exclusive Rights in Mask Works.

The owner of a mask work provided protection under this chapter has the exclusive rights to do and to authorize any of the following:

(1) to reproduce the mask work by optical, electronic, or any other means;

(2) to import or distribute a semiconductor chip product in which the mask work is embodied; and

(3) to induce or knowingly to cause another person to do any of the acts described in paragraphs (1) and (2).

SECTION 906. Limitation on Exclusive Rights: Reverse Engineering; First Sale.

(a) Notwithstanding the provisions of section 905, it is not an infringement of the exclusive rights of the owner of a mask work for—

(1) a person to reproduce the mask work solely for the purpose of teaching, analyzing, or evaluating the concepts or techniques embodied in the mask work or the circuitry, logic flow, or organization of components used in the mask work; or

(2) a person who performs the analysis or evaluation described in paragraph (1) to incorporate the results of such conduct in an original mask work which is made to be distributed.

(b) Notwithstanding the provisions of section 905(2), the owner of a particular semiconductor chip product made by the owner of the mask work, or by any person authorized by the owner of the mask work, may import, distribute, or otherwise dispose of or use, but not reproduce, that particular semiconductor chip product without the authority of the owner of the mask work.

SECTION 907. Limitation on Exclusive Rights: Innocent Infringement.

(a) Notwithstanding any other provision of this chapter, an innocent purchaser of an infringing semiconductor chip product—

(1) shall incur no liability under this chapter with respect to the importation or distribution of units of the infringing semiconductor chip product that occurs before the innocent purchaser has notice of protection with respect to the mask work embodied in the semiconductor chip product; and

(2) shall be liable only for a reasonable royalty on each unit of the infringing semiconductor chip product that the innocent purchaser imports or distributes after having notice of protection with respect to the mask work embodied in the semiconductor chip product.

(b) The amount of the royalty referred to in subsection (a)(2) shall be determined by the court in a civil action for infringement unless the parties resolve the issue by voluntary negotiation, mediation, or binding arbitration.

(c) The immunity of an innocent purchaser from liability referred to in subsection (a)(1) and the limitation of remedies with respect to an innocent purchaser referred to in subsection (a)(2) shall extend to any person who directly or indirectly purchases an infringing semiconductor chip product from an innocent purchaser.

(d) The provisions of subsections (a), (b), and (c) apply only with respect to those units of an infringing semiconductor chip product that an innocent purchaser purchased before having notice of protection with respect to the mask work embodied in the semiconductor chip product.

SECTION 908. Registration of Claims of Protection.

(a) The owner of a mask work may apply to the Register of Copyrights for registration of a claim of protection in a mask work. Protection of a mask work under this chapter shall terminate if application for registration of a claim of protection in the mask work is not made as provided in this chapter within two years after the date on which the mask work is first commercially exploited anywhere in the world.

(b) The Register of Copyrights shall be responsible for all administrative functions and duties under this chapter. Except for section 708, the provisions of chapter 7 of this title relating to the general responsibilities, organization, regulatory authority, actions, records, and publications of the Copyright Office shall apply to this chapter, except that the Register of Copyrights may make such changes as may be necessary in applying those provisions to this chapter.

(c) The application for registration of a mask work shall be made on a form prescribed by the Register of Copyrights. Such form may require any information regarded by the Register as bearing upon the preparation or identification of the mask work, the existence or duration of protection of the mask work under this chapter, or ownership of the mask work. The application shall be accompanied by the fee set pursuant to subsection (d) and the identifying material specified pursuant to such subsection.

(d) The Register of Copyrights shall by regulation set reasonable fees for the filing of applications to register claims of protection in mask works under this chapter, and for other services relating to the administration of this chapter or the rights under this chapter, taking into consideration the cost of providing those services, the benefits of a public record, and statutory fee schedules under this title. The Register shall also specify the identifying material to be deposited in connection with the claim for registration.

(e) If the Register of Copyrights, after examining an application for registration, determines, in accordance with the provisions of this chapter, that the application relates to a mask work which is entitled to protection under this chapter, then the Register shall register the claim of protection and issue to the applicant a certificate of registration of the claim of protection under the seal of the Copyright Office. The effective date of registration of a claim of protection shall be the date on which an application, deposit of identifying material, and fee, which are determined by the Register of Copyright or by a court of competent jurisdiction to be acceptable for registration of the claim, have all been received in the Copyright Office.

(f) In any action for infringement under this chapter, the certificate of registration of a mask work shall constitute prima facie evidence (1) of the facts stated in the certificate, and (2) that the applicant issued the certificate has met the requirements of this chapter, and the regulations issued under this chapter, with respect to the registration of claims.

(g) Any applicant for registration under this section who is dissatisfied with the refusal of the Register of Copyrights to issue a certificate of registration under this section may seek judicial review of that refusal by bringing an action for such review in an appropriate United States district court not later than sixty days after the refusal. The provisions of chapter 7 of title 5 shall apply to such judicial review. The failure of the Register of Copyrights to issue a certificate of registration within four months after an application for registration is purposes of this subsection and section 910(b)(2), except that, upon a showing of good cause, the district court may shorten such four-month period.

SECTION 909. Mask Work Notice.

(a) The owner of a mask work provided protection under this chapter may affix notice to the mask work, and to masks and semiconductor chip products embodying the mask work, in such manner and location as to give reasonable notice of such protection. The Register of Copyrights shall prescribe by regulation, as examples, specific methods of affixation and positions of notice for purposes of this section, but these specifications shall not be considered exhaustive. The affixation of such notice is not a condition of protection under this chapter, but shall constitute *prima facie* evidence of notice of protection.

(b) The notice referred to in subsection (a) shall consist of—

(1) the words "mask force", the symbol * M *, or the symbol M (the letter M in a circle); and

(2) the name of the owner or owners of the mask work or an abbreviation by which the name is recognized or is generally known.

SECTION 910. Enforcement of Exclusive Rights.

(a) Except as otherwise provided in this chapter, any person who violates any of the exclusive rights of the owner of a mask work under this chapter, by conduct in or affecting commerce, shall be liable as an infringer of such rights.

(b)(1) The owner of a mask work protected under this chapter, or the exclusive licensee of all rights under this chapter with respect to the mask work, shall, after a certificate of registration of a claim of protection in that mask work has been issued under section 908, be entitled to institute a civil action for any infringement with respect to the mask work which is committed after the commencement of protection of the mask work under section 904(a).

(2) In any case in which an application for registration of a claim of protection in a mask work and the required deposit of identifying material and fee have been received in the Copyright Office in proper form and registration of the mask work has been refused, the applicant is entitled to institute a civil action for infringement under this chapter with respect to the mask work if notice of the action, together with a copy of the complaint, is served on the Register of Copyrights, in accordance with the Federal Rules of Civil Procedure. The Register may, at his or her option, become a party to the action with respect to the issue of whether the claim of protection is eligible for registration by entering an appearance within sixty days after such service, but the failure of the Register to become a party to the action shall not deprive the court of jurisdiction to determine that issue.

(c)(1) The Secretary of the Treasury and the United States Postal Service shall separately or jointly issue regulations for the enforcement of the rights set forth in section 905 with respect to importation. These regulations may require, as a condition for the exclusion of articles from the United States, that the person seeking exclusion take any one or more of the following actions:

(A) Obtain a court order enjoining, or an order of the International Trade Commission under section 337 of the Tariff Act of 1930 excluding, importation of the articles.

(B) Furnish proof that the mask work involved is protected under this chapter and that the importation of the articles would infringe the rights in the mask work under this chapter.

(C) Post a surety bond for any injury that may result if the detention or exclusion of the articles proves to be unjustified.

(2) Articles imported in violation of the rights set forth in section 905 are subject to seizure and forfeiture in the same manner as property imported in violation of the customs laws. Any such forfeited articles shall

be destroyed as directed by the Secretary of the Treasury or the court, as the case may be, except that the articles may be returned to the country of export whenever it is shown to the satisfaction of the Secretary of the Treasury that the importer had no reasonable grounds for believing that his or her acts constituted a violation of the law.

SECTION 911. Civil Actions.

(a) Any court having jurisdiction of a civil action arising under this chapter may grant temporary restraining orders, preliminary injunctions, and permanent injunctions on such terms as the court may deem reasonable to prevent or restrain infringement of the exclusive rights in a mask work under this chapter.

(b) Upon finding an infringer liable, to a person entitled under section 910(b)(1) to institute a civil action, for an infringement of any exclusive right under this chapter, the court shall award such person actual damages suffered by the person as a result of the infringement. The court shall also award such person the infringer's profits that are attributable to the infringement and are not taken into account in computing the award of actual damages. In establishing the infringer's profits, such person is required to present proof only of the infringer's gross revenue, and the infringer is required to prove his or her deductible expenses and the elements of profit attributable to factors other than the mask work.

(c) At any time before final judgment is rendered, a person entitled to institute a civil action for infringement may elect, instead of actual damages and profits as provided by subsection (b), an award of statutory damages for all infringements involved in the action, with respect to any one mask work for which any one infringer is liable individually, or for which any two or more infringers are liable jointly and severally, in an amount not more than $250,000 as the court considers just.

(d) An action for infringement under this chapter shall be barred unless the action is commenced within three years after the claim accrues.

(e)(1) At any time while an action for infringement of the exclusive rights in a mask work under this chapter is pending, the court may order the impounding, on such terms as it may deem reasonable, of all semiconductor chip products, and any drawings, tapes, masks, or other products by means of which such products may be reproduced, that are claimed to have been made, imported, or used in violation of those exclusive rights. Insofar as practicable, applications for orders under this paragraph shall be heard and determined in the same manner as an application for a temporary restraining order or preliminary injunction.

(2) As part of a final judgment or decree, the court may order the destruction or other disposition of any infringing semiconductor chip products, and any masks, tapes, or other articles by means of which such products may be reproduced.

(f) In any civil action arising under this chapter, the court in its discretion may allow the recovery of full costs, including reasonable attorneys' fees, to the prevailing party.

SECTION 912. Relation to Other Laws.

(a) Nothing in this chapter shall affect any right or remedy held by any person under chapters 1 through 8 or 10 of this title, or under title 35.

(b) Except as provided in section 908(b) of this title, references to "this title" or "title 17" in chapters 1 through 8 or 10 of this title shall be deemed not to apply to this chapter.

(c) The provisions of this chapter shall preempt the laws of any State to the extent those laws provide any rights or remedies with respect to a mask work which are equivalent to those rights or remedies provided by this chapter, except that such preemption shall be effective only with respect to actions filed on or after January 1, 1986.

(d) Notwithstanding subsection (c), nothing in this chapter shall detract from any rights of a mask work owner, whether under Federal law (exclusive of this chapter) or under the common law or the statutes of a State, heretofore or hereafter declared or enacted, with respect to any mask work first commercially exploited before July 1, 1983.

SECTION 913. Transitional Provisions.

(a) No application for registration under section 908 may be filed, and no civil action under section 910 or other enforcement proceeding under this chapter may be instituted, until sixty days after the date of the enactment of this chapter.

(b) No monetary relief under section 911 may be granted with respect to any conduct that occurred before the date of the enactment of this chapter, except as provided in subsection (d).

(c) Subject to subsection (a), the provisions of this chapter apply to all mask works that are first commercially exploited or are registered under this chapter, or both, on or after the date of the enactment of this chapter.

(d)(1) Subject to subsection (a), protection is available under this chapter to any mask work that was first commercially exploited on or after July 1, 1983, and before the date of the enactment of this chapter, if a claim of protection in the mask work is registered in the Copyright Office before July 1, 1985, under section 908.

(2) In the case of any mask work described in paragraph (1) that is provided protection under this chapter, infringing semiconductor chip product units manufactured before the date of the enactment of this chapter may, without liability under sections 910 and 911, be imported into or distributed in the United States, or both, until two years after the date of registration of the mask work under section 908, but only if the importer or distributor, as the case may be, first pays or offers to pay the reasonable royalty referred to in section 907(a)(2) to the mask work owner, on all such units imported or distributed, or both, after the date of the enactment of this chapter.

(3) In the event that a person imports or distributes infringing semiconductor chip product units described in paragraph (2) of this subsection without first paying or offering to pay the reasonable royalty specified in such paragraph, or if the person refuses or fails to make such payment, the mask work owner shall be entitled to the relief provided in sections 910 and 911.

SECTION 914. International Transitional Provisions.

(a) Notwithstanding the conditions set forth in subparagraphs (A) and (C) of section 902(a)(1) with respect to the availability of protection under this chapter to nationals, domiciliaries, and sovereign authorities of a foreign nation, the Secretary of Commerce may, upon the petition of any person, or upon the Secretary's own motion, issue an order extending protection under this chapter to such foreign nationals, domiciliaries, and sovereign authorities if the Secretary finds—

(1) that the foreign nation is making good faith efforts and reasonable progress toward—

(A) entering into a treaty described in section 902(a)(1)(A); or

(B) enacting legislation that would be in compliance with subparagraph (A) or (B) of section 902(a)(2); and

(2) that the nationals, domiciliaries, and sovereign authorities of the foreign nation, and persons controlled by them, are not engaged in the misappropriation, or unauthorized distribution or commercial exploitation, of mask works; and

(3) that issuing the order would promote the purposes of this chapter and international comity with respect to the protection of mask works.

(b) While an order under subsection (a) is in effect with respect to a foreign nation, no application for registration of a claim for protection in a mask work under this chapter may be denied solely because the owner of the mask work is a national, domiciliary, or sovereign authority of that foreign nation, or solely because the mask work was first commercially exploited in that foreign nation.

(c) Any order issued by the Secretary of Commerce under subsection (a) shall be effective for such period as the Secretary designates in the order, except that no such order may be effective after the date on which the authority of the Secretary of Commerce terminates under subsection (e).

The effective date of any such order shall also be designated in the order. In the case of an order issued upon the petition of a person, such effective date may be no earlier than the date on which the Secretary receives such petition.

(d)(1) Any order issued under this section shall terminate if—

(A) the Secretary of Commerce finds that any of the conditions set forth in paragraphs (1), (2), and (3) of subsection (a) no longer exist; or

(B) mask works of nationals, domiciliaries, and sovereign authorities of that foreign nation or mask works first commercially exploited in that foreign nation become eligible for protection under subparagraph (A) or (C) of section 902(a)(1).

(2) Upon the termination or expiration of an order issued under this section, registrations of claims of protection in mask works made pursuant to that order shall remain valid for the period specified in section 904.

(e) The authority of the Secretary of Commerce under this section shall commence on the date of the enactment of this chapter, and shall terminate on July 1, 1991.

(f)(1) The Secretary of Commerce shall promptly notify the Register of Copyrights and the Committees on the Judiciary of the Senate and the House of Representatives of the issuance or termination of any order under this section, together with a statement of the reasons for such action. The Secretary shall also publish such notification and statement of reasons in the Federal Register.

(2) Two years after the date of the enactment of this chapter, the Secretary of Commerce, in consultation with the Register of Copyrights, shall transmit to the Committees on the Judiciary of the Senate and the House of Representatives a report on the actions taken under this section and on the current status of international recognition of mask work protection. The report shall include such recommendations for modifications of the protection accorded under this chapter to mask works owned by nationals, domiciliaries, or sovereign authorities of foreign nations as the Secretary, in consultation with the Register of Copyrights, considers would promote the purposes of this chapter and international comity with respect to mask work protection. Not later than July 1, 1990, the Secretary of Commerce, in consultation with the Register of Copyrights, shall transmit to the Committees on the Judiciary of the Senate and the House of Representatives a report updating the matters contained in the report transmitted under the preceding sentence.

APPENDIX 16:

AUDIO HOME RECORDING ACT OF 1992

CHAPTER 10—DIGITAL AUDIO RECORDING DEVICES AND MEDIA

SUBCHAPTER A: DEFINITIONS

SECTION 1001. Definitions

As used in this chapter, the following terms have the following meanings:

(1) A "digital audio copied recording" is a reproduction in a digital recording format of a digital musical recording, whether that reproduction is made directly from another digital musical recording or indirectly from a transmission.

(2) A "digital audio interface device" is any machine or device that is designed specifically to communicate digital audio information and related interface data to a digital audio recording device through a nonprofessional interface.

(3) A "digital audio recording device" is any machine or device of a type commonly distributed to individuals for use by individuals, whether or not included with or as part of some other machine or device, the digital recording function of which is designed or marketed for the primary purpose of, and that is capable of, making a digital audio copied recording for private use, except for—

(A) professional model products, and

(B) dictation machines, answering machines, and other audio recording equipment that is designed and marketed primarily for the creation of sound recordings resulting from the fixation of nonmusical sounds.

(4)(A) A "digital audio recording medium" is any material object in a form commonly distributed for use by individuals, that is primarily marketed or most commonly used by consumers for the purpose of making digital audio copied recordings by use of a digital audio recording device.

(B) Such term does not include any material object—

(i) that embodies a sound recording at the time it is first distributed by the importer or manufacturer; or

(ii) that is primarily marketed and most commonly used by consumers either for the purpose of making copies of motion pictures or other audiovisual works or for the purpose of making copies of nonmusical literary works, including computer programs or data bases.

(5)(A) A "digital musical recording" is a material object—

(i) in which are fixed, in a digital recording format, only sounds, and material, statements, or instructions incidental to those fixed sounds, if any, and

(ii) from which the sounds and material can be perceived, reproduced, or otherwise communicated, either directly or with the aid of a machine or device.

(B) A "digital musical recording" does not include a material object.

(i) in which the fixed sounds consist entirely of spoken word recordings, or

(ii) in which one or more computer programs are fixed, except that a digital musical recording may contain statements or instructions constituting the fixed sounds and incidental material, and statements or instructions to be used directly or indirectly in order to bring about the perception, reproduction, or communication of the fixed sounds and incidental material.

(C) For purposes of this paragraph—

(i) a "spoken word recording" is a sound recording in which are fixed only a series of spoken words, except that the spoken words may be accompanied by incidental musical or other wounds, and

(ii) the term "incidental" means related to and relatively minor by comparison.

(6) "Distribute" means to sell, lease, or assign a product to consumers in the United States, or to sell, lease, or assign a product in the United States for ultimate transfer to consumers in the United States.

(7) An "interested copyright party" is—

(A) the owner of the exclusive right under section 106(1) of this title to reproduce a sound recording of a musical work that has been embodied in a digital musical recording or analog musical recording lawfully made under this title that has been distributed;

(B) the legal or beneficial owner of, or the person that controls, the right to reproduce in a digital musical recording or analog musical recording a musical work that has been embodied in a digital musical recording or analog musical recording lawfully made under this title that has been distributed;

(C) a featured recording artist who performs on a sound recording that has been distributed; or

(D) any association or other organization—

(i) representing persons specified in subparagraph (A), (B), or (C), or

(ii) engaged in licensing rights in musical works to music users on behalf of writers and publishers.

(8) To "manufacture" means to produce or assemble a product in the United States. A "manufacturer" is a person who manufactures.

(9) A "music publisher" is a person that is authorized to license the reproduction of a particular musical work in a sound recording.

(10) A "professional model product" is an audio recording device that is designed, manufactured, marketed, and intended for use by recording professionals in the ordinary course of a lawful business, in accordance with such requirements as the Secretary of Commerce shall establish by regulation.

(11) The term "serial copying" means the duplication in a digital format of a copyrighted musical work or sound recording from a digital reproduction of a digital musical recording. The term "digital reproduction of a digital musical recording" does not include a digital musical recording as distributed, by authority of the copyright owner, for ultimate sale to consumers.

(12) The "transfer price" of a digital audio recording device or a digital audio recording medium—

(A) is, subject to subparagraph (B)—

(i) in the case of an imported product, the actual entered value at United States Customs (exclusive of any freight, insurance, and applicable duty), and

(ii) in the case of a domestic product, the manufacturer's transfer price (FOB the manufacturer, and exclusive of any direct sales taxes or excise taxes incurred in connection with the sale); and

(B) shall, in a case in which the transferor and transferee are related entities or within a single entity, not be less than a reasonable arms-length price under the principles of the regulations adopted pursuant to section 482 of the Internal Revenue Code of 1986, or any successor provision to such section.

(13) A "writer" is the composer or lyricist of a particular musical work.

SUBCHAPTER B: COPYING CONTROLS

SECTION 1002. Incorporation of Copying Controls

(a) Prohibition on Importation, Manufacture, and Distribution.—No person shall import, manufacture, or distribute any digital audio recording device or digital audio interface that does not conform to—

(1) the Serial Copy Management System;

(2) a system that has the same functional characteristics as the Serial Copy Management System and requires that copyright and generation status information be accurately sent, received, and acted upon between devices using the system's method of serial copying regulation and devices using the Serial Copy Management System; or

(3) any other system certified by the Secretary of Commerce as prohibiting unauthorized serial copying.

(b) Development of Verification Procedure.—The Secretary of Commerce shall establish a procedure to verify, upon the petition of an interested party, that a system meets the standards set forth in subsection (a)(2).

(c) Prohibition on Circumvention of the System.—No person shall import, manufacture, or distribute any device, or offer or perform any service, the primary purpose or effect of which is to avoid, bypass, remove, deactivate, or otherwise circumvent any program or circuit which implements, in whole or in part, a system described in subsection (a).

(d) Encoding of Information on Digital Musical Recordings.—

(1) Prohibition on Encoding Inaccurate Information.—No person shall encode a digital musical recording of a sound recording with inaccurate information relating to the category code, copyright status, or generation status of the source material for the recording.

(2) Encoding of Copyright Status Not Required.—Nothing in this chapter requires any person engaged in the importation or manufacture

of digital musical recordings to encode any such digital musical recording with respect to its copyright status.

(e) Information Accompanying Transmissions in Digital Format.—Any person who transmits or otherwise communicates to the public any sound recording in digital format is not required under this chapter to transmit or otherwise communicate the information relating to the copyright status of the sound recording. Any such person who does transmit or otherwise communicate such copyright status information shall transmit or communicate such information accurately.

SUBCHAPTER C: ROYALTY PAYMENTS

SECTION 1003. Obligation to Make Royalty Payments

(a) Prohibition on Importation and Manufacture.—No person shall import into and distribute, or manufacture and distribute, any digital audio recording device or digital audio recording medium unless such person records the notice specified by this section and subsequently deposits the statements of account and applicable royalty payments for such device or medium specified in section 1004.

(b) Filing of Notice.—The importer or manufacturer of any digital audio recording device or digital audio recording medium, within a product category or utilizing a technology with respect to which such manufacturer or importer has not previously filed a notice under this subsection, shall file with the Register of Copyrights a notice with respect to such device or medium, in such form and content as the Register shall prescribe by regulation.

(c) Filing of Quarterly and Annual Statements of Account.—

(1) Generally.—Any importer or manufacturer that distributes any digital audio recording device or digital audio recording medium that it manufactured or imported shall file with the Register of Copyrights, in such form and content as the Register shall prescribe by regulation, such quarterly and annual statements of account with respect to such distribution as the Register shall prescribe by regulation.

(2) Certification, Verification, and Confidentiality.—Each such statement shall be certified as accurate by an authorized officer or principal of the importer or manufacturer. The Register shall issue regulations to provide for the verification and audit of such statements and to protect the confidentiality of the information contained in such statements. Such regulations shall provide for the disclosure, in confidence, of such statements to interested copyright parties.

(3) Royalty Payments.—Each such statement shall be accompanied by the royalty payments specified in section 1004.

SECTION 1004. Royalty Payments

(a) Digital Audio Recording Devices.—

(1) Amount of Payment.—The royalty payment due under section 1003 for each digital audio recording device imported into and distributed in the United States, or manufactured and distributed in the United States, shall be 2 percent of the transfer price. Only the first person to manufacture and distribute or import and distribute such device shall be required to pay the royalty with respect to such device.

(2) Calculation for Devices Distributed with Other Devices.— With respect to a digital audio recording device first distributed in combination with one or more devices, either as a physically integrated unit or as a separate components, the royalty payment shall be calculated as follows:

(A) If the digital audio recording device and such other devices are part of a physically integrated unit, the royalty payment shall be based on the transfer price of the unit, but shall be reduced by any royalty payment made on any digital audio recording device included within the unit that was not first distributed in combination with the unit.

(B) If the digital audio recording device is not part of a physically integrated unit and substantially similar devices have been distributed separately at any time during the preceding 4 calendar quarters, the royalty payment shall be based on the average transfer price of such devices during those 4 quarters.

(C) If the digital audio recording device is not part of a physically integrated unit and substantially similar devices have not been distributed separately at any time during the preceding 4 calendar quarters, the royalty payment shall be based on a constructed price reflecting the proportional value of such device to the combination as a whole.

(3) Limits on Royalties.— Notwithstanding paragraph (1) or (2), the amount of the royalty payment for each digital audio recording device shall not be less than $1 nor more than the royalty maximum. The royalty maximum shall be $8 per device, except that in the case of a physically integrated unit containing more than 1 digital audio recording device, the royalty maximum for such unit shall be $12. During the 6th year after the

effective date of this chapter, and not more than once each year thereafter, any interested copyright party may petition the Copyright Royalty
Tribunal to increase the royalty maximum and, if more than 20 percent
of the royalty, payments are at the relevant royalty maximum, the Tribunal shall prospectively increase such royalty maximum with the goal of
having no more than 10 percent of such payments at the new royalty
maximum; however the amount of any such increase as a percentage of
the royalty maximum shall in no event exceed the percentage increase in
the Consumer Price Index during the period under review.

(b) Digital Audio Recording Media.—The royalty payment due under
section 1003 for each digital audio recording medium imported into and distributed in the United States, or manufactured and distributed in the United
States, shall be 3 percent of the transfer price. Only the first person to manufacture and distribute or import and distribute such medium shall be required to pay the royalty with respect to such medium.

SECTION 1005. Deposit of Royalty Payments and Deduction of Expenses

The Register of Copyrights shall receive all royalty payments deposited
under this chapter and, after deducting the reasonable costs incurred by the
Copyright Office under this chapter, shall deposit the balance in the Treasury of the United States as offsetting receipts, in such manner as the Secretary of the Treasury directs. All funds held by the Secretary of the Treasury
shall be invested in interest-bearing United States securities for later distribution with interest under section 1007. The Register may, in the Register's
discretion, 4 years after the close of any calendar year, close out the royalty
payments account for that calendar year, and may treat any funds remaining
in such account and any subsequent deposits that would otherwise be attributable to that calendar year as attributable to the succeeding calendar year.
The Register shall submit to the Copyright Royalty Tribunal, on a monthly
basis, a financial statement reporting the amount of royalties under this
chapter that are available for distribution.

SECTION 1006. Entitlement to Royalty Payments

(a) Interested Copyright Parties. — The royalty payments deposited pursuant to section 1005 shall, in accordance with the procedures specified in
section 1007, be distributed to any interested copyright party—

(1) whose musical work or sound recording has been—

(A) embodied in a digital musical recording or an analog musical recording lawfully made under this title that has been distributed, and

(B) distributed in the form of digital musical recordings or analog musical recordings or disseminated to the public in transmissions, during the period to which such payments pertain; and

(2) who has filed a claim under section 1007.

(b) Allocation of Royalty Payments to Groups.—The royalty payments shall be divided into 2 funds as follows:

(1) The Sound Recordings Fund.—66 2/3 percent of the royalty payments shall be allocated to the Sound Recordings Fund. 2 5/8 percent of the royalty payments allocated to the Sound Recordings Fund shall be placed in an escrow account managed by an independent administrator jointly appointed by the interested copyright parties described in section 1001(7)(A) and the American Federation of Musicians (or any successor entity) to be distributed to nonfeatured musicians (whether or not members of the American Federation of Musicians or any successor entity) who have performed on sound recordings distributed in the United States. 1 3/8 percent of the royalty payments allocated to the Sound Recordings Fund shall be placed in an escrow account managed by an independent administrator jointly appointed by the interested copyright parties described in section 1001(7)(A) and the American Federation of Television and Radio Artists (or any successor entity) to be distributed to nonfeatured vocalists (whether or not members of the American Federation Television and Radio Artists or any successor entity) who have performed on sound recordings distributed in the United States. 40 percent of the remaining royalty payments in the Sound Recordings Fund shall be distributed to the interested copyright parties described in section 1001(7)(C), and 60 percent of such remaining royalty payments shall be distributed to the interested copyright parties described in section 1001(7)(A).

(2) The Musical Works Fund.—

(A) 33 1/3 percent of the royalty payments shall be allocated to the Musical Works Fund for distribution to interested copyright parties described in section 1001(7)(B).

(B)(i) Music publishers shall be entitled to 50 percent of the royalty payments allocated to the Musical Works Fund.

(ii) Writers shall be entitled to the other 50 percent of the royalty payments allocated to the Musical Works Fund.

(c) Allocation of Royalty Payments Within Groups.—If all interested copyright parties within a group specified in subsection (b) do not agree on a voluntary proposal for the distribution of the royalty payments within each group, the Copyright Royalty Tribunal shall, pursuant to the procedures specified under section 1007(c), allocate royalty payments under this section based on the extent to which, during the relevant period—

(1) for the Sound Recordings Fund, each sound recording was distributed in the form of digital musical recordings or analog musical recordings; and

(2) for the Musical Works Fund, each musical work was distributed in the form of digital musical recordings or analog musical recordings or disseminated to the public in transmissions.

SECTION 1007. Procedures for Distributing Royalty Payments

(a) Filing of Claims and Negotiations.—

(1) Filing of Claims.—During the first 2 months of each calendar year after the calendar year in which this chapter takes effect, every interested copyright party seeking to receive royalty payments to which such party is entitled under section 1006 shall file with the Copyright Royalty Tribunal a claim for payments collected during the preceding year in such form and manner as the Tribunal shall prescribe by regulation.

(2) Negotiations.—Notwithstanding any provision of the antitrust laws, for purposes of this section interested copyright parties within each group specified in section 1006(b) may agree among themselves to the proportionate division of royalty payments, may lump their claims together and file them jointly or as a single claim, or may designate a common agent, including any organization described in section 1001(7)(D), to negotiate or receive payment on their behalf; except that no agreement under this subsection may modify the allocation of royalties specified in section 1006(b).

(b) Distribution of Payments in the Absence of a Dispute.—Within 30 days after the period established for the filing of claims under subsection (a), in each year and after the year in which this section takes effect, the Copyright Royalty Tribunal shall determine whether there exists a controversy concerning the distribution of royalty payments under section 1006(c). If the tribunal determines that no such controversy exists, the Tribunal shall, within 30 days after such determination, authorize the distribution of the royalty payments as set forth in the agreements regarding the distribution of royalty payments entered into pursuant to subsection (a), after deducting its reasonable administrative costs under this section.

(c) Resolution of Disputes.—If the Tribunal finds the existence of a controversy, it shall, pursuant to chapter 8 of this title, conduct a proceeding to determine the distribution of royalty payments. During the pendency of such a proceeding, the Tribunal shall withhold from distribution an amount sufficient to satisfy all claims with respect to which a controversy exists, but shall, to the extent feasible, authorize the distribution of any amounts that are not in controversy. The Tribunal shall, before authorizing the distribution of such royalty payments, deduct its reasonable administrative costs under this section.

SUBCHAPTER D: PROHIBITION ON CERTAIN INFRINGEMENT ACTIONS, REMEDIES, AND ARBITRATION

SECTION 1008. Prohibition on certain infringement actions

No action may be brought under this title alleging infringement of copyright based on the manufacture, importation, or distribution of a digital audio recording device, a digital audio recording medium, analog recording device, or an analog recording medium, or based on the noncommercial use by a consumer of such as device or medium for making digital musical recordings or analog musical recordings.

SECTION 1009. Civil remedies

(a) Civil Actions.—Any interested copyright party injured by a violation of section 1002 or 1003 may bring a civil action in an appropriate United States district court against any person for such violation.

(b) Other Civil Actions.—Any person injured by a violation of this chapter may bring a civil action in an appropriate United States district court for actual damages incurred as a result of such violation.

(c) Powers of the Court.—In an action brought under subsection (a), the court—

(1) may grant temporary and permanent injunctions on such terms as it deems reasonable to prevent or restrain such violation; (2) in the case of a violation of section 1002, or in the case of an injury resulting from a failure to make royalty payments required by section 1003, shall award damages under subsection (d); (3) in is discretion may allow the recovery of costs by or against any party other than the United States or an officer thereof; and

(4) in its discretion may award a reasonable attorney's fee to the prevailing party.

(d) Award of Damages.—

(1) Damages for Section 1002 or 1003 Violations.—

(A) Actual Damages.—

(i) In an action brought under subsection (a), if the court finds that a violation of section 1002 or 1003 has occurred, the court shall award to the complaining party its actual damages if the complaining party elects such damages at any time before final judgment is entered.

(ii) In the case of section 1003, actual damages shall constitute the royalty payments that should have been paid under section 1004 and deposited under section 1005. In such a case, the court, in its discretion, may award an additional amount of not to exceed 50 percent of the actual damages.

(B) Statutory Damages for Section 1002 Violations.—

(i) Device.—A complaining party may recover an award of statutory damages for each violation of section 1002(a) or (c) in the sum of not more than $2,500 per device involved in such violation or per device on which a service prohibited by section 1002(c) has been performed, as the court considers just.

(ii) Digital Musical Recording.—A complaining party may recover an award of statutory damages for each violation of section 1002(d) in the sum of not more than $25 per digital musical recording involved in such violation, as the court considers just.

(iii) Transmission.—A complaining party may recover an award of damages for each transmission or communication that violates section 1002(e) in the sum of not more than violates section 1002(e) in the sum of not more than $10,000, as the court considers just.

(2) Repeated Violations.—In any case in which the courts finds that a person has violated section 1002 or 1003 within years after a final judgment against that person for another such violation was entered, the court may increase the award of damages to not more than double the amounts that would otherwise be awarded under paragraph (1), as the court considers just.

(3) Innocent Violations of Section 1002.—The court in its discretion may reduce the total award of damages against a person violating section 1002 to a sum of not less than $250 in any case in which the court finds that the violator was not aware and had no reason to believe that its acts constituted a violation of section 1002.

(e) Payment of Damages.—Any award of damages under subsection (d) shall be deposited with the Register pursuant to section 1005 for distribution to interested copyright parties as though such funds were royalty payments made pursuant to section 1003.

(f) Impounding of Articles.—At any time while an action under subsection (a) is pending, the court may order the impounding, on such terms as it deems reasonable, of any digital audio recording device, digital musical recording, or device specified in section 1002(c) that is in the custody or control of the alleged violator and that the court has reasonable cause to believe does not comply with, or was involved in a violation of, section 1002.

(g) Remedial Modification and Destruction of Articles.—In an action brought under subsection (a), the court may, as part of a final judgment or decree finding a violation of section 1002, order the remedial modification or the destruction of any digital audio recording device, digital musical recording, or device specified in section 1002(c) that—

(1) does not comply with, or was involved in a violation of, section 1002, and

(2) is in the custody or control of the violator or has been impounded under subsection (f).

SECTION 1010. Arbitration of certain disputes

(a) Scope of Arbitration.—Before the date of first distribution in the United States of a digital audio recording device or a digital audio interface device, any party manufacturing, importing, or distributing such device, and any interested copyright party may mutually agree to binding arbitration for the purpose of determining whether such device is subject to section 1002, or the basis on which royalty payments for such device are to be made under section 1003.

(b) Initiation of Arbitration Proceedings.—Parties agreeing to such arbitration shall file a petition with the Copyright Royalty Tribunal requesting the commencement of an arbitration proceeding. The petition may include the names and qualifications of potential arbitrators. Within 2 weeks after receiving such a petition, the Tribunal shall cause notice to be published in the Federal Register of the initiation of an arbitration proceeding. Such notice shall include the names and qualifications of 3 arbitrators chosen by the Tribunal from a list of available arbitrators obtained from the American Arbitration Association or such similar organization as the Tribunal shall select, and from potential arbitrators listed in the parties' petition. The arbitrators selected under this subsection shall constitute an Arbitration Panel.

(c) Stay of Judicial Proceedings.—Any civil action brought under section 1009 against a party to arbitration under this section shall, on application of one of the parties to the arbitration, be stayed until completion of the arbitration proceeding.

(d) Arbitration Proceeding.—The Arbitration Panel shall conduct an arbitration proceeding with respect to the matter concerned, in accordance with such procedures as it may adopt. The Panel shall act on the basis of a fully documented written record. Any party to the arbitration may submit relevant information and proposals to the Panel. The parties to the proceeding shall bear the entire cost thereof in such manner and proportion as the Panel shall direct.

(e) Report to Copyright Royalty Tribunal.—Not later than 60 days after publication of the notice under subsection (b) of the initiation of an arbitration proceeding, the Arbitration Panel shall report to the Copyright Royalty Tribunal its determination concerning whether the device concerned is subject to section 1002, or the basis on which royalty payments for the device are to be made under section 1003. Such report shall be accompanied by the written record, and shall set forth the facts that the Panel found relevant to its determination.

(f) Action by the Copyright Royalty Tribunal.—Within 60 days after receiving the report of the Arbitration Panel under subsection (e), the Copyright Royalty Tribunal shall adopt or reject the determination of the Panel. The Tribunal shall adopt the determination of the Panel unless the Tribunal finds that the determination is clearly erroneous. If the Tribunal rejects the determination of the Panel, the Tribunal shall, before the end of that 60-day period, and after full examination of the record created in the arbitration proceeding, issue an order setting forth its decision and the reasons therefore. The Tribunal shall cause to be published in the Federal Register the determination of the Panel and the decision of the Tribunal under this subsection with respect to the determination (including any order issued under the preceding sentence).

(g) Judicial Review.—Any decision of the Copyright Royalty Tribunal under subsection (f) with respect to a determination of the Arbitration Panel may be appealed, by a party to the arbitration, to the United States Court of Appeals for the District of Columbia Circuit, within 30 days after the publication of the decision in the Federal Register. The pendency of an appeal under this subsection shall not stay the Tribunal's decision. The court shall have jurisdiction to modify or vacate a decision of the Tribunal only if it finds, on the basis of the record before the Tribunal, that the Arbitration Panel or the Tribunal acted in an arbitrary manner. If the court modifies the decision of the Tribunal, the court shall have jurisdiction to enter its own decision in accordance with its final judgment. The court may further vacate the decision of the Tribunal and remand the case for arbitration proceedings as provided in this section.

APPENDIX 17:

UCC CONVENTION SIGNATORIES
(NON-BERNE PARTICIPATING)

Algeria
Andorra
Bangladesh
Belize
Cuba
Dominican Republic
Ecuador
El Salvador
Guatemala
Haiti
Kampuchea
(Cambodia)

Kenya
Korea (North)
Laos
Liberia
Malawi
Mauritius
Nigeria
Panama
Paraguay
Peru
Soviet Union
Zambia

APPENDIX 18:

BERNE CONVENTION COUNTRIES

Argentina	Fiji	Madagascar	Slovak Republic
Australia	Finland	Mali	South Africa
Austria	France	Malta	Spain
Bahamas	Gabon	Mauritania	Sri Lanka
Barbados	Germany	Mexico	Surinam
Belgium	Ghana	Monaco	Sweden
Benin	Greece	Morocco	Switzerland
Brazil	Guinea	Netherlands	Thailand
Bulgaria	Hungary	New Zealand	Togo
Cameroon	Iceland	Niger	Tunisia
Canada	India	Nigeria	Turkey
Central Africa Republic	Ireland	Norway	United Kingdom
Chad	Israel	Pakistan	United States
Chile	Italy	Peru	Burkina Faso
China	Ivory Coast	Philippines	Uraguay
Colombia	Japan	Poland	Vatican City
Costa Rica	Lebanon	Portugal	Venezuela
Cyprus	Libya	Romania	Yugoslavia
Czech Republic	Liechtenstein	Rwanda	Zaire
Denmark	Luxembourg	Senegal	Zimbabwe

APPENDIX 19:

GATT SIGNATORY COUNTRIES

GATT Signatories:

People's Democratic Republic of Algeria

Antigua and Barbuda

Argentine Republic

Australia

Republic of Austria

State of Bahrain

People's Republic of Bangladesh

Barbados

Kingdom of Belgium

Belize

Republic of Benin

Republic of Bolivia

Republic of Botswana

Federative Republic of Brazil

Brunei Darussalam

Burkina Faso

Republic of Burundi

Republic of Cameroon

Canada

Central African Republic

Republic of Chad

Republic of Chile

People's Republic of China

Republic of Colombia

Republic of the Congo

Republic of Costa Rica

Republic of the Côte d'Ivroire

Republic of Cuba

Republic of Cyprus

Czech Republic

Kingdom of Denmark

Commonwealth of Dominica

Malaysia

Dominican Republic

Arab Republic of Egypt

Republic of El Salvador

Republic of Fiji

Republic of Finland

French Republic

Gabonese Republic

Republic of Gambia

Federal Republic of Germany

Republic of Ghana

Hellenic Republic

Republic of Guatemala

Republic of Guyana

Republic of Haiti

Republic of Honduras

Hong Kong

Republic of Hungary

Republic of Iceland

Republic of India

Republic of Indonesia

Ireland

State of Israel

Italian Republic

Jamaica

Japan

Republic of Kenya

Republic of Korea

State of Kuwait

Kingdom of Lesotho

Grand Duchy of Luxembourg

Macau

Republic of Madagascar

Republic of Malawi

Kingdom of Swaziland

Republic of Maldives

Republic of Mali

Republic of Malta

Islamic Republic of Mauritania

Republic of Mauritius

United Mexican States

Kingdom of Morocco

Republic of Mozambique

Union of Myanmar

Republic of Namibia

Kingdom of the Netherlands

New Zealand

Republic of Nicaragua

Republic of the Niger

Federal Republic of Nigeria

Kingdom of Norway

Islamic Republic of Pakistan

Republic of Paraguay

Republic of Peru

Republic of the Philippines

Republic of Poland

Portuguese Republic

Romania

Rwandese Republic

Saint Lucia

Saint Vincent and the Grenadines

Republic of Senegal

Republic of Sierra Leone

Republic of Singapore

Slovak Republic

Republic of South Africa

Kingdom of Spain

Democratic Socialist Republic of Sri Lanka

Republic of Surinarne

Kingdom of Sweden

Swiss Confederation

United Republic of Tanzania

Kingdom of Thailand

Togolese Republic

Republic of Trinidad and Tobago

Republic of Tunisia

Republic of Turkey

Republic of Uganda

United Kingdom of Great Britain and Northern Ireland

United States of America

Eastern Republic of Uruguay

Republic of Venezuela

Republic of Zaire

Republic of Zambia

Republic of Zimbabwe

European Communities

APPENDIX 20:

SELECTED PROVISIONS OF THE NORTH AMERICAN FREE TRADE AGREEMENT (NAFTA) CONCERNING INTELLECTUAL PROPERTY RIGHTS

PART 6. NAFTA INTELLECTUAL PROPERTY PROVISIONS

CHAPTER 17. Intellectual Property

Article 1701: Nature and Scope of Obligations

1. Each Party shall provide in its territory to the nationals of another Party adequate and effective protection and enforcement of intellectual property rights, while ensuring that measures to enforce intellectual property rights do not themselves become barriers to legitimate trade.

2. To provide adequate and effective protection and enforcement of intellectual property rights, each Party shall, at a minimum, give effect to this Chapter and to the substantive provisions of:

(a) the Geneva Convention for the Protection of Producers of Phonograms Against Unauthorized Duplication of their Phonograms, 1971 (Geneva Convention);

(b) the Berne Convention for the Protection of Literary and Artistic Works, 1971 (Berne Convention);

(c) the Paris Convention for the Protection of Industrial Property, 1967 (Paris Convention); and

(d) the International Convention for the Protection of New Varieties of Plants, 1978 (UPOV Convention), or the International Convention for the Protection of New Varieties of Plants, 1991 (UPOV Convention).

If a Party has not acceded to the specified text of any such Conventions on or before the date of entry into force of this Agreement, it shall make every effort to accede.

3. Paragraph 2 shall apply, except as provided in Annex 1701.3.

Article 1702: More Extensive Protection

A Party may implement in its domestic law more extensive protection of intellectual property rights than is required under this Agreement, provided that such protection is not inconsistent with this Agreement.

Article 1703: National Treatment

1. Each Party shall accord to nationals of another Party treatment no less favorable than that it accords to its own nationals with regard to the protection and enforcement of all intellectual property rights. In respect of sound recordings, each Party shall provide such treatment to producers and performers of another Party, except that a Party may limit rights of performers of another Party in respect of secondary uses of sound recordings to those rights its nationals are accorded in the territory of such other Party.

2. No Party may, as a condition of according national treatment under this Article, require right holders to comply with any formalities or conditions in order to acquire rights in respect of copyright and related rights.

3. A Party may derogate from paragraph 1 in relation to its judicial and administrative procedures for the protection or enforcement of intellectual property rights, including any procedure requiring a national of another Party to designate for service of process an address in the Party's territory or to appoint an agent in the Party's territory, if the derogation is consistent with the relevant Convention listed in Article 1701(2), provided that such derogation:

　　(a) is necessary to secure compliance with measures that are not inconsistent with this Chapter; and

　　(b) is not applied in a manner that would constitute a disguised restriction on trade.

4. No Party shall have any obligation under this Article with respect to procedures provided in multilateral agreements concluded under the auspices of the World Intellectual Property Organization relating to the acquisition or maintenance of intellectual property rights.

Article 1704: Control of Abusive or Anticompetitive Practices or Conditions

Nothing in this Chapter shall prevent a Party from specifying in its domestic law licensing practices or conditions that may in particular cases constitute an abuse of intellectual property rights having an adverse effect on competition in the relevant market. A Party may adopt or maintain, consistent with the other provisions of this Agreement, appropriate measures to prevent or control such practices or conditions.

Article 1705: Copyright

1. Each Party shall protect the works covered by Article 2 of the Berne Convention, including any other works that embody original expression within the meaning of that Convention. In particular:

(a) all types of computer programs are literary works within the meaning of the Berne Convention and each Party shall protect them as such; and

(b) compilations of data or other material, whether in machine readable or other form, which by reason of the selection or arrangement of their contents constitute intellectual creations, shall be protected as such.

The protection a Party provides under subparagraph (b) shall not extend to the data or material itself, or prejudice any copyright subsisting in that data or material.

2. Each Party shall provide to authors and their successors in interest those rights enumerated in the Berne Convention in respect of works covered by paragraph 1, including the right to authorize or prohibit:

(a) the importation into the Party's territory of copies of the work made without the right holder's authorization;

(b) the first public distribution of the original and each copy of the work by sale, rental or otherwise;

(c) the communication of a work to the public; and

(d) the commercial rental of the original or a copy of a computer program.

Subparagraph (d) shall not apply where the copy of the computer program is not itself an essential object of the rental. Each Party shall provide that putting the original or a copy of a computer program on the market with the right holder's consent shall not exhaust the rental right.

3. Each Party shall provide that for copyright and related rights:

(a) any person acquiring or holding economic rights may freely and separately transfer such rights by contract for purposes of their exploitation and enjoyment by the transferee; and

(b) any person acquiring or holding such economic rights by virtue of a contract, including contracts of employment underlying the creation of works and sound recordings, shall be able to exercise those rights in its own name and enjoy fully the benefits derived from those rights.

4. Each Party shall provide that, where the term of protection of a work, other than a photographic work or a work of applied art, is to be calculated on a basis other than the life of a natural person, the term shall be not less than 50 years from the end of the calendar year of the first authorized publication of the work or, failing such authorized publication within 50 years from the making of the work, 50 years from the end of the calendar year of making.

5. Each Party shall confine limitations or exceptions to the rights provided for in this Article to certain special cases that do not conflict with a normal exploitation of the work and do not unreasonably prejudice the legitimate interests of the right holder.

6. No Party may grant translation and reproduction licenses permitted under the Appendix to the Berne Convention where legitimate needs in that Party's territory for copies or translations of the work could be met by the right holder's voluntary actions but for obstacles created by the Party's measures.

7. Annex 1705.7 applies to the Parties specified in that Annex.

Article 1706: Sound Recordings

1. Each Party shall provide to the producer of a sound recording the right to authorize or prohibit:

(a) the direct or indirect reproduction of the sound recording;

(b) the importation into the Party's territory of copies of the sound recording made without the producer's authorization;

(c) the first public distribution of the original and each copy of the sound recording by sale, rental or otherwise; and

(d) the commercial rental of the original or a copy of the sound recording, except where expressly otherwise provided in a contract between the producer of the sound recording and the authors of the works fixed therein.

Each Party shall provide that putting the original or a copy of a sound recording on the market with the right holder's consent shall not exhaust the rental right.

2. Each Party shall provide a term of protection for sound recordings of at least 50 years from the end of the calendar year in which the fixation was made.

3. Each Party shall confine limitations or exceptions to the rights provided for in this Article to certain special cases that do not conflict with a normal exploitation of the sound recording and do not unreasonably prejudice the legitimate interests of the right holder.

Article 1707: Protection of Encrypted Program-Carrying Satellite Signals

Within one year from the date of entry into force of this Agreement, each Party shall make it:

(a) a criminal offense to manufacture, import, sell, lease or otherwise make available a device or system that is primarily of assistance in decoding an encrypted program-carrying satellite signal without the authorization of the lawful distributor of such signal; and

(b) a civil offense to receive, in connection with commercial activities, or further distribute, an encrypted program-carrying satellite signal that has been decoded without the authorization of the lawful distributor of the signal or to engage in any activity prohibited under subparagraph (a).

Each Party shall provide that any civil offense established under subparagraph (b) shall be actionable by any person that holds an interest in the content of such signal.

Article 1708: Trademarks [Omitted]

Article 1709: Patents [Omitted]

Article 1710: Layout Designs of Semiconductor Integrated Circuits [Omitted]

Article 1711: Trade Secrets [Omitted]

Article 1712: Geographical Indications [Omitted]

Article 1713: Industrial Designs [Omitted]

Article 1714: Enforcement of Intellectual Property Rights: General Provisions

1. Each Party shall ensure that enforcement procedures, as specified in this Article and Articles 1715 through 1718, are available under its domestic law so as to permit effective action to be taken against any act of infringement of intellectual property rights covered by this Chapter, including expeditious remedies to prevent infringements and remedies to deter further

infringements. Such enforcement procedures shall be applied so as to avoid the creation of barriers to legitimate trade and to provide for safeguards against abuse of the procedures.

2. Each Party shall ensure that its procedures for the enforcement of intellectual property rights are fair and equitable, are not unnecessarily complicated or costly, and do not entail unreasonable time-limits or unwarranted delays.

3. Each Party shall provide that decisions on the merits of a case in judicial and administrative enforcement proceedings shall:

(a) preferably be in writing and preferably state the reasons on which the decisions are based;

(b) be made available at least to the parties in a proceeding without undue delay; and

(c) be based only on evidence in respect of which such parties were offered the opportunity to be heard.

4. Each Party shall ensure that parties in a proceeding have an opportunity to have final administrative decisions reviewed by a judicial authority of that Party and, subject to jurisdictional provisions in its domestic laws concerning the importance of a case, to have reviewed at least the legal aspects of initial judicial decisions on the merits of a case. Notwithstanding the above, no Party shall be required to provide for judicial review of acquittals in criminal cases.

5. Nothing in this Article or Articles 1715 through 1718 shall be construed to require a Party to establish a judicial system for the enforcement of intellectual property rights distinct from that Party's system for the enforcement of laws in general.

6. For the purposes of Articles 1715 through 1718, the term "right holder" includes federations and associations having legal standing to assert such rights.

Article 1715: Specific Procedural and Remedial Aspects of Civil and Administrative Procedures

1. Each Party shall make available to right holders civil judicial procedures for the enforcement of any intellectual property right provided in this Chapter. Each Party shall provide that:

(a) defendants have the right to written notice that is timely and contains sufficient detail, including the basis of the claims;

(b) parties in a proceeding are allowed to be represented by independent legal counsel;

(c) the procedures do not include imposition of overly burdensome requirements concerning mandatory personal appearances;

(d) all parties in a proceeding are duly entitled to substantiate their claims and to present relevant evidence; and

(e) the procedures include a means to identify and protect confidential information.

2. Each Party shall provide that its judicial authorities shall have the authority:

(a) where a party in a proceeding has presented reasonably available evidence sufficient to support its claims and has specified evidence relevant to the substantiation of its claims that is within the control of the opposing party, to order the opposing party to produce such evidence, subject in appropriate cases to conditions that ensure the protection of confidential information;

(b) where a party in a proceeding voluntarily and without good reason refuses access to, or otherwise does not provide relevant evidence under that party's control within a reasonable period, or significantly impedes a proceeding relating to an enforcement action, to make preliminary and final determinations, affirmative or negative, on the basis of the evidence presented, including the complaint or the allegation presented by the party adversely affected by the denial of access to evidence, subject to providing the parties an opportunity to be heard on the allegations or evidence;

(c) to order a party in a proceeding to desist from an infringement, including to prevent the entry into the channels of commerce in their jurisdiction of imported goods that involve the infringement of an intellectual property right, which order shall be enforceable at least immediately after customs clearance of such goods;

(d) to order the infringer of an intellectual property right to pay the right holder damages adequate to compensate for the injury the right holder has suffered because of the infringement where the infringer knew or had reasonable grounds to know that it was engaged in an infringing activity;

(e) to order an infringer of an intellectual property right to pay the right holder's expenses, which may include appropriate attorney's fees; and

(f) to order a party in a proceeding at whose request measures were taken and who has abused enforcement procedures to provide adequate compensation to any party wrongfully enjoined or restrained in the proceeding for the injury suffered because of such abuse and to pay that party's expenses, which may include appropriate attorney's fees.

3. With respect to the authority referred to in subparagraph 2(c), no Party shall be obliged to provide such authority in respect of protected subject matter that is acquired or ordered by a person before that person knew or had reasonable grounds to know that dealing in that subject matter would entail the infringement of an intellectual property right.

4. With respect to the authority referred to in subparagraph 2(d), a Party may, at least with respect to copyrighted works and sound recordings, authorize the judicial authorities to order recovery of profits or payment of pre-established damages, or both, even where the infringer did not know or had no reasonable grounds to know that it was engaged in an infringing activity.

5. Each Party shall provide that, in order to create an effective deterrent to infringement, its judicial authorities shall have the authority to order that:

(a) goods that they have found to be infringing be, without compensation of any sort, disposed of outside the channels of commerce in such a manner as to avoid any injury caused to the right holder or, unless this would be contrary to existing constitutional requirements, destroyed; and

(b) materials and implements the predominant use of which has been in the creation of the infringing goods be, without compensation of any sort, disposed of outside the channels of commerce in such a manner as to minimize the risks of further infringements.

In considering whether to issue such an order, judicial authorities shall take into account the need for proportionality between the seriousness of the infringement and the remedies ordered as well as the interests of other persons. In regard to counterfeit goods, the simple removal of the trademark unlawfully affixed shall not be sufficient, other than in exceptional cases, to permit release of the goods into the channels of commerce.

6. In respect of the administration of any law pertaining to the protection or enforcement of intellectual property rights, each Party shall only exempt both public authorities and officials from liability to appropriate remedial measures where actions are taken or intended in good faith in the course of the administration of such laws.

7. Notwithstanding the other provisions of Articles 1714 through 1718, where a Party is sued with respect to an infringement of an intellectual property right as a result of its use of that right or use on its behalf, that Party may limit the remedies available against it to the payment to the right holder of adequate remuneration in the circumstances of each case, taking into account the economic value of the use.

8. Each Party shall provide that, where a civil remedy can be ordered as a result of administrative procedures on the merits of a case, such procedures shall conform to principles equivalent in substance to those set out in this Article.

Article 1716: Provisional Measures

1. Each Party shall provide that its judicial authorities shall have the authority to order prompt and effective provisional measures:

(a) to prevent an infringement of any intellectual property right, and in particular to prevent the entry into the channels of commerce in their jurisdiction of allegedly infringing goods, including measures to prevent the entry of imported goods at least immediately after customs clearance; and

(b) to preserve relevant evidence in regard to the alleged infringement.

2. Each Party shall provide that its judicial authorities shall have the authority to require any applicant for provisional measures to provide to the judicial authorities any evidence reasonably available to that applicant that the judicial authorities consider necessary to enable them to determine with a sufficient degree of certainty whether:

(a) the applicant is the right holder;

(b) the applicant's right is being infringed or such infringement is imminent; and

(c) any delay in the issuance of such measures is likely to cause irreparable harm to the right holder, or there is a demonstrable risk of evidence being destroyed.

Each Party shall provide that its judicial authorities shall have the authority to require the applicant to provide a security or equivalent assurance sufficient to protect the interests of the defendant and to prevent abuse.

3. Each Party shall provide that its judicial authorities shall have the authority to require an applicant for provisional measures to provide other

information necessary for the identification of the relevant goods by the authority that will execute the provisional measures.

4. Each Party shall provide that its judicial authorities shall have the authority to order provisional measures on an ex parte basis, in particular where any delay is likely to cause irreparable harm to the right holder, or where there is a demonstrable risk of evidence being destroyed.

5. Each Party shall provide that where provisional measures are adopted by that Party's judicial authorities on an ex parte basis:

(a) a person affected shall be given notice of those measures without delay but in any event no later than immediately after the execution of the measures;

(b) a defendant shall, on request, have those measures reviewed by that Party's judicial authorities for the purpose of deciding, within a reasonable period after notice of those measures is given, whether the measures shall be modified, revoked or confirmed, and shall be given an opportunity to be heard in the review proceedings.

6. Without prejudice to paragraph 5, each Party shall provide that, on the request of the defendant, the Party's judicial authorities shall revoke or otherwise cease to apply the provisional measures taken on the basis of paragraphs 1 and 4 if proceedings leading to a decision on the merits are not initiated:

(a) within a reasonable period as determined by the judicial authority ordering the measures where the Party's domestic law so permits; or

(b) in the absence of such a determination, within a period of no more than 20 working days or 31 calendar days, whichever is longer.

7. Each Party shall provide that, where the provisional measures are revoked or where they lapse due to any act or omission by the applicant, or where the judicial authorities subsequently find that there has been no infringement or threat of infringement of an intellectual property right, the judicial authorities shall have the authority to order the applicant, on request of the defendant, to provide the defendant appropriate compensation for any injury caused by these measures.

8. Each Party shall provide that, where a provisional measure can be ordered as a result of administrative procedures, such procedures shall conform to principles equivalent in substance to those set out in this Article.

Article 1717: Criminal Procedures and Penalties

1. Each Party shall provide criminal procedures and penalties to be applied at least in cases of willful trademark counterfeiting or copyright piracy on a commercial scale. Each Party shall provide that penalties available include imprisonment or monetary fines, or both, sufficient to provide a deterrent, consistent with the level of penalties applied for crimes of a corresponding gravity.

2. Each Party shall provide that, in appropriate cases, its judicial authorities may order the seizure, forfeiture and destruction of infringing goods and of any materials and implements the predominant use of which has been in the commission of the offense.

3. A Party may provide criminal procedures and penalties to be applied in cases of infringement of intellectual property rights, other than those in paragraph 1, where they are committed wilfully and on a commercial scale.

Article 1718: Enforcement of Intellectual Property Rights at the Border

1. Each Party shall, in conformity with this Article, adopt procedures to enable a right holder, who has valid grounds for suspecting that the importation of counterfeit trademark goods or pirated copyright goods may take place, to lodge an application in writing with its competent authorities, whether administrative or judicial, for the suspension by the customs administration of the release of such goods into free circulation. No Party shall be obligated to apply such procedures to goods in transit. A Party may permit such an application to be made in respect of goods that involve other infringements of intellectual property rights, provided that the requirements of this Article are met. A Party may also provide for corresponding procedures concerning the suspension by the customs administration of the release of infringing goods destined for exportation from its territory.

2. Each Party shall require any applicant who initiates procedures under paragraph 1 to provide adequate evidence:

(a) to satisfy that Party's competent authorities that, under the domestic laws of the country of importation, there is prima facie an infringement of its intellectual property right; and

(b) to supply a sufficiently detailed description of the goods to make them readily recognizable by the customs administration.

The competent authorities shall inform the applicant within a reasonable period whether they have accepted the application and, if so, the period for which the customs administration will take action.

3. Each Party shall provide that its competent authorities shall have the authority to require an applicant under paragraph 1 to provide a security or equivalent assurance sufficient to protect the defendant and the competent authorities and to prevent abuse. Such security or equivalent assurance shall not unreasonably deter recourse to these procedures.

4. Each Party shall provide that, where pursuant to an application under procedures adopted pursuant to this Article, its customs administration suspends the release of goods involving industrial designs, patents, integrated circuits or trade secrets into free circulation on the basis of a decision other than by a judicial or other independent authority, and the period provided for in paragraphs 6 through 8 has expired without the granting of provisional relief by the duly empowered authority, and provided that all other conditions for importation have been complied with, the owner, importer or consignee of such goods shall be entitled to their release on the posting of a security in an amount sufficient to protect the right holder against any infringement. Payment of such security shall not prejudice any other remedy available to the right holder, it being understood that the security shall be released if the right holder fails to pursue its right of action within a reasonable period of time.

5. Each Party shall provide that its customs administration shall promptly notify the importer and the applicant when the customs administration suspends the release of goods pursuant to paragraph 1.

6. Each Party shall provide that its customs administration shall release goods from suspension if, within a period not exceeding 10 working days after the applicant under paragraph 1 has been served notice of the suspension, the customs administration has not been informed that:

(a) a party other than the defendant has initiated proceedings leading to a decision on the merits of the case, or

(b) a competent authority has taken provisional measures prolonging the suspension,

provided that all other conditions for importation or exportation have been met. Each Party shall provide that, in appropriate cases, the customs administration may extend the suspension by another 10 working days.

7. Each Party shall provide that if proceedings leading to a decision on the merits of the case have been initiated, a review, including a right to be

heard, shall take place on request of the defendant with a view to deciding, within a reasonable period, whether these measures shall be modified, revoked or confirmed.

8. Notwithstanding paragraphs 6 and 7, where the suspension of the release of goods is carried out or continued in accordance with a provisional judicial measure, Article 1716(6) shall apply.

9. Each Party shall provide that its competent authorities shall have the authority to order the applicant under paragraph 1 to pay the importer, the consignee and the owner of the goods appropriate compensation for any injury caused to them through the wrongful detention of goods or through the detention of goods released pursuant to paragraph 6.

10. Without prejudice to the protection of confidential information, each Party shall provide that its competent authorities shall have the authority to give the right holder sufficient opportunity to have any goods detained by the customs administration inspected in order to substantiate the right holder's claims. Each Party shall also provide that its competent authorities have the authority to give the importer an equivalent opportunity to have any such goods inspected. Where the competent authorities have made a positive determination on the merits of a case, a Party may provide the competent authorities the authority to inform the right holder of the names and addresses of the consignor, the importer and the consignee, and of the quantity of the goods in question.

11. Where a Party requires its competent authorities to act on their own initiative and to suspend the release of goods in respect of which they have acquired prima facie evidence that an intellectual property right is being infringed:

(a) the competent authorities may at any time seek from the right holder any information that may assist them to exercise these powers;

(b) the importer and the right holder shall be promptly notified of the suspension by the Party's competent authorities, and where the importer lodges an appeal against the suspension with competent authorities, the suspension shall be subject to the conditions, with such modifications as may be necessary, set out in paragraphs 6 through 8; and

(c) the Party shall only exempt both public authorities and officials from liability to appropriate remedial measures where actions are taken or intended in good faith.

12. Without prejudice to other rights of action open to the right holder and subject to the defendant's right to seek judicial review, each Party shall pro-

vide that its competent authorities shall have the authority to order the destruction or disposal of infringing goods in accordance with the principles set out in Article 1715(5). In regard to counterfeit goods, the authorities shall not allow the re-exportation of the infringing goods in an unaltered state or subject them to a different customs procedure, other than in exceptional circumstances.

13. A Party may exclude from the application of paragraphs 1 through 12 small quantities of goods of a non-commercial nature contained in travellers' personal luggage or sent in small consignments that are not repetitive.

Article 1719: Cooperation and Technical Assistance

1. The Parties shall provide each other on mutually agreed terms with technical assistance and shall promote cooperation between their competent authorities. Such cooperation shall include the training of personnel.

2. The Parties shall cooperate with a view to eliminating trade in goods that infringe intellectual property rights. For this purpose, each Party shall establish and notify the other Parties by January 1, 1994 of contact points in its federal government and shall exchange information concerning trade in infringing goods.

Article 1720: Protection of Existing Subject Matter

1. Except as required under Article 1705(7), this Agreement does not give rise to obligations in respect of acts that occurred before the date of application of the relevant provisions of this Agreement for the Party in question.

2. Except as otherwise provided for in this Agreement, each Party shall apply this Agreement to all subject matter existing on the date of application of the relevant provisions of this Agreement for the Party in question and that is protected in a Party on such date, or that meets or subsequently meets the criteria for protection under the terms of this Chapter. In respect of this paragraph and paragraphs 3 and 4, a Party's obligations with respect to existing works shall be solely determined under Article 18 of the Berne Convention and with respect to the rights of producers of sound recordings in existing sound recordings shall be determined solely under Article 18 of that Convention, as made applicable under this Agreement.

3. Except as required under Article 1705(7), and notwithstanding the first sentence of paragraph 2, no Party may be required to restore protection to subject matter that, on the date of application of the relevant provisions of this Agreement for the Party in question, has fallen into the public domain in its territory.

4. In respect of any acts relating to specific objects embodying protected subject matter that become infringing under the terms of laws in conformity with this Agreement, and that were begun or in respect of which a significant investment was made, before the date of entry into force of this Agreement for that Party, any Party may provide for a limitation of the remedies available to the right holder as to the continued performance of such acts after the date of application of this Agreement for that Party. In such cases, the Party shall, however, at least provide for payment of equitable remuneration.

5. No Party shall be obliged to apply Article 1705(2)(d) or 1706(1)(d) with respect to originals or copies purchased prior to the date of application of the relevant provisions of this Agreement for that Party.

6. No Party shall be required to apply Article 1709(10), or the requirement in Article 1709(7) that patent rights shall be enjoyable without discrimination as to the field of technology, to use without the authorization of the right holder where authorization for such use was granted by the government before the text of the Draft Final Act Embodying the Results of the Uruguay Round of Multilateral Trade Negotiations became known.

7. In the case of intellectual property rights for which protection is conditional on registration, applications for protection that are pending on the date of application of the relevant provisions of this Agreement for the Party in question shall be permitted to be amended to claim any enhanced protection provided under this Agreement. Such amendments shall not include new matter.

Article 1721: Definitions

1. For purposes of this Chapter:

confidential information includes trade secrets, privileged information and other materials exempted from disclosure under the Party's domestic law.

2. For purposes of this Agreement:

encrypted program-carrying satellite signal means a program-carrying satellite signal that is transmitted in a form whereby the aural or visual characteristics, or both, are modified or altered for the purpose of preventing the unauthorized reception, by persons without the authorized equipment that is designed to eliminate the effects of such modification or alteration, of a program carried in that signal;

geographical indication means any indication that identifies a good as originating in the territory of a Party, or a region or locality in that territory, where a particular quality, reputation or other characteristic of the good is essentially attributable to its geographical origin;

in a manner contrary to honest commercial practices means at least practices such as breach of contract, breach of confidence and inducement to breach, and includes the acquisition of undisclosed information by other persons who knew, or were grossly negligent in failing to know, that such practices were involved in the acquisition;

intellectual property rights refers to copyright and related rights, trademark rights, patent rights, rights in layout designs of semiconductor integrated circuits, trade secret rights, plant breeders' rights, rights in geographical indications and industrial design rights;

nationals of another Party means, in respect of the relevant intellectual property right, persons who would meet the criteria for eligibility for protection provided for in the Paris Convention (1967), the Berne Convention (1971), the Geneva Convention (1971), the International Convention for the Protection of Performers, Producers of Phonograms and Broadcasting Organizations (1961), the UPOV Convention (1978), the UPOV Convention (1991) or the Treaty on Intellectual Property in Respect of Integrated Circuits, as if each Party were a party to those Conventions, and with respect to intellectual property rights that are not the subject of these Conventions, "nationals of another Party" shall be understood to be at least individuals who are citizens or permanent residents of that Party and also includes any other natural person referred to in Annex 201.1 (Country-Specific Definitions);

public includes, with respect to rights of communication and performance of works provided for under Articles 11, 11 *bis*(1) and 14(1)(ii) of the Berne Convention, with respect to dramatic, dramatico-musical, musical and cinematographic works, at least, any aggregation of individuals intended to be the object of, and capable of perceiving, communications or performances of works, regardless of whether they can do so at the same or different times or in the same or different places, provided that such an aggregation is larger than a family and its immediate circle of acquaintances or is not a group comprising a limited number of individuals having similarly close ties that has not been formed for the principal purpose of receiving such performances and communications of works; and

secondary uses of sound recordings means the use directly for broadcasting or for any other public communication of a sound recording.

Annex 1701.3. Intellectual Property Conventions

1. Mexico shall:

(a) make every effort to comply with the substantive provisions of the 1978 or 1991 UPOV Convention as soon as possible and shall do so no later than two years after the date of signature of this Agreement; and

(b) accept from the date of entry into force of this Agreement applications from plant breeders for varieties in all plant genera and species and grant protection, in accordance with such substantive provisions, promptly after complying with subparagraph (a).

2. Notwithstanding Article 1701(2)(b), this Agreement confers no rights and imposes no obligations on the United States with respect to Article 6 *bis* of the Berne Convention, or the rights derived from that Article.

Annex 1705.7. Copyright

The United States shall provide protection to motion pictures produced in another Party's territory that have been declared to be in the public domain pursuant to 17 U.S.C. section 405. This obligation shall apply to the extent that it is consistent with the Constitution of the United States, and is subject to budgetary considerations.

Annex 1710.9. Layout Designs [Omitted]

Annex 1718.14. Enforcement of Intellectual Property Rights

Mexico shall make every effort to comply with the requirements of Article 1718 as soon as possible and shall do so no later than three years after the date of signature of this Agreement.

GLOSSARY

GLOSSARY

Action at Law - A judicial proceeding whereby one party prosecutes another for a wrong done.

Acknowledgement - A formal declaration of one's signature before a notary public.

Acquiescence - Conduct that may imply consent.

Actual Damages - Actual damages are those damages directly referable to the breach or tortious act, and which can be readily proven to have been sustained, and for which the injured party should be compensated as a matter of right.

Agency - The relationship between a principal and an agent who is employed by the principal, to perform certain acts dealing with third parties.

Agent - One who represents another known as the principal.

American Arbitration Association (AAA) - National organization of arbitrators from whose panel arbitrators are selected for labor and civil disputes.

Anonymous Work - A work for which no natural person is identified as author.

Arbitration - The reference of a dispute to an impartial person chosen by the parties to the dispute who agree in advance to abide by the arbitrator's award issued after a hearing at which both parties have an opportunity to be heard.

Arbitration Acts - Federal and state laws which provide for submission of disputes to the process of arbitration.

Arbitration Board - A panel of arbitrators appointed to hear and decide a dispute according to the rules of arbitration.

Arbitration Clause - A clause inserted in a contract providing for compulsory arbitration in case of a dispute as to the rights or liabilities under such contract.

Arbitrator - A private, disinterested person, chosen by the parties to a disputed question, for the purpose of hearing their contention, and awarding judgment to the prevailing party.

Architectural Work - The design of a building as embodied in any tangible medium of expression, including a building, architectural plans, or drawings. The work includes the overall form as well as the arrangement and composition of spaces and elements in the design, but does not include individual standard features.

Asset - The entirety of a person's property, either real or personal.

Assignee - An assignee is a person to whom an assignment is made, also known as a grantee.

Assignment - An assignment is the transfer of an interest in a right or property from one party to another.

Audiovisual Works - Works that consist of a series of related images which are intrinsically intended to be shown by the use of machines or devices such as projectors, viewers, or electronic equipment, together with accompanying sounds, if any, regardless of the nature of the material objects, such as films or tapes, in which the works are embodied.

Award - The final and binding decision of an arbitrator, made in writing and enforceable in court under state and federal statutes.

Berne Convention - The Convention for the Protection of Literary and Artistic Works, signed at Berne, Switzerland, on September 9, 1886, and all acts, protocols, and revisions thereto.

Best Edition of a Work - The edition, published in the United States at any time before the date of deposit, that the Library of Congress determines to be most suitable for its purposes.

Best Evidence Rule - The rule of law which requires the original of a writing, recording or photograph to be produced in order to prove its authenticity.

Boilerplate - Refers to standard language found almost universally in certain documents.

Breach of Contract - The failure, without any legal excuse, to perform any promise which forms the whole or the part of a contract.

Burden of Proof - The duty of a party to substantiate an allegation or issue to convince the trier of fact as to the truth of their claim.

Capacity - Capacity is the legal qualification concerning the ability of one to understand the nature and effects of one's acts.

Collective Work - A work, such as a periodical issue, anthology, or encyclopedia, in which a number of contributions, constituting separate and independent works in themselves, are assembled into a collective whole.

Commission - Compensation for services performed which is based on a percentage of an agreed amount.

Common Law - Common law is the system of jurisprudence which originated in England and was later applied in the United States.

Compensatory Damages - Compensatory damages are those damages directly referable to a breach or tortious act, and which can be readily proven to have been sustained, and for which the injured party should be compensated as a matter of right.

Compilation - A work formed by the collection and assembling of preexisting materials or of data that are selected, coordinated, or arranged in such a way that the resulting work as a whole constitutes an original work of authorship. The term "compilation" includes collective works.

Compulsory Arbitration - Arbitration which occurs when the consent of one of the parties is enforced by statutory provisions.

Consideration - Something of value exchanged between parties to a contract, which is a requirement of a valid contract.

Contract - A contract is an agreement between two or more persons which creates an obligation to do or not to do a particular thing.

Conveyance - A conveyance is the transfer of property, or title to property, from one person to another, by means of a written instrument and other formalities.

Copies - Material objects, other than phonorecords, in which a work is fixed by any method now known or later developed, and from which the work can be perceived, reproduced, or otherwise communicated, either directly or with the aid of a machine or device. The term "copies" includes the material object, other than a phonorecord, in which the work is first fixed.

Copyright - Refers to the legal protection given to the works of authors and artists, granting them exclusive control over the right to publish their works.

Copyright Owner - With respect to any one of the exclusive rights comprised in a copyright, refers to the owner of that particular right.

Created - A work is considered "created" when it is fixed in a copy or phonorecord for the first time; where a work is prepared over a period of time, the portion of it that has been fixed at any particular time constitutes the work as of that time, and where the work has been prepared in different versions, each version constitutes a separate work.

Damages - In general, damages refers to monetary compensation which the law awards to one who has been injured by the actions of another, such as in the case of tortious conduct or breach of contractual obligations.

Decedent - A deceased person.

Derivative Work - A work based upon one or more preexisting works, such as a translation, musical arrangement, dramatization, fictionalization, motion picture version, sound recording, art reproduction, abridgment, condensation, or any other form in which a work may be recast, transformed, or adapted. A work consisting of editorial revisions, annotations, elaborations, or other modifications, which, as a whole, represent an original work of authorship, is a "derivative work".

Device - A "device", "machine", or "process" is one now known or later developed.

Digital Audio Copied Recording - A reproduction in a digital recording format of a digital musical recording, whether that reproduction is made directly from another digital musical recording or indirectly from a transmission.

Digital Audio Interface Device - Any machine or device that is designed specifically to communicate digital audio information and related interface data to a digital audio recording device through a nonprofessional interface.

Digital Audio Recording Device - Any machine or device of a type commonly distributed to individuals for use by individuals, whether or not included with or as part of some other machine or device, the digital recording function of which is designed or marketed for the primary purpose of, and that is capable of, making a digital audio copied recording for private use, except for—(A) professional model products, and (B) dictation machines, answering machines, and other audio recording equipment that is designed and marketed primarily for the creation of sound recordings resulting from the fixation of nonmusical sounds.

Digital Audio Recording Medium - Any material object in a form commonly distributed for use by individuals, that is primarily marketed or most commonly used by consumers for the purpose of making digital audio copied recordings by use of a digital audio recording device. Such term does not include any material object—(i) that embodies a sound recording at the time it is first distributed by the importer or manufacturer; or (ii) that is primarily marketed and most commonly used by consumers either for the purpose of making copies of motion pictures or other audiovisual works or for the purpose of making copies of nonmusical literary works, including computer programs or data bases.

Digital Musical Recording - A material object—(i) in which are fixed, in a digital recording format, only sounds, and material, statements, or instructions incidental to those fixed sounds, if any, and (ii) from which the sounds and material can be perceived, reproduced, or otherwise communicated, either directly or with the aid of a machine or device. A "digital musical recording" does not include a material object—(i) in which the fixed sounds consist entirely of spoken word recordings, or (ii) in which one or more computer programs are fixed, except that a digital musical recording may contain statements or instructions constituting the fixed sounds and incidental material, and statements or instructions to be used directly or indirectly in order to bring about the perception, reproduction, or communication of the fixed sounds and incidental material.

Digital Transmission - A transmission in whole or in part in a digital or other non-analog format.

Display a Work - Means to show a copy of the work, either directly or by means of a film, slide, television image, or any other device or process or, in the case of a motion picture or other audiovisual work, to show individual images nonsequentially.

Federal Courts - The courts of the United States.

Financial Gain - Includes receipt, or expectation of receipt, of anything of value, including the receipt of other copyrighted works.

Fixed In a Tangible Medium of Expression - Refers to a work when it is embodied in a copy or phonorecord, by or under the authority of the author, and is sufficiently permanent or stable to permit it to be perceived, reproduced, or otherwise communicated for a period of more than transitory duration. A work consisting of sounds, images, or both, that are being transmitted, is "fixed" if a fixation of the work is being made simultaneously with its transmission.

Fraud - A false representation of a matter of fact, whether by words or by conduct, by false or misleading allegations, or by concealment of that which should have been disclosed, which deceives and is intended to deceive another, and thereby causes injury to that person.

Fraudulent Conveyance - The transfer of property for the purpose of delaying or defrauding creditors.

Freedom of Information Act (FOIA) - A federal law which requires federal agencies to disclose information in its possession which is not exempt from the law.

General Damages - General damages are those damages directly referable to the breach or tortious act and which can be readily proven to have been sustained, and for which the injured party should be compensated as a matter of right.

Heirs - Those individuals who, by law, inherit an estate of an ancestor who dies without a will.

Hereditament - Anything which can be inherited.

Illegal - Against the law.

Implied Consent - Consent which is manifested by signs, actions or facts, or by inaction or silence, which raises a presumption that consent has been given.

Infancy - The state of a person who is under the age of legal majority.

Inherit - To take as an heir at law by descent rather than by will.

Inheritance - Property inherited by heirs according to the laws of descent and distribution.

Injunction - A judicial remedy either requiring a party to perform an act, or restricting a party from continuing a particular act.

Intentional Tort - A tort or wrong perpetrated by one who intends to do that which the law has declared wrong, as contrasted with negligence in which the tortfeasor fails to exercise that degree of care in doing what is otherwise permissible.

International Law - The law which governs the relationship among the nations.

Intestate - The state of dying without having executed a valid will.

Intestate Succession - The manner of disposing of property according to the laws of descent and distribution when the decedent died without leaving a valid will.

Joint and Several - The rights and liabilities shared among a group of people individually and collectively.

Joint Work - A work prepared by two or more authors with the intention that their contributions be merged into inseparable or interdependent parts of a unitary whole.

Literary Works - Works, other than audiovisual works, expressed in words, numbers, or other verbal or numerical symbols or indicia, regardless of the nature of the material objects, such as books, periodicals, manuscripts, phonorecords, film, tapes, disks, or cards, in which they are embodied.

Material Breach - A material breach refers to a substantial breach of contract which excuses further performance by the innocent party and gives rise to an action for breach of contract to make a binding decision.

Motion Pictures - Audiovisual works consisting of a series of related images which, when shown in succession, impart an impression of motion, together with accompanying sounds, if any.

Music publisher - Refers to a person or entity that is authorized to license the reproduction of a particular musical work in a sound recording.

Obscene Material - Material which lacks serious literary, artistic, political or scientific value and, taken as a whole, appeals to the prurient interest and, as such, is not protected by the free speech guarantee of the First Amendment.

Perform a Work - Means to recite, render, play, dance, or act it, either directly or by means of any device or process or, in the case of a motion picture or other audiovisual work, to show its images in any sequence or to make the sounds accompanying it audible.

Phonorecords - Material objects in which sounds, other than those accompanying a motion picture or other audiovisual work, are fixed by any method now known or later developed, and from which the sounds can be perceived, reproduced, or otherwise communicated, either directly or with the aid of a machine or device.

Pictorial, Graphic, and Sculptural Works - Includes two-dimensional and three-dimensional works of fine, graphic, and applied art, photographs, prints and art reproductions, maps, globes, charts, diagrams, models, and technical drawings, including architectural plans.

Piracy - The illegal reproduction and distribution of property which is protected by copyright, patent, trademark or trade secret law.

Plagiarism - The appropriation of another's literary works by claiming credit for having produced those works on one's own.

Professional Model Product - An audio recording device that is designed, manufactured, marketed, and intended for use by recording professionals in the ordinary course of a lawful business, in accordance with such requirements as the Secretary of Commerce shall establish by regulation.

Pseudonymous work - A work in which the author is identified under a fictitious name.

Publication - The distribution of copies or phonorecords of a work to the public by sale or other transfer of ownership, or by rental, lease, or lending.

Punitive Damages - Compensation in excess of compensatory damages which serves as a form of punishment to the wrongdoer who has exhibited malicious and willful misconduct.

Quantum Meruit - Quantum meruit is an equitable doctrine based on unjust enrichment which refers to the extent of liability in a contract implied by law wherein the court infers a reasonable amount payable by the willing recipient of services rendered or goods furnished.

Quasi-Contract - Quasi contract refers to the legal obligation invoked in the absence of an agreement where there has been unjust enrichment.

Quid Pro Quo - Latin for "something for something." Refers to the exchange of promises or performances between two parties. Also refers to the legal consideration necessary to create a binding contract.

Recording - The process of filing of certain legal instruments or documents with the appropriate government office.

Reformation - An equitable remedy which calls for the rewriting of a contract involving a mutual mistake or fraud.

Registration - Means a registration of a claim in the original or the renewed and extended term of copyright.

Rescission - The cancellation of a contract which returns the parties to the positions they were in before the contract was made.

Right of Survivorship - The automatic succession to the interest of a deceased joint owner in a joint tenancy.

Serial copying - The duplication in a digital format of a copyrighted musical work or sound recording from a digital reproduction of a digital musical recording. The term "digital reproduction of a digital musical recording" does not include a digital musical recording as distributed, by authority of the copyright owner, for ultimate sale to consumers.

Sound Recordings - Works that result from the fixation of a series of musical, spoken, or other sounds, but not including the sounds accompanying a motion picture or other audiovisual work, regardless of the nature of the material objects, such as disks, tapes, or other phonorecords, in which they are embodied.

Succession - The process by which a decedent's property is distributed, either by will or by the laws of descent and distribution.

Successor - One who takes the place of another and continues in their position.

Trademark - Refers to any mark, word, symbol or other device used by a manufacturer to identify its products.

Transfer of Copyright Ownership - An assignment, mortgage, exclusive license, or any other conveyance, alienation, or hypothecation of a copyright or of any of the exclusive rights comprised in a copyright, whether or not it is limited in time or place of effect, but not including a nonexclusive license.

Transmission Program - A body of material that, as an aggregate, has been produced for the sole purpose of transmission to the public in sequence and as a unit.

Transmit a Performance or Display - To communicate it by any device or process whereby images or sounds are received beyond the place from which they are sent.

Treaty - In international law, refers to an agreement made between two or more independent nations.

Unconscionable - Refers to a bargain so one-sided as to amount to an absence of meaningful choice on the part of one of the parties, together with terms which are unreasonably favorable to the other party.

Uniform Laws - Laws that have been approved by the Commissioners on Uniform State Laws, and which are proposed to all state legislatures for consideration and adoption.

Useful Article - An article having an intrinsic utilitarian function that is not merely to portray the appearance of the article or to convey information. An article that is normally a part of a useful article is considered a "useful article".

Void - Having no legal force or binding effect.

Will - A legal document which a person executes setting forth their wishes as to the distribution of their property upon death.

Work of Visual Art - (1) a painting, drawing, print or sculpture, existing in a single copy, in a limited edition of 200 copies or fewer that are signed and consecutively numbered by the author, or, in the case of a sculpture, in multiple cast, carved, or fabricated sculptures of 200 or fewer that are consecutively numbered by the author and bear the signature or other identifying mark of the author; or (2) a still photographic image produced for exhibition purposes only, existing in a single copy that is signed by the author, or in a limited edition of 200 copies or fewer that are signed and consecutively numbered by the author. A work of visual art does not include—(A)(i) any poster, map, globe, chart, technical drawing, diagram, model, applied art, motion picture or other audiovisual work, book, magazine, newspaper, periodical, data base, electronic information service, electronic publication, or similar publication; (ii) any merchandising item or advertising, promotional, descriptive, covering, or packaging material or container; (iii) any portion or part of any item described in clause (i) or (ii); (B) any work made for hire; or (C) any work not subject to copyright protection under this title.

Work of the United States Government - A work prepared by an officer or employee of the United States Government as part of that person's official duties.

Work Made for Hire" - (1) a work prepared by an employee within the scope of his or her employment; or (2) a work specially ordered or commissioned for use as a contribution to a collective work, as a part of a motion picture or other audiovisual work, as a translation, as a supplementary work, as a compilation, as an instructional text, as a test, as answer material for a test, or as an atlas, if the parties expressly agree in a written instrument signed by them that the work shall be considered a work made for hire.

Writer - The composer or lyricist of a particular musical or literary work.